This is for me. I've waited forty years for it. What to do, when and why. At a glance and with scarcely any page hopping.

It's also for the gardeners who are returning to the gardening ways of their forefathers, to the moon-gardening ways of head gardener and Cornishman R J Harris.

It's for Cousin Jacks, too, at R J Harris's special request. To Cousin Jacks the world over — gorhemm ynn adon!

Front cover picture

*Head gardener R J Harris with the exhibit that won
for him the Chairman's Award for the best exhibit in
the Cornwall county championship onion section of
one of the annual Newquay Chrysanthemum Shows.
The twenty-four matched* Bedfordshire Champion
*onions weighed 44.5kg. They were sown in a feed-
free, unfed nursery bed when the September moon
was in its first quarter. They were then planted out at
the same moon time in the following March in one of
Mr Harris's single-dug beds during the first year of
the bed's four-year life span (see* ONION/1 *and* -/2).
*This onion variety first appeared in British
nurserymen's catalogues in 1869. The hay-padded
frame was crafted for the head gardener by a
Cornish wood turner using elm retrieved from the end
of a pew which was put out as scrap when one of
Cornwall's redundant chapels was demolished.*
Photo: B White Press Photography, Newquay, Cornwall

With thanks to Mr Brian L Dunsby, Secretary and Public
Relations Officer, John Innes Manufacturers Association, and
to Dr Ray Mathias, Head of Science Communication and
Education, John Innes Centre, for their comments on the
SUPPLIERS and *COMPOST: John Innes* sections of this manual.
And to Mr Bob Parker and Dr Serge Six, M D, for their advice
on the *pH* section. Mrs Olive Harris, Mrs Diana Summers and
Miss Anne Summers, also, must be thanked for their endlessly
supportive endeavours including emending proofs and —
invaluably and indispensably — standing in as guinea-pig
users of the manual. Thanks must go to
Mr and Mrs David Willis for fundamental aid, and to the
visitors to the manual's web site who, during a three-year
period, e-mailed their reactions to the authors' plans for the
manual and to the sample pages of it that were displayed for
critical discussion. Mr and Mrs George Robinson's permission
to refer to the Tresillian estate, and to its horticultural projects,
must also be acknowledged.

R J Harris's

MOON
Gardening

The *A-to-Z* of the Cornish head gardener's
way of producing common soft fruits
and vegetables, with 127 tips and
130 panels of associated information

For beginners at gardening
For beginners at moon gardening

Reportage and compilation: WILL SUMMERS

a really useful book from

Really Useful
Gardening
Books

An imprint of Really Useful Books

R J Harris's Moon Gardening is published by
 Really Useful Books, Shrewsbury, Shropshire,
 +44 01743 246469,
 reallyusefulbooks@boltblue.com,
 a division of The Really Useful Partnership

First published in Great Britain by
 Really Useful Books July 2002
 First impression July 2002
 Second impression February 2003
 Third impression June 2003

British Library Cataloguing in Publication Data
A catalogue record for this book is available from the
 British Library

ISBN 0-9542394-0-7

Design by Perfect Graphics. Typeset in Bookman and
 Avant Garde by Keyboard Wonders

Printed and bound in Great Britain by
 The Cromwell Press, Trowbridge, Wiltshire.

TOPICS LISTED IN THIS MANUAL

See the back pages for a full index

Where it is appropriate, instructions regarding soil preparation and plant management are repeated throughout the manual to save the user the inconvenience of cross-referencing

R J Harris is a professional horticulturist who grows vegetables, fruit and flowers with the help of three of horticulture's oldest and least-used tools: the moon; knowledge of the plants' ability to help each other to thrive or to perish; knowledge of how gardeners worked before the arrival of today's technology. He was discovered nationally by BBC2's *Garden Stories*, and was, until recently, the head gardener of three major horticultural undertakings: the 20-acre Tresillian estate near Newquay, Cornwall; an adjacent 70-acre conservation area; one of Cornwall's largest tourist attractions. Tresillian is now a consolidated, 200-acre estate in non-commercial ownership. Cornishman R J Harris remains its head gardener.

Mr Harris began his career as an apprentice in the mid '50s. He has practised in the public and the private sectors, his studies of the moon's influence on the management of plants dating from the '60s.

He is a poet, a story-teller, a regularly-employed local radio broadcaster, a parish councillor, a show judge and the chairman of several of the West Country's horticultural societies.

A special charge on him has been the recovery from dereliction and the restoration to its original state of Tresillian's Victorian walled kitchen garden. Standing in the shoes and occupying the minds of those who were head gardeners before him, he pursues a programme of research into yesterday's plants and yesterday's ways with them. As word has spread of his efforts, the garden has become a Mecca for writers, publishers, producers, educationists and students at all levels of horticultural training.

Upon a number of fundamental, practical levels his restoration work does not emulate the practice of his Victorian predecessors. They dared admit no constraint in their fight to send up to the big house nothing other than a comprehensive supply of unblemished produce and flowers. Anticipating the onset of pests and diseases, they did not hesitate to order the application of poisons that were harmful to humans, animals, birds and insects. He has not revived that example.

With a half-century-long career behind him — and with having witnessed mid-20th-century gardening's limitations and penalties — he is of sufficiently senior status to be able to jettison the practices that he sees as undesirable, whether they be of the past or of the present. He applies in their place his own combination of positive organic horticulture (seeing that as more than solely a rejection of what, patently, is undesirable), compatible planting and folk memories of the influence of the moon's phases that reach out to us from the days of the Romans, the Greeks and the Romanies.

This manual is about that combination. It is for the beginner in gardening and for the beginner in moon gardening. It is the product of more than three years of talks with a retired journalist whose life has left time and opportunity to do little more than contain the maraudings of a series of suburban patches.

WS: March 2002

B EAN: *broad* — **preparation, sowing, management, harvesting.** Of the antique and modern broad beans grown at Tresillian, the head gardener recommends the one variety that brings with it the least risk of — and the most easily dealt with — blackfly attack. It is the longpod type known as *Aquadulce*. Its seeds are available at most garden centres, usually as from August or September.

In the walled kitchen garden it is sown in a section of Mr Harris's single-dug bed (*BED/3*) in the first year of the bed's four-year life span. It occupies the section during the bed's first Winter. This is when the nutrients and the moisture of the bed's 30cm or so thickness of fully-composted animal manure, placed a spade's depth beneath its surface, are untapped.

Accompanying the broad bean in the following Spring and Summer of the first-year single-dug bed (*BED/3*) are broccoli, the cabbage family, cauliflower, kale, kohlrabi, leek, savoy, spinach, swede and turnip as well as this manual's highlighted dwarf french bean, onion and pea. Each is in its own, adjacent section of the first-year single-dug bed (*BED/3*).

To apply R J Harris's method of growing the longpod *Aquadulce* broad bean, do as follows

1 well before sowing time, procure seeds of the longpod *Aquadulce* broad bean

2 create the head gardener's single-dug bed. See *BED/3* for a full instruction. Complete the bed by **the end of the September moon's third quarter**

3 immediately earmark a section of the bed for broad-bean production

REQUIRED FOR BEAN: broad

- A section of a first-year, single-dug bed (*BED/3*) immediately after the bed's completion, for use as a broad-bean producer.

- Longpod *Aquadulce* broad bean seeds sown 20cm apart in 20cm-wide double-rank rows spaced 90cm apart at **the start of the October and the November moons' second quarters**.

- 60g to the square metre of fish-blood-and-bone fertiliser, applied to the broad-bean section at **the start of the September moon's fourth quarter**.

- A hoe, garden lines, stakes, soft string, a rake, a garden fork, a garden spade, secateurs, a compost bin or heap, garden shears, garden labels, a four-tined cultivator (if possible), a trench for a deep-trench bed (*BED/1*) or shallow-trench bed (*BED/2*) if either is available, fine-mesh, wire-netting arches to protect plantlets.

4 ensure that the section is

— no more than large enough to accommodate the required number of broad-bean plants. [*Considerations: 1 — broad-bean plants deliver a harvest that extends over a two-to-three-month period in late Spring/early Summer thanks to two successive, monthly sowings during the previous Autumn. A single, successful plant produces between 750g and 1000g of de-podded beans; 2 — the bean plants grow*

1

Freezing, probably, is the best way to preserve broad beans. Pick the beans before they are fully mature, de-pod them immediately after harvesting (retaining the pods as compostable, waste vegetable matter), spread a single layer of them on a baking sheet, place the loaded sheet in a freezer for a day or so, and then store the frozen beans in identified, dated, plastic bags. Keep the filled bags in a freezer.

The beans are added into dishes or steamed as a separate vegetable in their frozen state.

20cm apart in rows. Two single rows, 20cm apart, support each other in a double-rank row. The double-rank rows are spaced 90cm apart. The calculation that decides how much ground is earmarked for broad-bean production takes account of the weight of produce required per day plus the weight required for the freezer — plus, possibly, the total weight of donations to friends, relatives and neighbours]

— sheltered, if there is a choice of location, so that Winter's and early Spring's harsh conditions have as little impact as possible upon, initially, the broad-bean seedlings and, finally, upon the plantlets that develop from the seedlings

— provided with access to each of its four sides for easy management and

harvesting.
[***Consideration:*** *the access acknowledges that adjacent sections within the single-dug bed (BED/3) are, or are to be, earmarked for other crop production*]

5 at **the start of the September moon's fourth quarter**, level the surface of the broad-bean section. Begin with a garden fork. Break up the large clods formed by the use of a garden spade during the bed's installation and completion

6 follow by using a rake. Move the surface of the ground backwards and forwards with the rake's tines. Criss-cross it in the process. Use the full length of the rake's handle. Aim for a rake-tine depth of very coarse earth crumbs, evenly laid out

7 de-earth the rake frequently, to keep its tines unblocked

8 remove the stones that are trapped by the rake's unblocked tines. Store these

TIP 1
➜ **Eat the pods as well as the beans when the very young *Aquadulces* are harvested. Cut the topped, tailed and washed pods into short pieces without first de-podding the very young beans. Place the pieces in a steamer basket in a saucepan containing a few centimetres of boiling water and steam them for ten minutes or so until they are tender. The fully-grown pod is not for consumption. The beans are de-podded before being steamed.**

for use in connection with other projects in the garden. [*Considerations:* **1** — *cost-conscious gardening aims always to conserve useful resources that may be difficult to obtain at some point in the future. Sometimes, stones are an irreplaceable ingredient in garden projects, and merit the small amount of storage space that they occupy when conserved;* **2** — *the stones that slip through the rake's unblocked tines are of the size that is required by the soil. They are an aid to drainage. They act as a moisture-retaining mulch. At all times, but especially in Summer, they release during the night the heat that they absorb during the day, relatively warming the section and its contents;* **3** — *the stones that are gathered by the rake's regularly de-earthed tines are likely to be too large to be wanted in the soil;* **4** — *generally, if no stone removal is desired, use a hoe when a bed's surface is being turned. The hoe's shape prevents it from gathering stones of any size*]

9 still at **the start of the September moon's fourth quarter**, dress the raked-level surface of the broad-bean section with 60g to the square metre of fish-blood-and-bone fertiliser. Work it in lightly. Use the rake. Restore the level surface

10 achieve a less coarse tilth on the broad-bean section's surface. Do so by re-applying the rake if no other tool is available. Move its head in all directions methodically. Seek a greater

breaking down of the coarse particles of surface earth

11 for a better, more easily achieved breaking down of the surface particles, use R J Harris's preferred four-tined cultivator. Do so as if it were a rake. Reduce the coarse crumbs of the soil to crumbs which are as fine as the four-tined cultivator is capable of producing. Whether a rake or a cultivator is applied, penetrate the surface with it as deeply as its tines permit. [*Consideration:* of the many manually-operated cultivators that are available for this purpose, the head gardener uses the long-

TIP 2
➔ **Crimson Flower is the head gardener's favourite broad bean for Spring sowing. It and other Spring-sown broad bean varieties often bring with them the need to combat serious blackfly infestations. This is a messy, thankless, time-consuming task involving the use of sprayed pest killer. The planting method is precisely as for *Aquadulce*, with the moon and other key stages being programmed to cater for a March, April or May sowing (whichever month brings workable soil and warmed conditions). Sow buckwheat seeds in the bed at the same time. This pink-flowered, red-stemmed plant draws in the hoverfly. So does the poached egg plant. The hoverfly feeds on blackfly. Even so, the blackfly persists, encouraging a policy decision to grow the head gardener's recommended, Autumn-sown bean in preference to any other variety.**

handled tool that has three, four or five long, curved tines. In the hands of a practised operator, the three-tined cultivator provides a coarse tilth, the four-tined a less coarse tilth, and the five-tined a fine tilth. Also, being much less prone to clogging and having far fewer and more widely-spaced tines than the rake, all three cultivators ignore the essential small stones that the initial raking leaves in situ]

12 do not extend this Autumn conditioning of the broad-bean section's surface to the remainder of *BED/3*. This larger area retains the ploughed field appearance that resulted from spade digging when the whole of the single-dug bed (*BED/3*) was made.

*[**Consideration:** Winter requires the coarse, lumpy, open texture that is attained by spade digging in the Autumn if it is to succeed in penetrating the surface with its rains and frosts. The penetration creates the*

Visit *R J Harris's Moon Gardening's* companion web site **www.moongardening.fsnet.co.uk** to keep in touch with the results of the head gardener's latest experimental archaeological projects and developmental work in the walled kitchen garden at Tresillian in Cornwall.

2

The broad bean that is planted in October and November, and carries excellent, usable beans before any serious arrival of the blackfly in the following mid-Spring, was first mentioned by Suttons, the seeds merchants, in the mid 1800s. This firm's catalogues referred to it as the *Aquadulce*, and identified it as being one of the Longpod varieties. It was known and valued in Britain long before Suttons noticed it, being viewed in mediaeval times as a prime winter-time feed for horses

Probably, the early Egyptians must be thanked for these important legumes, and the Romans for adding them to the British diet.

In Victorian days, the beans' delicate blossom, a thing of no little beauty, was prized for cosmetic purposes. Its petals were distilled into a lotion, which was thought to improve the complexion.

conditions that increase soil fertility and introduce a measure of pest control]

13 at **the start of the October moon's second quarter**, position a garden line on the section's surface where the first double-rank sowing is to be made

14 using the garden line as a guide, create a 20cm-wide, 8cm-deep channel of the required length. Use a garden spade. Deposit the removed soil as it arises to one side of the channel for the whole of the channel's length.

*[**Consideration:** by this means, achieve relatively effortless reinstatement, later]*

15 remove the garden line. Drive a 30cm-long marker

stick into the ground at the ends of the two, parallel edges of the open channel. Leave a half of each of the four marker sticks showing above the surface

16 post two rows of the broad-bean seeds in the channel — one row along each of the channel's two edges. Space the seeds 20cm apart in each of the two rows

17 stagger the seeds' postings opposite to each other, so that each seed faces a blank space.
[**Consideration:** *the staggered seed sowing ensures that most of the double-rank, fully-grown plants support each other without additional aid*]

18 backfill the channel. Use the rake. Cover the posted seeds carefully with an 8cm thickness of soil, so that they are not dislodged from their positions

19 compress the channel's top gently and slightly with the back of a rake. Create a shallow, rain-collecting depression along the length of the double-rank row for the full width of the row

20 mark one end of each of the two rows in the double-rank row with a durable label recording what has been sown and when

21 adjust fine-mesh wire netting arches over the double-rank row, to protect

the broad beans' young, tender, green shoots from bird attack when they appear above ground

22 with effect from the initial sowing, at weekly intervals remove the protective wire-netting arches. Tie garden lines between the marker sticks and over the invisible rows of sown seeds. Hoe alongside and adjacent to the sown rows. Be guided by the garden lines where not to apply the hoe. Replace the protective wire-netting arches.
[**Considerations: 1** — *hoeing prevents weed-seed germination and, thus, keeps the bed weed-free;* **2** — *it makes nutrients available to the plants alone;* **3** — *it deprives the slugs and the snails of food;* **4** — *it raises extra moisture to the surface, where the developing plants' roots await it*]

23 at **the start of the November moon's second**

If further explanation is required, e-mail
R J Harris on
rjh@moongardening.fsnet.co.uk

TIP 3
➜ **Mark a few developing broad beans with soft-string ties. Permit them to dry on the plant, when their pods become paper-thin, brown and brittle. Store them for a few days in paper bags in a cool, dry, dark place to complete the drying. De-pod the beans, keep them as when first stored, and use them next season as seeds. Put the unsown surplus into stews, soups and casseroles. Soak them, beforehand, for twenty-four hours. Do not keep them any longer than this, either as seeds or as food. Generally, they deteriorate and become unsuitable for either purpose.**

quarter, repeat the entire sowing operation minus the fertiliser application. Position the second double-rank row parallel to and 90cm from the first. Continue the weekly hoeing

24 be alert, as from December, for the appearance of broad-bean shoots. When they bear at least four leaves and have become plantlets, remove the protective wire-netting arches. Remove the end-of-row marker sticks

25 at this stage, draw earth up around each affected double-rank row of plantlets to form a ridge along the length of the double-rank row. Make the ridge as high as the plantlets. Use a rake. [*Consideration: this offers protection should Winter and Spring be exceptionally harsh. It also encourages extra root formation. The plantlets continue to extend in height, despite the presence around them of the protective earth barrier*]

26 be alert in the Spring, as the plants achieve a maximum height of about 90cm, for pods that bear usable beans. Test by opening one or two each day or two. Harvest the pods every other day once this stage is reached, whether or not they are required in the kitchen. Pick from ground level up

3

Autumn/Winter-sown broad beans go into the ground at Tresillian at monthly intervals between October and January.

"We could sow in February as well," says head gardener R J Harris, "but the bean harvest, in total, would be too great."

The monthly sowing is done even when deep Winter forces the gardeners to keep off the beds. Trays or individual pots filled with John Innes No 2 potting compost are used, and then are posted in cold frames.

With the compost kept moist and the frames properly ventilated and protected against the cold, the beans are ready for planting out the moment that conditions improve. This is monthly — always at the start, or thereabouts, of the moon's second quarter.

The broad beans are harvested between April and the end of July, which is when spring cabbage plantlets — May/June sown in trayed John Innes No 2 potting compost — take their place.

27 at the same time, insert one or two plant-high-plus-30cm stakes into the ground at the ends of the double-rank rows to support individual plants should they evince a tendency to flop. Drive the stakes some 30cm into the

TIP 4
➔ **If local knowledge warns that weather conditions render a November sowing of *Aquadulce* broad beans not possible, sow in October instead (preferably), or in September. Create BED/3 one month or two months earlier accordingly. Observe the same moon quarters in the prescribed ways. The general effectiveness of the bed itself is in no way diminished by an earlier bed construction.**

soil. Avoid the plants roots. Attach the flopping plants to them with soft string

28 freeze, give away to the neighbours or compost the unwanted surplus. Or place it in the bottom of the trench that awaits conversion into a deep-trench bed (*BED/1*) or shallow-trench bed (*BED/2*), if there is one in the garden. [*Consideration: the broad bean plant's cropping season is six weeks or so in length. This is from when the first young pod is ready to be picked. The pod's contents develop rapidly. As they mature, the plant devotes most of its energies to them. This induces a general reduction in the plant's readiness to bear pods. At the same time, its quickly over-maturing pods are of reducing interest to the kitchen. Harvesting aims never to permit the bean-bearing plant to bring its seeds to the stage of fulfilment. This applies to all bean and pea plants*]

29 with the arrival of the very young pods, be alert for the slightest sign of blackfly on the highest part of each plant's stem. Examine daily. When ants are seen hurrying from ground level to plants' tops, look closely at the stems' tips

30 on identifying blackfly, instantly remove as much of the tip as is carrying the pest. Cut if off with secateurs or scissors. Drop the removed, blackfly-covered pieces into a plastic bag as they are removed from the plant. Knot the bag

tightly the moment the job is done. Dispose of the bag in the kitchen rubbish bin. [*Consideration: the blackfly can feed only on the plant's most tender extremities. These are, first, the plant's stem tip and then, after that, the tips of its youngest pods and leaves. A removal of the portion of the stem tip that is affected the moment it is affected — and the whole of the only slightly affected pod and/or leaf — prevents the black fly from spreading throughout the plant. It does this rapidly when not challenged. Speedy reaction to the blackfly arrival also results in the plant losing as little body matter as possible to the secateurs*]

31 continue the vigilance and the corrective treatment for as long as pods are on the plant

32 hoe the broad-bean section's surface regularly from start

TIP 5
➜ **Another way to sow broad-bean seeds: 1) position two parallel garden lines 20cm apart where a double-rank row is required; 2) using a trowel (not a dibber), and being guided by the two garden lines, excavate all of the required 8cm-deep seed holes; 3) space them 20cm apart; 4) stagger their positions in relation to each other in the double-rank row; 5) drop a seed into each hole; 6) return to the start and fill in the holes. The method calls for less physical effort than first channelling with a garden spade. It also guarantees that no 'blanks' are left in the sown row.**

to finish, for the reasons stated earlier

33 when all of the pods have been harvested, cut the plants' stems at ground level with secateurs or garden shears. Leave their roots in the ground

34 either

— spread out to dry and then burn the bean-plant vegetation on unused ground or an empty bed, turning its cold ashes into the ground's or the bed's surface

or

— destroy it off site

or

— place it in a trench that awaits development into a deep-trench bed (*BED/1*) or shallow-trench bed (*BED/2*). [**Consideration:** *the standard practice is to compost this kind of redundant vegetation. The head gardener does not do so. He believes that the material almost certainly harbours pests. Also, it may carry the beginnings of disease — and not only disease appertaining to the original plant. These conditions may not be destroyed by the composting process. Better and safer, he is certain, to burn it, or to bury it and all that it may harbour beneath either bed's dense filling*]

35 turn the surface of the now unemployed broad-bean section of the single-dug bed (*BED/3*) with a fork in

readiness for its second crop. Insert the fork as deep as the whole length of its tines. If the broad-bean roots are lifted by this process, turn them back into the depths of the soil. [**Consideration:** *in the head gardener's crop-rotation system, the follow-on crop in the ex-broad-bean section is spring cabbage. This plant is ravenously nitrogen-hungry. The need is met by the nitrogen that is secreted by the bean plants' roots.*]

for background information, see *FERTILISER, MOON, ROTATION.*

BEAN: *climbing french* — **preparation, planting/sowing, management, harvesting.** For climbing-french-bean production, the head gardener uses a section of his deep-trench bed (*BED/1*) in the first year of its four-year life span. This is when the nutrients of the metre-deep, layered 'sponge' beneath its surface are untapped. It is also when the 'sponge' has maximum ability to catch and to retain the moisture that descends to it from the ground's surface and ascends to it from the moon-attracted, rising water table, holding it in readiness for the climbing-french-bean plants' roots.

Accompanying the climbing french bean in the first-year deep-trench bed (*BED/1*) are marrows, courgettes, pumpkins and sweet peas and this manual's highlighted runner bean. Each is in its own, adjacent section of the first-year deep-trench bed (*BED/1*).

Whilst R J Harris opts for the deep-trench bed (*BED/1*) for climbing-french-bean production, it must be noted that his shallow-trench bed (*BED/2*) is an alternative medium. Equally, it must be noted that the results of using this lesser

REQUIRED FOR *BEAN: climbing french*

- A 1m-long section of a first-year, deep-trench bed (*BED/1*) for use as a climbing-french-bean producer.

- 115g to the square metre of fish-blood-and-bone fertiliser, applied to the climbing-french-bean section at **the start of the April moon's fourth quarter**.

- Climbing-french-bean seeds, sown in 8cm pots in early April and planted out as plantlets at **the start of the May moon's second quarter**. Additional seeds sown alongside the plantlets — one per plantlet — at planting out time.

- 60g to the square metre of fish-blood-and-bone fertiliser, applied to the climbing-french-bean section at **the start of the June moon's fourth quarter**.

- 8cm pots, John Innes No 2 potting compost, a bean-sized dibber, water, a watering can with a fine rose, a cold frame, cold greenhouse or conservatory, fleece or redundant blankets, 2m-to-3m-long garden canes, a garden fork, a compost bin or heap, a rake, a hoe, garden string, a trowel, labels, lengths of heavy-duty, bared copper wire or redundant copper tubing (if possible), a trench that awaits conversion into a deep-trench bed (*BED/1*) or shallow-trench bed (*BED/2*), if either is available, sheets of brown paper, a metal container, a paper bag, secateurs or garden shears, a sharpened garden spade.

bed do not equal those of using the other.

For crops of climbing french beans of the Tresillian quality, proceed as follows

1   create the head gardener's deep-trench bed. See *BED/1* for a full instruction. Complete it by **the end of the September, October or November moon's third quarter** — depending upon weather/soil conditions and upon plans for adjacent cultivations within the total area of the bed

2   earmark a 1m-long section of the 1m-wide deep-trench bed (*BED/1*) for use as a 1m x 1m climbing-french-bean bed capable of bearing eight climbing-french-bean plants growing upon a wigwam made of eight garden canes and constructed above the 1m-square section.
[***Consideration:*** *the length of the 1m-wide section is increased when a larger number of producing plants is required. In this event, an elongated rig in the traditional style is the alternative to a wigwam, with climbing-french-bean plants spaced 30cm apart along each of its two sides. For instructional purposes, this section focuses upon the development and management of an eight-cane wigwam bearing eight plants*]

3   ensure that the section

    — is accompanied by access to each of its sides for easy management and harvesting. The access acknowledges that adjacent sections for other crop production are demarcated within the first-year deep-trench bed (*BED/1*)

— is sheltered as much as possible to provide protection against the wind. [**Considerations: 1** — *this reduces the risk in freak weather conditions of a blowing-over of the cane wigwam;* **2** — *the climbing french bean's blossom is more effective when not exposed to the wind. The pollinators tend to avoid wind-tossed blossom. Without pollination, there can be no beans*]

— is sited so that the 2m-to-3m tall, laden, cane wigwam surmounting it and bearing climbing-french-bean vines does not cast shadow where shadow is not welcome

4 leave the earmarked section to Winter undisturbed, along with the remainder of the deep-trench bed (*BED/1*)

5 at the earliest moment in the New Year, procure the seeds of the chosen variety of climbing french bean

6 in early April in the New Year (there is no moon-

4

The *Cherokee Trail of Tears* is one of the head gardener's current favourite climbing french beans. It is said to be named after the early 1800s event when the Cherokee North American Indians were required by Government order to vacate their land for reservations in other, poorer and distant territory.

Their long march became known as the Trail of Tears. Legend has it that as they journeyed, they sprinkled in their wake the bean that both formed an important part of their diet and was a central entity of their society, culture and religious beliefs.

Perhaps they looked to the day when they would return, and find awaiting them the plant that was so basic to their ability to survive.

They never did return.

The bean — purple-black, pencil-thin, about 9cm long and hailing from that mysterious time when the European was not a part of North American life — is of the variety that is known today as climbing french bean. The native North American name for it is not recorded.

---

quarter involvement at this stage), loosely and completely fill an 8cm pot — or a pot of a similarly small size — with John Innes No 2 potting compost. Do not place drainage stones in the pot first of all. [**Consideration:** *in so small a pot, a drainage aid is unnecessary*]

7 brush a hand across the top of the pot to level off the compost

8 tap the base of the pot, gently yet firmly, two or three times, upon the workbench top. By this means, settle the surface of the compost until it is level with the base of the rim that

is moulded into the top of the pot

9 add more compost, if necessary, to compensate for under-filling

10 gently and without pause, add water to the compost's surface until it threatens to overspill from the top of the pot. Use a can fitted with a fine rose. Do not disturb the surface of the compost as the water is added

11 produce twelve compost-filled, watered pots in this way.
[**Consideration:** *the number of pots prepared is decided by the size of the eventual planting out of climbing-french-bean plantlets and the gardener's judgement of his/her ability to raise potted plantlets successfully. Twelve is suggested as a probably sensible total for most gardeners and kitchen gardens*]

12 group together the twelve pots upon the workbench top. Cover them with a folded newspaper. Place alongside them the climbing-french-bean seeds that are to be sown in them. Leave the assembly undisturbed for at least twenty-four hours.
[**Considerations:** 1 — *this enables the compost to become comprehensively moistened. It also enables compost and seeds to arrive at a common ambient temperature. This encourages seed germination;* 2 — *the newspaper reduces evaporation. It is folded to increase its rigidity and to reduce its area to one that is slightly larger than the total area of the tops of the grouped pots. Newspaper is cheaper, safer and more convenient than a sheet of glass. Unlike condensation-dripping glass, it does not encourage any kind of undesirable condition of the compost's surface*]

13 after a minimum twenty-four-hour pause, make a 5cm-deep hole in the centre of each pot's compost. Use an appropriately-sized dibber or improvised equivalent

14 drop a climbing-french-bean seed into each hole. Close the compost over it

15 station the sown pots in a cold frame, cold greenhouse or conservatory until planting-out time arrives and plantlets 7cm to 8cm high have developed

16 keep the compost in the sown pots moist at all times. Use a can with a fine rose. Apply the water as gently as possible, to leave undisturbed compost surfaces.

TIP 6
➔ The bumble bee willingly pollinates the climbing french bean. The household bee does so reluctantly. Avoid the risk of non-pollination (bumble bees are getting scarcer and scarcer) by planting sweet peas alongside or among the climbing french beans. Their scent brings in the household bee, which then does not differentiate between the two kinds of blossom.

5

Among the climbing french beans being grown in the walled kitchen garden at Tresillian are *Cherokee Trail of Tears* (see other panel), golden-podded and -leafed *Lazy Housewife* from Spain, *Pea Bean Inca*, brought in from Inca, Majorca, by a sparetime gardener, and *Romanian*, from Romania.

Whilst being different from each other in habit and produced bean, they have one thing in common: seeds which — although as different from each other as are their parents — display remarkably attractive and contrasted colours.

They, and many other climbing french beans, have been released by the HDRA's Heritage Seed Library (see *SUPPLIERS*).

[***Consideration:*** *over-watering is to be avoided. It is a greater fault than slight under-watering. Wait for the compost's surface to show faint traces of dusty dryness before applying water*]

17 if frost threatens, protect the cold frame and the small cold greenhouse by night with fleece or redundant blankets

18 if the pots are placed on a conservatory window sill, turn them daily to correct the plantlets' tendency to lean towards and to stretch up to the light.
[***Consideration:*** *this results in distorted stems*]

19 at **the start of the April moon's fourth quarter**, empty the surface of the climbing-french-bean section-to-be of its Winter/Spring-developed weed growth. Use a garden fork to do so

20 compost the arising annual weeds that have not set seeds, with their roots

21 off site, destroy or dispose of the arising annual and perennial weeds that have set seeds, together with their roots, and the grass growth and its roots

22 continue the use of the garden fork to level the surface of the climbing-french-bean-section-to-be. Break up the large clods formed by the use of a garden spade when the deep-trench bed (*BED/1*) was installed and completed during the previous Autumn, and which have thwarted Winter's attempts to reduce their size

23 follow the forking with a raking. De-earth the rake frequently, to keep its tines unblocked

24 remove the stones that are trapped by the rake's unblocked tines. Store these for use in connection with other projects in the garden.

TIP 7
➔ **Grow buckwheat or poached egg plant alongside the climbing-french-bean wigwam. It attracts the hover fly. This predator feeds on black fly, the scourge of all beans and peas. Grow borage, also. It brings in the bees and other pollinators, which are attracted to the climbing french bean.**

[*Considerations:* **1** — *cost-conscious gardening aims always to conserve useful resources that may be difficult to obtain at some point in the future. Sometimes, stones are an irreplaceable ingredient in garden projects, and merit the small amount of storage space that they occupy when conserved;* **2** — *the stones that slip through the rake's unblocked tines are of the size that is required by the soil. They are an aid to drainage. They act as a moisture-retaining mulch. At all times, but especially in Summer, they release during the night the heat that they absorb during the day, relatively warming the section and its contents;* **3** — *the stones that are gathered by the rake's regularly de-earthed tines are likely to be too large to be wanted in the soil;* **4** — *generally, if no stone removal is desired, use a hoe when a bed's surface is being turned. The hoe's shape prevents it from gathering stones of any size*]

25 still at **the start of the April moon's fourth quarter**, dress the raked-level surface of the climbing-french-bean section-to-be with 115g to the square metre of fish-blood-and-bone fertiliser. Work it in lightly. Use a rake

26 achieve a less coarse tilth on the surface of the climbing-french-bean section-to-be. Do so by re-applying the rake. Move its head in all directions methodically. Seek a greater breaking down of the coarse particles of surface earth

27 for a better, more easily achieved breaking down of the surface particles, use R J Harris's preferred four-tined cultivator. Do so as if it were a rake. Reduce the coarse crumbs of the soil to crumbs which are as fine as the four-tined cultivator is capable of producing. Whether a rake or a cultivator is applied, penetrate the surface with it as deeply as its tines permit. [*Consideration: of the many manually-operated cultivators that are available for this purpose, the head gardener uses the long-handled tool that has three, four or five long, curved tines. In the hands of a practised operator, the three-tined cultivator provides a coarse tilth, the four-tined a less coarse tilth, and the five-tined a fine tilth. Also, being much less prone to clogging and having far fewer and more widely-spaced tines than the rake, all three cultivators ignore the essential small stones that the initial raking leaves in situ*]

28 whilst treating and preparing the surface of the earmarked climbing-french-bean section of the deep-trench bed (*BED/1*), maintain as far as possible the rain-collecting depression that is a feature of this type of bed.

TIP 8
➜ **A large jam jar filled with water keeps surplus climbing-french-bean pods — and any other bean or pea pods — fresh for days. Put the pods into the water stalks first.**

[**Consideration:** *the depression is caused by bed settlement during the Winter months. Retaining it enhances the bed's ability to remain moisture-charged in the least rainy of weather conditions*]

29 **at the start of the May moon's second quarter**, transfer the pots to an earth surface. Gently water them thoroughly. Use a can with a fine rose. Ensure that the surplus water drains wholly onto the earth, not also onto hard standing. [**Considerations: 1** — *thoroughly moistened compost playing host to a plantlet's roots slides effortlessly and without breakage from the pot containing it. This makes for a successful transplantation from pot to garden soil; 2 — potentially, water drained onto a hard surface in the garden, whether deliberately or accidentally, creates habitat for diseases and/or pests. Drained onto and absorbed by earth, it does not*]

30 park the drained, watered pots for a few hours in a sheltered, protected place for their compost to become comprehensively moistened

31 whilst waiting for this process to complete, erect an eight-cane wigwam of 300-cm long garden canes above the earmarked, prepared, 1m-square climbing-french-bean section. Do so as follows

For the starting dates of each month's moon quarters see almost any diary — but it is essential to consult *MOON* first of all.

— insert one cane a few centimetres into the earth just outside each of the four corners of the section

— angle each cane inwards as it is inserted, so that the four canes' tops meet and cross each other

— fill in each of the four sides of the resultant wigwam with a single cane. The cane is equidistant from the two adjacent corner canes. Insert it into the earth just outside the section's side. Angle it inwards as it is inserted, so that the four canes' tops meet and cross and touch the tops of the corner canes

— thrust the eight canes fully into the earth. Tie them securely at their tops with garden string. Do so, preferably, with the help of a step ladder and another person to steady the ladder as it is used

32 still at **the start of the May moon's second quarter**, select the eight strongest-looking climbing-french-bean plantlets. Earmark the unselected balance for further plantings or as

TIP 9
➔ **A climbing french bean's vine climbs up its supportive cane or string in an anti-clockwise direction. Be sure to emulate this performance when re-winding an errant stem or branch, or when introducing a plantlet to its supportive cane or string.**

presentations to friends, neighbours, relatives or the next church bazaar

33 insert one plantlet into the ground on the inside of each of the wigwam's eight canes. To do so, in each case

— excavate an approximately pot-size, pot-shape hole in the appropriate place. Use a trowel

— place an empty 8cm pot in the hole (or an empty pot that is the same size as the pots in which the plantlets grow). Adjust the depth of the hole so that the rim of the empty pot's top levels with the surrounding ground surface

— firm gathered-in earth around the empty pot

— remove the empty pot, with care. Leave a pot-shaped, pot-sized hollow in the ground

— loosen the earth at the base of the hollow. Use a hand fork.
[*Consideration: this prevents poor drainage. Poor drainage results in accumulated water, which is anathema to the developing plantlets' roots*]

— working as close as possible to the waiting hollow, place a potted plantlet upright in the palm of one hand

— place the fingers of the other hand over the top of the pot. Spread the

fingers, so that they pass around the stem of the plantlet. By this means avoid touching and possibly damaging what is the plant's most sensitive feature — which, if harmed, will incur death for the plantlet

— grip the top of the pot with the tips of the spread fingers. Turn the pot upside down

— supporting the surface of the compost, still with the fingers spread out to avoid touching the plantlet's stem, permit the pot's contents to slide out slowly. If necessary, initiate this and encourage it to happen by first tapping the upturned base of the pot gently once or twice

— hold and support the pot-shaped, glistening compost root ball upside down in the palm of the hand. Place the empty pot to one side with the other hand

— using both hands, turn the compost root ball

TIP 10
➜   **Where the local weather pattern dictates a later start to gardening in general, start off the climbing-french-bean plantlets in pots in early May — not in early April — and advance every other stage by one month. Much less crucially, the harvesting may or may not be delayed by the same period. This depends upon the length of the local gardening season.**

upright. Do so with utmost gentleness and without compressing it. Immediately slip the root ball into the waiting hollow. It fits the hollow perfectly

— gently firm in the compost root ball. Depress its surface slightly below that of the surrounding ground in order to create a rain-collecting depression

34 immediately insert a climbing-french-bean seed 5cm into the soil alongside each transplanted plantlet. Site it at the edge of the compost root ball, as close as possible to the adjacent cane. Close the soil over the seed. [**Consideration:** *the reward, in the event of successful germination and the development of plantlet to mature, producing plant, is a climbing-french-bean season that is doubled in length and a wigwam that doubles its productivity*]

35 if frost threatens, protect each inserted climbing-french-bean plantlet with fleece. Tuck the fleece around the plantlet with care to avoid damage to the plantlet's stem. Place

weights on the fleece's edges — or pin it down — to hold it in situ in windy conditions. Remove the fleece the moment the day-time weather improves. Continue to have it in readiness against the onset of night-time frost

36 mark the wigwam with a label stating what has been planted/sown and when

37 within the perimeter of the base of the wigwam place lengths of heavy-duty, bared copper wire or redundant copper tubing close to the plantlets' stems to ward off the slugs and the snails. Clean the empty pots and return them to store

38 at the start of **the June moon's fourth quarter**, dress the surface of the May-planted climbing-french-bean bed with 60g of fish-blood-and-bone fertiliser. Turn it in lightly. Use a hoe, if possible and with care. Otherwise, use a hand fork

39 if climbing-french-bean production is desired in stages until the season ends, prepare for, construct

TIP 11
➔ **The deep-trench bed (BED/1) needs no watering except in the very driest of dry conditions. At such times, use 1:80 strength comfrey solution once or twice per week. Apply it in the cooler conditions of the day's end. The shallow-trench bed (BED/2) is more likely than the deep-trench bed (BED/1) to require to be watered in an abnormally dry Summer.**

and plant up/sow in the same way a June wigwam and a July wigwam

40 for **a June wigwam**

— sow seeds in pots in early May

— prepare an earmarked section of the deep-trench bed's surface and feed it with 115g to the square metre of fish-blood-and-bone fertiliser at **the start of the May moon's fourth quarter**

— build a wigwam and plant it up/sow it at **the start of the June moon's second quarter**

— give the June bed a booster feed of 60g to the square metre of fish-blood-and-bone fertiliser at **the start of the July moon's fourth quarter**

41 for **a July wigwam**

— sow seeds in pots in early June

— prepare an earmarked section of the deep-trench bed's surface and feed it with 115g to the square metre of fish-blood-and-bone fertiliser at **the start of the June moon's fourth quarter**

— build an eight-cane wigwam and plant it up at **the start of the July moon's second quarter**. Do not also sow it with seeds. [***Consideration:*** *planted at this advanced point in the season, the seeds cannot be expected to*

evolve into mature plants capable of bearing an acceptable harvest]

— give the July bed a booster feed of 60g to the square metre of fish-blood-and-bone fertiliser at **the start of the August moon's fourth quarter**

42 note that, in the North of the British Isles and where very cold conditions are experienced at the close of the season, a July wigwam requires anti-frost protection with all-over fleece as it bears harvestable pods in September and October

43 harvest the climbing french beans when they are young and not yet fully-formed. Harvest them every other day whether or not they are required in the kitchen. Pick from ground level up. [***Considerations:* 1** — *the climbing french bean's cropping season is six weeks or so in length. This is from when the first young pod is ready to be picked. The seeds within the pods develop rapidly. As they do so, the plant devotes most of its energies to them. This induces a general reduction*

TIP 12
➜ **If slug/snail attack removes the climbing-french-bean plantlet's leaves, do not remove the bare stem from the ground and re-sow. In due course, the stem produces new leaves and suffers only a check to its development. Use the head gardener's copper wire/tube way of keeping the slugs/snails at bay. See Tip 122.**

in the plant's ability to bear pods. At the same time, its quickly over-maturing pods are of reducing interest to the kitchen. Harvesting aims never to permit the pea- or bean-bearing plant to bring its seeds to the stage of fulfilment; 2 — try using the very young beans raw and chopped into short pieces, as a salad ingredient. Equally, raw, they are excellent as an occasional 'nibble']

44 give away, freeze or compost-bin the unwanted surplus of climbing french beans. Or place it in the bottom of the trench that awaits conversion into a deep-trench bed (*BED/1*) or shallow-trench bed (*BED/2*), if there is one in the garden

45 keep the ground surface at the base of the wigwam turned on a weekly basis. Use a hoe, if possible, or a hand fork.
[*Considerations: 1 — this prevents weed-seed germination. As a result, it makes nutrients available to the bean plants alone. It deprives the slugs and the snails of food. Additionally, the turning raises extra moisture to the surface, where the developing plants' roots await it; 2 — weed growth is prevented, in the main, by the developing climbing-french-bean vines as they mount to the top of the wigwam and prevent light from reaching the bed surface upon which the laden wigwam stands*]

46 as the harvesting progresses, leave a few beans on the vines to mature fully so that their

seeds may be collected for sowing in the following season. Mark them with ties of garden string, to avoid accidental removal. Pluck them when the pods have turned brown and have become paperlike in texture.

47 complete the drying of the pods by placing them between sheets of brown paper and storing them in a dry, cool, airy place

48 de-pod the seeds. Add the pods to the compost-matter collection. Place the seeds in a metal container. Shake the container. If the seeds rattle with a metallic sound, they are dry. If they do not, continue to dry them between sheets of brown paper and test them again

49 store the fully-dried seeds in a paper bag in a cool, dry, dark place. Do so until the next planting season.
[*Consideration: this presumes that cross-pollination with a different variety of climbing french bean has not taken place. If it has, the outcome is a type that is other than the type the beans of which are saved. Only the responsible gardener can judge whether or not this matters*]

TIP 13
➔ **For variety, more diverse colour at blossom time and to help to draw in the pollinators, mix two or three runner-bean plantlets and/or seeds into the planting up of the climbing-french-bean wigwam. The two bean types make similar demands on soil and gardener. See *BEAN: runner.***

6

Sweet corn and the climbing french bean make good companions when planted together in the same bed, advises R J Harris. The bean requires no wigwam or other supportive trellis.

The sweet corn is sown first of all, earlier by one month.

It is well established by the time the bean begins to look for support for its vines. This the sweet corn provides readily, along with the partial shade that makes the pencil-like beans a little more tender, a little more flavoursome.

"A point to watch," says the head gardener, "is that for best results all round the sweet corn is grown in four-row blocks.

"This because it is pollinated by the wind, not by insects.

"With four parallel rows sown a mere 35cm to 40cm from each other, you can be sure that pollination takes place.

"The bean is planted on the outside of the four-row block, to make sure that it does not impede the transfer of the sweet corn pollen."

bed and burn them, and then turn their cold ashes into the bed's surface

or

— destroy the vines off site

or

— place the vines in a trench that awaits development into a deep-trench bed (*BED/1*) or shallow-trench bed (*BED/2*).
[**Consideration:** *the standard practice is to compost this kind of redundant vegetable matter. The head gardener does not do so. He believes that the material almost certainly harbours pests. Also, it may carry the beginnings of disease — and not only disease which is related to the original plant. These conditions may not be destroyed by the composting process. Better and safer, he is certain, to burn it, or to bury it and all that it may harbour beneath either bed's dense filling*]

50 when the wigwam is denuded of beans, cut the vines at ground level. Use secateurs or garden shears. Leave their roots in the ground, so that their nitrogen secretions remain in the soil

51 dismantle the wigwam. Clean the canes and return them to store

52 either

— permit the vines to dry thoroughly on an empty

53 at **the start of the soonest moon's third quarter** (in September or October or November), give the surface of the unemployed climbing-french-bean section its pre-Winter dig. Use a sharpened garden spade. Dig to the full length of the spade's blade. If the climbing french beans' roots are lifted by this process, turn them back into the depths of the soil.

54 make this a part of the total deep-trench bed (*BED/1*) end-of-year, pre-Winter dig.

Aim for the surface finish that resembles the surface finish of a ploughed field. Aim to complete the dig by **the start of the moon's fourth quarter**

55 permit the section's highly broken surface — along with the other, now unemployed, highly broken surfaces of the deep-trench bed (*BED/1*) — to Winter unused and exposed to the elements in preparation for its second year's work. In R J Harris's crop rotation programme, this is the development and production of the harvest of annual flowers. In this it is joined by the similarly-treated shallow-trench beds (*BED/2*) and single-dug beds (*BED/3*) that have been installed as elements of the Tresillian rotation programme.

for background information, see
BED/1 & -/2,
COMPOST: John Innes/1 & -/2,
COMPOST: vegetable waste,
FERTILISER, MOON,
ROTATION.

B EAN: *dwarf french/1* — **preparation, sowing, management, harvesting.** The dwarf french bean grows in a section of Mr Harris's single-dug bed (*BED/3*) in the first year of the bed's four-year life span. This is when the nutrients and moisture of the bed's 30cm or so thickness of fully-composted animal manure, placed a spade's depth beneath its surface, are untapped.

He sows seeds and plants plantlets at monthly intervals from May to July.

Accompanying the dwarf french bean in the first-year single-dug bed

REQUIRED FOR *BEAN: dwarf french/1*

● A section of a first-year single-dug bed (*BED/3*) for use as a dwarf-french-bean producer.

● 115g to the square metre of fish-blood-and-bone fertiliser, applied to the dwarf-french-bean section at **the start of the April moon's fourth quarter**.

● Dwarf-french-bean seeds, sown 30cm apart in 30cm-wide double-rank rows spaced 75cm apart in the dwarf-french-bean section at **the start of the May, June and July moons' second quarters**.

● 60g to the square metre of fish-blood-and-bone fertiliser, applied to the dwarf-french-bean May, June and July sowings at **the start of the fourth quarter of the June, July and August moons**.

● A hoe, a rake, a garden line, a garden spade, a garden fork, fine-mesh wire netting, stakes, soft string, garden labels, a compost bin or heap, copper wire or tubing (optional), a trench for a deep-trench bed or a shallow-trench bed (optional), secateurs or garden shears, a four-tined cultivator (optional).

For the complete instruction, see *BEAN: dwarf french/1 to -/3.*

(*BED/3*) are broccoli, the cabbage family, cauliflower, kale, kohlrabi, leek, savoy, spinach, swede and turnip as well as this manual's highlighted onion and pea and — for a part of the tenure of these two — the broad bean sown in the previous Autumn. Each is in its own, adjacent section of first-year single-dug bed (*BED/3*).

Inter-planted between the dwarf-french-bean plants' rows (and those of the pea plants) are catch crops, which include this manual's highlighted lettuce.

Seeking the results with dwarf french beans that the head gardener achieves in the walled kitchen garden at Tresillian, proceed as follows

1 create the head gardener's single-dug bed. See *BED/3* for a full instruction. Complete it by **the end of the September, October or November moon's third quarter** — depending upon weather/soil conditions and upon plans for adjacent cultivations within the total area of the single-dug bed (*BED/3*)

2 earmark a section of the bed for dwarf-french-bean production

3 ensure that the section

— is no more than large enough to accommodate the desired number of dwarf-french-bean plants. [**Consideration:** *these deliver a harvest that extends through the Summer thanks to three successive, monthly sowings. For working purposes, assume — until a harvested result declares a firm weight — that a single, successful plant produces about 500g of beans. The bean plants grow 30cm apart in rows. Two rows are established 30cm apart to form a double-rank row. The double-rank rows are spaced 75cm apart. The calculation that decides how much ground is*

earmarked for bean production takes account of the weight of produce required per day plus the weight required for the freezer, friends, neighbours and 'give away' purposes]

— provides access to each of its four sides for unhampered management and harvesting. [**Consideration:** *the access acknowledges that adjacent sections within the single-dug bed (BED/3) are, or are to be, earmarked for other crop production*]

4 leave the earmarked section to Winter undisturbed, along with the remainder of the single-dug bed (*BED/3*)

5 at the earliest moment in the New Year, procure the desired variety of dwarf-french-bean seed

6 at **the start of the April moon's fourth quarter**, clear the section of weeds. Use a garden fork

TIP 14
➔ **Stop mice from digging up sown dwarf-french-bean seeds (and pea seeds) in two ways: 1) bathe the seeds in a small bowl of paraffin just before sowing them; 2) place short lengths of the herb catnip in the seed channels as the seeds are sown and cover them as the seeds are covered. The herb's smell attracts cats. In turn, these — or their smell — keep the mice at bay. Another explanation is that mice associate the catnip aroma with cats, and, thus, are repelled.**

7 compost the annual weeds that have not set seeds, with their roots — or place them in the trench that awaits development into a deep-trench bed (*BED/1*) or shallow-trench bed (*BED/2*), if there is one in the garden

8 off site, destroy or dispose of the arising annual and perennial weeds that have set seeds, together with their roots, and the grass growth and its roots

9 at the same time as de-weeding the dwarf-french-bean section-to-be, use the garden fork to level its surface. Break up the large clods formed by the use of a garden spade when the single-dug bed (*BED/3*) was created, and that have thwarted Winter's attempts to reduce them in size

10 follow by using a rake. Move the surface of the ground backwards and forwards with the rake's tines. Criss-cross it in the process. Use the full length of the rake's handle. Aim for a rake-tine depth of very coarse earth crumbs, evenly laid out

11 de-earth the rake frequently, to keep its tines unblocked

12 remove the stones that are trapped by the rake's unblocked tines. Store these for use in connection with other projects in the garden. [*Considerations: 1 — cost-conscious gardening aims always to conserve useful resources that may be difficult to obtain at some point in the future. Sometimes, stones are an irreplaceable ingredient in garden projects, and merit the small amount of storage space that they occupy when conserved; 2 — the stones that slip through the rake's unblocked tines are of the size that is required by the soil. They are an aid to drainage. They act as a moisture-retaining mulch. At all times, but especially in Summer, they release during the night the heat that they absorb during the day, relatively warming the section and its contents; 3 — the stones that are gathered by the rake's regularly de-earthed tines are likely to be too large to be wanted in the soil; 4 — generally, if no stone removal is desired, use a hoe when a bed's surface is being turned. The hoe's shape prevents it from gathering stones of any size*]

13 still at **the start of the April moon's fourth quarter**, dress the raked-level surface of the dwarf-french-bean section-to-be with 115g to the square metre of fish-blood-and-bone fertiliser. Work it in. Use the rake. Restore the level surface

14 achieve a less coarse tilth on the dwarf-french-bean section's surface. Do so by re-applying the rake if no other tool is available. Move its head in all directions methodically. Seek a greater breaking down of the coarse particles of surface earth

15 for a better, more easily achieved breaking down of the surface particles, use R J Harris's preferred four-tined cultivator. Do so as if

it were a rake. Reduce the coarse crumbs of the soil to crumbs which are as fine as the four-tined cultivator is capable of producing. Whether a rake or a cultivator is applied, penetrate the surface with it as deeply as its tines permit. [**Consideration:** *of the many manually-operated cultivators that are available for this purpose, the head gardener uses the long-handled tool that has three, four or five long, curved tines. In the hands of a practised operator, the three-tined cultivator provides a coarse tilth, the four-tined a less coarse tilth, and the five-tined a fine tilth. Also, being much less prone to clogging and having far fewer and more widely-spaced tines than the rake, all three cultivators ignore the essential small stones that the initial raking leaves in situ*]

16 at **the start of the May moon's second quarter**, position a garden line on the section's surface where the first sowing is to be made

17 using the garden line as a guide, create a 30cm-wide, 5cm-deep channel of the required length. Use a garden spade. Deposit the removed soil as it arises to one side of the channel for the whole of the channel's length.
[**Consideration:** *by this means, achieve relatively effortless reinstatement, later*]

18 remove the garden line. Drive a 20cm-to-30cm-long row-marker stick into the ground at the ends of the two, parallel edges of the open channel. Leave a half of each of the four row-marker sticks showing above the surface

19 post two rows of the dwarf-french-bean seeds in the channel — one row along each of the channel's two edges. Space the seeds 30cm apart in each of the two rows

20 stagger the seeds' postings opposite to each other, so that each seed faces a blank space

21 backfill the channel. Use the rake. Cover the posted seeds with a 5cm thickness of soil. Take care not to dislodge them from their positions

22 compress the channel's top gently and slightly with the back of a rake. Create a shallow, rain-collecting depression along the length of the double-rank row for the full width of the row

---

TIP 15
➔ **An alternative way to sow dwarf-french-bean seeds: 1) position two parallel garden lines 30cm apart where a double-rank row is required; 2) using a trowel (not a dibber), and being guided by the two garden lines, excavate all of the required 5cm-deep seed holes 30cm apart; 3) stagger their positions in relation to each other in the double-rank row; 4) drop a seed into each hole; 5) go back and fill in the holes. Insert end-of-row marker sticks. Use a garden-line when hoeing before emergent seedlings show where not to ply the hoe.**

23 mark one end of each of the two rows in the double-rank row with a durable label recording what has been sown and when

24 adjust fine-mesh wire-netting arches over the double-rank row, to protect the dwarf french beans' young, tender, green shoots from bird attack when they appear above ground

25 drive a stake at least 30cm into the earth at each end of the double-rank row, in between the two rows of sown seeds. The two stakes stand about 70cm above the earth's surface

26 at **the start of the June moon's second quarter**, repeat the entire operation minus the fertiliser application. Position the second double-rank row parallel to and 75cm from the first

27 at **the start of the July moon's second quarter**, repeat the entire operation — minus the fertiliser application — if an enlarged crop is wanted. Position this third double-rank row parallel to and 75cm from the June sowing

28 with effect from the initial sowing, at weekly intervals remove the protective wire-netting arches. Tie garden

7

Among the dwarf french beans being grown in the walled garden at Tresillian are *Jersey,* from the Channel Isles, where it has been known for centuries, *May Beans,* sown in May, perhaps from Normandy and at least 200 years old, and white-podded *Navy Bean Edmund,* to which nobody and nothing lays recorded claim.

In common with almost all of the vegetables and fruits that are grown by head gardener R J Harris in the Cornish Victorian kitchen garden, the produce of these legumes is of days gone by and is unobtainable in today's retail outlets.

They serve to remind gardeners of the vast loss that has been made inevitable by official dictat and commercial pressures. Thanks to the HDRA's Heritage Seed Library (see *SUPPLIERS*) it has not been placed beyond correction. When sanity returns, the Library's seed collections will be there to be tapped into.

lines between the end-of-row row-marker sticks and over the invisible rows of sown seeds. Hoe alongside and adjacent to the sown rows. Be guided by the garden lines where not to apply the hoe. Replace the protective wire-netting arches. **[*Considerations:* 1 —** *hoeing prevents weed-seed germination and, thus, keeps the bed weed-free;* **2** *— it makes nutrients available to the plants alone;* **3** *— it deprives the slugs and the snails of food;* **4** *— it raises extra moisture to the surface, where the developing plants' roots await it*]

29 as the season progresses, remove the anti-bird guards the moment they threaten to hamper plantlet development

30 at this stage, tie lengths of garden string tautly from stake to stake. Vertically space the lengths 10cm apart. Position the first length 10cm from ground level. By this means provide support for the dwarf-french-bean plants as they develop and mature

31 be alert for when the plantlets need to be guided onto the garden string ladder support. Carefully and gently introduce their tendrils to the first string rung

32 place short lengths of bare, heavy-duty copper wire or copper tubing in the section generally to ward off the slugs and the snails

33 give the May, June and July sowings booster feeds of 60g to the square metre of fish-blood-and-bone fertiliser, at the following timings

— the May sowing: at **the start of the June moon's fourth quarter**

— the June sowing: at **the start of the July moon's fourth quarter**

— the July sowing: at **the start of the August moon's fourth quarter**

34 harvest the dwarf-french-bean pods when they are young and just short of being fully-formed. Take them every other day whether or not they are required for the kitchen. Pick from ground level up

35 freeze, give away to the neighbours or compost the unwanted surplus. Or place it in the bottom of the trench that awaits conversion into a deep-trench bed (*BED/1*) or shallow-trench bed (*BED/2*), if there is one in the garden. [***Considerations: 1*** — *the dwarf french beans' cropping season is only six weeks or so in length. This is from when the first young bean is ready to be picked. The bean's contents — the plant's seeds — develop rapidly. As they mature, the plant devotes most of its energies to them. This induces a general reduction in the plant's ability to bear anew. At the same time, its quickly over-maturing produce is of reducing interest to the kitchen. This is especially so when the individual bean becomes yellow and large:* **2** — *harvesting aims never to permit the bean- or pea-bearing plant to bring its seeds to the stage of fulfilment*]

36 as the dwarf-french-bean plants become denuded of pods, cut their stems at ground level. Use secateurs or garden shears. Leave their roots in the ground, so that their nitrogen additions remain where it can be of benefit

37 progressively dismantle the string/stakes support. Clean and return the stakes to store

38 also progressively, either

— spread out to dry and then burn the dwarf-french-bean-plant vegetation on unused ground or an empty bed, turning its cold ashes into the ground's or the bed's surface

or

— destroy it off site

or

— place it in a trench that awaits development into a deep-trench bed (*BED/1*) or shallow-trench bed (*BED/2*).
[**Consideration:**
the standard practice is to compost this kind of redundant vegetable matter. The head gardener does not do so. He believes that the material almost certainly harbours pests. Also, it may carry the beginnings of disease — and not only disease which is related to the original plant. These conditions may not be destroyed by the composting process. Better and safer, he is certain, to burn it, or to bury it and all that it may harbour beneath either bed's dense filling]

39 complete the emptying of the dwarf-french-bean section by the **start of the September or October moon's third quarter**

40 at the **start of the chosen moon's third quarter,** methodically dig over the ex-dwarf-french-bean section's empty surface. Use a garden

---

8

The range of modern dwarf-french-bean varieties that is now available in Britain has widened considerably in step with the widening of the EC. French (not surprisingly, perhaps) and Italian varieties are being imported by the seed merchants, who continue to bring in the bean from what was its country of origin in the 1500s, the Netherlands.

R J Harris rates the modern French varieties especially highly, noting the range of bean colours that they now make available to the sparetime gardener.

"Yellow, red, green, black," he says. "With planned planting, one can have a marvellously contrasted crop from the bean beds."

See *SUPPLIERS* for the head gardener's sources of supply.

---

spade. Do so to the depth of the spade's blade. If the dwarf french beans' roots are lifted by this process, turn them back into the depths of the soil. Overall, achieve a surface appearance that is as close as possible to that of the surface of a ploughed field

41 make this spade-dig a part of the Autumn spade dig of the total single-dug bed (*BED/3*) area. Ideally, complete the overall dig by **the start of the moon's fourth quarter**

42 permit the section's highly broken surface — along with the other, now unemployed, highly broken other surfaces of the single-dug bed (*BED/3*) — to Winter unused and exposed to the elements in preparation for its second year's work. In

R J Harris's crop rotation programme, this is the development and production of the harvest of annual flowers. In this it is joined by the similarly-treated deep-trench beds (*BED/1*) and shallow-trench beds (*BED/2*) that have been installed as elements of the Tresillian rotation programme.

for background information, see
COMPOST: vegetable waste,
COMPOST: John Innes/1 & -/2,
FERTILISER, MANURE/1 & -/2, MOON,
ROTATION,

B**EAN: *dwarf french/2* — plantlet production in plastic roof guttering, and plantlet planting out and management.** The head gardener uses dwarf-french-bean plantlets to secure an advanced start to his dwarf-french-bean production. He combines their use with the first sowing of seeds (see *BEAN: dwarf french/1*).

He produces plantlets in two ways

— as sets of four compost-rooted plantlets, each set assembled in planting mode in a length of plastic roof guttering

— as compost-rooted single plantlets in individual small pots (for the instruction on this, see (*BEAN: dwarf french/3*).

To apply R J Harris's plastic roof-guttering method

1 early in the year, procure the seeds of the chosen variety of dwarf french bean

2 at the beginning of April (there is no moon-quarter involvement at this stage)

REQUIRED FOR *BEAN: dwarf french/2*

● The section of a first-year single-dug bed (*BED/3*) that has received its first sowing of dwarf-french-bean seeds as described in *BEAN: dwarf french/1*. Or the section of a first-year single-dug bed (*BED/3*) which is to receive plantlets only and which has been prepared and fed, and will be maintained and moon-managed, as described in *BEAN: dwarf french/1*.

● Dwarf-french-bean seeds *1)* sown in early April 5cm deep at 30cm postings in plastic roof guttering filled with John Innes No 2 potting compost and *2)* planted out as plantlets at **the start of the May moon's second quarter**.

● 60g to the square metre of fish-blood-and-bone fertiliser, applied to the dwarf-french-bean plantlets' May planting out at **the start of the June moon's fourth quarter**.

● 130cm-long lengths of plastic roof guttering, newspaper plugs, sticky tape, John Innes No 2 potting compost, a watering can with a fine rose, water, a cold frame, cold greenhouse or conservatory, sacks, fleece or redundant blankets, stakes, soft string, a trowel, a hand fork.

For the complete instruction, see *BEAN: dwarf french/1 to -/3.*

— clean a 130cm-long (at least) length of plastic roof guttering. Ensure that its inner surface is perfectly smooth and offers no protrusions.

[**Consideration:** *half-round guttering is best. Guttering with a shaped profile can be equally suitable, depending upon the extent and complexity of the shaping of the profile*]

— place the guttering length flat on a workbench top

— block its two ends with plugs of newspaper

— secure the plugs to the guttering with sticky tape

— fill the guttering between the two plugs and to its top with John Innes No 2 potting compost

— rap the base of the guttering gently yet firmly, two or three times, on the workbench top to consolidate the compost

— add more compost and level off, if that is necessary

— moisten the compost thoroughly. Use a watering can with a fine rose

— cover the guttering assembly with sheets of folded newspaper. [**Consideration:** *this reduces evaporation*]

— leave the assembly and the seeds together on the workbench top for at least one day. [**Consideration:** *the compost moistens comprehensively. Seeds and compost achieve a common ambient*

temperature. This is an aid to germination]

— after the minimal one-day pause, insert four dwarf-french-bean seeds 5cm deep in the centre of the compost at 30cm postings. Begin and end the four postings 10cm or so away from the two newspaper plugs

3 produce two or four or a greater even number of this assembly

4 lodge the sown plastic roof-guttering assemblies in a cold frame, cold green house or conservatory. Balance good ventilation against cold infiltration in accordance with the weather's performance. In the case of the cold frame and the very small greenhouse, be ready with coverings such as sacks, fleece or redundant blankets to increase the night-time — and, if necessary, the day-time — protection. Weigh down the protective covering against the force of the wind

5 keep the compost moist all the time as the dwarf-french-bean plantlets develop and reach the stage

TIP 16
➜ If inserting only plantlets into the dwarf-french-bean section — not in addition to sown seeds, and whether by means of *BEAN: dwarf french/2*'s or *BEAN: dwarf french/3*'s method — prepare, feed, maintain and manage the section in every way as described in *BEAN: dwarf french/1*.

at which they bear at least four leaves

6 **at the start of the May moon's second quarter**, transfer the guttering assemblies to any earth surface. Gently water them thoroughly. Use a can with a fine rose. Ensure that the surplus water drains wholly onto the earth, not also onto hard standing.
[**Consideration:** *by this means avoid creating a habitat on the hard standing for diseases and/or pests development*]

7 park the drained, watered guttering assemblies for a few hours in a protected place for their compost to become comprehensively moistened

8 still **at the start of the May moon's second quarter**, take them to the sown dwarf-french-bean section that is described in *BEAN: dwarf french/1*

9 at a spot on the section's surface which establishes a new row, or which is 75cm away from, and parallel to, a sown double-rank row of dwarf-french-bean seeds, trowel out an excavation which, generously, is roughly the shape and length of one of the roof-guttering assemblies

10 place an empty length of the utilised plastic roof guttering in the excavation. Adjust the excavation's depth, if necessary, so that the top of

For the starting dates of each month's moon quarters see almost any diary — but it is essential to consult *MOON* first of all.

9

Summer spinach and lettuce do very well indeed when sown between rows of dwarf-french-bean plants — and of pea plants.

Both of these catch crops need the same preparation as does the bean, so the one bed, whatever its size or lack of size, may be made at least doubly or trebly productive.

The spinach dotes on the nitrogen that the beans' roots discharge into the soil. When germinating, the lettuce seed loves the shade that the bean plants cast (although the head gardener advocates lettuce development from seedlings, not seeds).

Small, successive sowings/plantings of the two guests are recommended by R J Harris: "It provides the ideal cropping pattern for the average size of family," he says.

"As the season wears on, use very young lettuce and spinach plantlets taken from trays sown earlier on.

"Once in the ground, they'll mature before the season ends."

the guttering levels with the surrounding ground

11 firm the earth around the empty length of guttering

12 with great care, remove the empty guttering length. Leave a channel formed in the section's surface that has the shape and size of any one of the guttering assemblies

13 loosen the floor of the formed channel to ensure adequate drainage. Use a hand fork, with care

14 lay a plastic guttering assembly into the formed channel

15 remove one of its newspaper plugs

16 cut the sticky tape around the other newspaper plug

17 with one hand, raise the end that is still plugged a few centimetres above the floor of the formed channel. Hold the plug firmly with the other hand

18 carefully and gently slide the plastic guttering away from beneath the length of compost and the plantlets growing in it. Hold the newspaper plug stationary. Permit the gutter-shaped length of moistened compost and its four plantlets to emerge from the unplugged end of the guttering and settle unbroken into the formed channel. Place the empty length of plastic guttering to one side. [*Consideration: the successful outcome of this operation is due to the comprehensive moistening of the compost and the smoothness of the interior of the plastic guttering. It underlines the importance of the watering stage. Dry or insufficiently moistened compost is unable to quit the plastic guttering without crumbling and breaking and dislodging the plantlets rooted in it*]

19 in the same way, place the contents of another length of plastic guttering immediately alongside and parallel to the first four plantlets. Install it 30cm away from them.

Position this second set of plantlets so that they are staggered in relation to the first set. The result is a double-rank row of eight staggered dwarf-french-bean plantlets

20 gently press the combined surfaces of the two lengths of plantlet-bearing compost to a slightly lower level than that of the surrounding surface to create a rain-catchment area at the base of the plantlets' stems. Do so without touching and possibly damaging the plantlets' stems

21 treat the remaining pairs of guttering assemblies in the same way. Continue the double-rank row until it is of the required length. Or create a new row. Maintain a 75cm space between the double-rank rows, whether the double-rank rows are of plantlets or sown seeds

22 if the plantlets appear to be vulnerable to bird attack, protect them with arches of fine-mesh wire netting

23 erect a stake-and-string ladder over the inserted plantlets, as described in *BEAN: dwarf french/1*. Be alert, subsequently, to guide the plantlets' tendrils onto the first rungs of the string ladder. Remove the wire-netting guards to make this possible

24 give the immediate area of the May planting out a booster feed of 60g to the square metre of fish-blood-and-bone fertiliser at **the start of the June moon's fourth quarter**

25 manage the augmented dwarf-french-bean section generally, and harvest the crop, as described in *BEAN: dwarf french/1*.
[**Consideration:** *a crop that is one month advanced can be expected, thanks to the May addition of the dwarf-french-bean plantlets to the initial sowing of seeds in May.*]

for background information, see
BED/3,
COMPOST: *John Innes/1 & -/2*,
MOON.

BEAN: *dwarf french/3* — **plantlet production in pots, plantlet planting out and management.** The head gardener uses plantlets to secure an advanced start to his dwarf-french-bean production. He combines their use with the first sowing of seeds (see *BEAN: dwarf french/1*).

He produces plantlets in two ways

— as sets of four compost-rooted plantlets, each set assembled in planting mode in a length of half-round plastic roof guttering (*BEAN: dwarf french/2*)

— as compost-rooted single plantlets in individual small pots.

To apply R J Harris's pot method, proceed as follows

1 as soon as possible early in the year, procure the seeds of the chosen variety of dwarf french bean

2 in early April in the New Year (there is no moon-quarter involvement at this

REQUIRED FOR *BEAN: dwarf french/3*

● The section of a first-year single-dug bed (*BED/3*) that has received its first sowing of dwarf-french-bean seeds as described in *BEAN: dwarf french/1*. Or the section of a first-year single-dug bed (*BED/3*) which is to receive plantlets only and which has been prepared and fed, and will be maintained and moon-managed, as described in *BEAN: dwarf french/1*.

● Dwarf-french-bean seeds, sown in early April 5cm deep in John Innes No 2 potting compost in individual 8cm pots and planted out as plantlets at **the start of the May moon's second quarter.**

● 60g to the square metre of fish-blood-and-bone fertiliser, applied to the dwarf-french-bean plantlets' May planting out at **the start of the June moon's fourth quarter.**

● A watering can with a fine rose, John Innes No 2 potting compost, 8cm pots, water, a cold frame, cold greenhouse or conservatory, stakes, soft string, a trowel, a hand fork.

For the complete instruction, see *BEAN: dwarf french/1 to -/3.*

stage), loosely and completely fill an 8cm pot — or a pot of a similarly small size — with John Innes No 2 potting compost. Do not place drainage stones in the pot first of all.

For the starting dates of each month's moon quarters see almost any diary — but it is essential to consult *MOON* first of all.

[**Consideration:** *in so small a pot, a drainage aid is unnecessary*]

3 brush a hand across the top of the pot to level off the compost

4 tap the base of the pot, gently yet firmly, two or three times upon the workbench top. By this means, settle the surface of the compost until it is level with the base of the rim that is moulded into the top of the pot

5 add more compost, if necessary, to compensate for under-filling

6 gently and without pause, add water to the compost's surface until it threatens to overspill from the top of the pot. Use a can fitted with a fine rose. Do not disturb the surface of the compost as the water is added

7 produce as many compost-filled, watered pots in this way as are required. [**Consideration:** *probably, the number of pots prepared is no more than between four and eight. This depends upon the gardener's judgement of his/her ability to raise potted plantlets successfully. It must be borne in mind, also, that no more is aimed for than an early start to dwarf-french-bean production. The early start is succeeded relatively swiftly by the results of sowing seeds*]

8 group together the pots upon the workbench top. Cover them with a folded newspaper. Place alongside them the dwarf-french-bean seeds that are to be sown in them. Leave the assembly undisturbed for at least twenty-four hours. [**Considerations: 1** *— this enables the compost to become comprehensively moistened. It also enables compost and seeds to arrive at a common ambient temperature. This encourages seed germination;* **2** *— the newspaper reduces evaporation. It is folded to increase its rigidity and to reduce its area to one that is slightly larger than the total area of the tops of the grouped pots. Newspaper is cheaper, safer and more convenient than a sheet of glass. Unlike condensation-dripping glass, it does not encourage any kind of undesirable condition of the compost's surface*]

9 after the at least twenty-four hour pause, make a 3cm-deep hole in the centre of each pot's compost. Use an appropriately-sized dibber or improvised equivalent

10 drop a dwarf-french-bean seed into each hole. Close the compost over it

11 station the sown pots in a cold frame, cold greenhouse or conservatory until planting-out time arrives. and plantlets 7cm to 8cm high have developed

12 keep the compost in the sown pots moist at all times. Use a can with a fine rose. Apply the water as gently as possible, to leave the compost's surfaces undisturbed.

[*Consideration: over-watering is to be avoided. It is a greater fault than slight under-watering. Wait for the compost's surface to show faint traces of dusty dryness before applying water*]

13 if frost threatens, protect the cold frame and the small cold greenhouse by night with fleece or redundant blankets

14 if the pots are placed on a conservatory window sill, turn them daily to correct the plantlets' desire to lean towards and to stretch up to the light.
[*Consideration: this results in distorted stems*]

15 **at the start of the May moon's second quarter**, transfer the pots to an earth surface. Gently water them thoroughly. Use a can with a fine rose. Ensure that the surplus water drains wholly onto the earth, not also onto hard standing.
[*Considerations: 1 — thoroughly moistened compost playing host to a plantlet's roots slides effortlessly and without breakage from the pot containing it. This makes for a successful transplantation from pot to garden soil; 2 — potentially, water drained onto a hard surface in the garden, whether deliberately or accidentally, creates habitat for diseases and/or pests. Drained onto and absorbed by earth, it does not*]

16 park the pots watered, drained pots for a few hours in a sheltered, protected place for their compost to become comprehensively moistened

17 after this pause, and still **at the start of the May moon's second quarter**, take the pots to the sown dwarf-french-bean section that is described in *BEAN: dwarf french/1*

18 position a garden line on the section's surface. Place it 75cm away from, and parallel to, a sown double-rank row of dwarf-french-bean seeds

19 at the line's starting point, on the other side of it from the sown row of seeds, trowel out an approximately pot-shape, pot-size excavation

20 place an empty 8cm pot in the hole. Adjust the depth of the hole so that the pot's rim levels with the surrounding ground surface

21 firm the earth around the empty pot

22 remove the empty pot, with care. Leave a pot-shaped, pot-sized hollow in the ground

TIP 17
➔ **Gardeners in the colder parts of the British Isles are advised to advance their dwarf-french-bean sowings — and the preparation for sowing — by one month and to reduce the sowings in number from three to two. Hence, the fish-blood-and-bone feed is applied in May, and the first and second sowings are made in June and July. The moon quarters remain the same throughout.**

23 loosen the earth at the base of the hollow. Use a hand fork.
[**Consideration:** *this prevents poor drainage. Poor drainage results in accumulated water, which is anathema to the developing plantlet's roots*]

24 working as close as possible to the waiting hollow, place a potted plantlet upright in the palm of one hand

25 place the fingers of the other hand over the top of the pot. Spread the fingers, so that they pass around the stem of the plantlet. By this means avoid touching and possibly damaging the stem, the plant's most sensitive feature — which, if harmed, brings death to the plantlet

26 grip the top of the pot with the tips of the spread fingers. Turn the pot upside down

27 supporting the surface of the compost, still with the fingers spread out to avoid touching the plantlet's stem, permit the pot's contents to slide out slowly. If necessary, initiate this and encourage it to happen by first tapping the upturned base of the pot gently once or twice

28 hold and support the pot-shaped, glistening compost root ball upside down in the palm of the hand. Place the empty pot to one side with the other hand

29 using both hands, turn the compost root ball upright. Do so with utmost gentleness and without compressing it. Immediately slip the root ball into the waiting hollow. It fits the hollow perfectly

30 gently firm in the compost root ball, depressing its surface slightly below that of the surrounding ground in order to create a rain-collecting depression

31 transplant one half of the potted plantlets in this way, along the positioned garden line. Post them at 30cm intervals

32 move the garden line 30cm away from, and parallel to, the newly-installed plantlets

33 transplant the other half of the potted plantlets as the first batch was transplanted. Use the newly-moved garden line as a guide. Position the plantlets 30cm apart.
[**Consideration:** *thus, overall, is created a double-rank row of dwarf-french-bean plantlets*]

34 if the plantlets appear to be vulnerable to bird attack, protect them with arches of fine-mesh wire netting

35 erect a stake-and-string ladder over the plantlets, as described in *BEAN: dwarf french/1*. Be alert, subsequently, to guide the plantlets' tendrils onto the first rungs of the string ladder. Remove the wire-netting guards to make this possible

36 give the immediate area of the May planting out a booster feed of 60g to the square metre of fish-blood-and-bone fertiliser at **the**

start of the June moon's fourth quarter

37 manage the dwarf-french-bean section generally, and harvest the crop, as described in *BEAN: dwarf french/1*.

[**Consideration:** *a crop that is one month advanced can be expected, thanks to the May addition of the dwarf-french-bean plantlets to the initial sowing of seeds in May.*]

for background information, see
COMPOST: John Innes/1 & -/2, MOON, ROTATION.

BEAN: *runner* — **preparation, planting/sowing, management, harvesting.** For runner-bean production, the head gardener uses a section of a Tresillian deep-trench bed (*BED/1*), that is in the first year of the bed's four-year life span. This is when the nutrients of the metre-deep, layered 'sponge' beneath its surface are untapped. It is also when the 'sponge' has maximum ability to catch and to retain the moisture that descends to it from the ground's surface and ascends to it from the moon-attracted, rising water table, holding it in readiness for the roots of the runner-bean plants.

Accompanying the runner bean in the first-year deep-trench bed (*BED/1*) are marrows, courgettes, pumpkins and sweet peas and this manual's highlighted climbing french bean. Each is in its own, adjacent section of the first-year deep-trench bed (*BED/1*).

Whilst R J Harris opts for the deep-trench bed (*BED/1*) for runner-bean production, it must be noted that his shallow-trench bed (*BED/2*) is an alternative medium. Equally, it must be noted that the results of using this lesser bed do

REQUIRED FOR *BEAN: runner*

- A 1m-long section of a first-year, deep-trench bed (*BED/1*) for use as a runner-bean producer.

- 115g to the square metre of fish-blood-and-bone fertiliser, applied to the runner-bean section at **the start of the April moon's fourth quarter**.

- Runner-bean seeds, sown in 8cm pots in early April and planted out as plantlets at **the start of the May moon's second quarter**. Additional seeds sown alongside the plantlets — one per plantlet — at planting out time.

- 60g to the square metre of fish-blood-and-bone fertiliser, applied to the runner-bean section at **the start of the June moon's fourth quarter**.

- 8cm pots, John Innes No 2 potting compost, a bean-sized dibber, water, a watering can with a fine rose, a cold frame, cold greenhouse or conservatory, fleece or redundant blankets, 2m-to-3m-long garden canes, a garden fork, a compost bin or heap, a rake, a hoe, garden string, a trowel, fleece, labels, lengths of heavy-duty, bared copper wire or redundant copper tubing (optional), a trench that awaits conversion into a deep-trench bed (*BED/1*) or shallow-trench bed (*BED/2*) if either is available, sheets of brown paper, a metal container, a paper bag, secateurs or garden shears, a sharpened garden spade.

not equal those of using the other.

Taking the head gardener's example as a guide, proceed as follows

1 create the head gardener's deep-trench bed. See *BED/1* for a full instruction. Complete it by **the end of the September, October or November moon's third quarter** — depending upon weather/soil conditions and upon plans for adjacent cultivations within the total area of the bed

2 earmark a 1m-long section of the 1m-wide deep-trench bed (*BED/1*) for use as a bed capable of bearing eight runner-bean plants growing upon a wigwam made of eight garden canes and constructed above the 1m-square section.
[***Consideration:*** *the length of the 1m-wide section is increased when a larger number of producing plants is required. In this event, an elongated rig in the traditional style is the alternative to a wigwam, with runner-bean plants spaced 30cm apart along each of its two sides. For instructional purposes, this section focuses upon the development and management of an eight-cane wigwam bearing eight plants*]

3 ensure that the section

— provides access to each of its sides for easy management and harvesting. The access acknowledges that adjacent sections for other crop production are demarcated within the

first-year deep-trench bed (*BED/1*)

— is sheltered as much as possible to provide protection against the wind.
[***Considerations:*** **1** — *this reduces the risk in freak weather conditions of a blowing-over of the cane wigwam;* **2** — *the runner bean's blossom is more effective when not exposed to the wind. The pollinators tend to avoid wind-tossed blossom. Without pollination, there can be no beans*]

— is sited so that the cane wigwam surmounting it and bearing runner-bean vines does not cast shadow where shadow is not welcome

4 leave the earmarked section to Winter undisturbed, along with the remainder of the deep-trench bed (*BED/1*)

5 at the earliest moment in the New Year, procure the seeds of the chosen variety of runner bean

6 in early April in the New Year (there is no moon-quarter involvement at this stage), loosely and completely fill an 8cm pot — or a pot of a similarly small size — with John Innes No 2 potting compost. Do not precede this by placing drainage stones in the pot.
[***Consideration:*** *in so small a pot, a drainage aid is unnecessary*]

7 brush a hand across the top of the pot to level off the compost

8 tap the base of the pot, gently yet firmly, two or three times, upon the workbench top. By this means, settle the surface of the compost until it is level with the base of the rim that is moulded into the top of the pot

9 add more compost to compensate for under-filling

10 gently and without pause, add water to the compost's surface until it threatens to overspill from the top of the pot. Use a can fitted with a fine rose. Do not disturb the surface of the compost as the water is added

11 produce twelve compost-filled, watered pots in this way.
[**Consideration:** *the number of pots prepared is decided by the size of the eventual planting out of runner-bean plantlets and the gardener's judgement of his/her ability to raise potted plantlets successfully. Twelve is suggested as a probably sensible total for most gardeners and kitchen gardens*]

12 group together the twelve pots upon the workbench top. Cover them with a folded newspaper. Place alongside them the runner-bean seeds that are to be sown in them. Leave the covered pots and seeds undisturbed for at least twenty-four hours.
[**Considerations: 1** — *this enables the compost to become comprehensively moistened. It also enables compost and seeds to arrive at a common ambient*

temperature. This encourages seed germination; **2** — *the newspaper reduces evaporation. It is folded to increase its rigidity and to reduce its area to one that is slightly larger than the total area of the tops of the grouped pots. Newspaper is cheaper, safer and more convenient than a sheet of glass. Unlike condensation-dripping glass, it does not encourage any kind of undesirable condition of the compost's surface*]

13 after the minimal twenty-four hour pause, make a 3cm-deep hole in the centre of each pot's compost. Use an appropriately-sized dibber or improvised equivalent

14 drop a runner-bean seed into each hole. Close the compost over it

15 station the sown pots in a cold frame, cold greenhouse or conservatory until planting-out time arrives and plantlets 7cm to 8cm high have developed

16 keep the compost in the sown pots moist at all times. Use a can with a fine rose. Apply the water gently, to leave the compost surface undisturbed
[**Consideration:** *over-watering is to be avoided. It is a greater fault than slight under-watering. Wait for the compost's surface to show faint traces of dusty dryness before applying water*]

17 if frost threatens, protect the cold frame and the small cold greenhouse by night

10

Thanks to regular seed collection during many years, an annual cropper in the walled kitchen garden at Tresillian is a runner bean the seeds of which were given to Mr Harris in the 1950s, when he was an apprentice.

It was a runner bean without a name — presented to him by the head gardener who was his tutor and mentor in horticulture.

Much later, as a qualified and senior practitioner, Mr Harris sent a sample of the runner bean's seeds to the Henry Doubleday Seed Library. This is the body that was set up with neither Government aid nor encouragement to try to maintain Britain's native stock of plants. It does so, currently, in the teeth of edicts from Brussels — where, clearly, no one understands that plant diversity is essential to mankind's survival.

At the Library, the nameless seed was dubbed *John's Best*, after R J Harris.

"Probably," says the head gardener, "it was a cross between Dobie's *Yardstick* and the same firm's *Long As Your Arm*. These were two well-known varieties produced by a company which no longer exists, except in the memories of today's older gardeners."

The bean is longer than a man's forearm when ready for picking (thanks, no doubt, to the *Long As Your Arm* genes). Despite that, attests R J Harris, when harvested before maturity, it has a full flavour and neither string nor toughness.

with fleece or redundant blankets

18 if the pots are placed on a conservatory window sill, turn them daily to correct the plantlets' tendency to lean towards and to stretch up to the light.
[**Consideration:** *this results in distorted stems*]

19 at **the start of the April moon's fourth quarter**, empty the surface of the runner-bean-section-to-be of its Winter/Spring-developed weed growth. Use a garden fork to do so

20 compost the arising annual weeds that have not set seeds, with their roots

21 off site, destroy or dispose of the arising annual and perennial weeds that have

set seeds, together with their roots, and the grass growth and its roots

22 continue the use of the garden fork to level the surface of the runner-bean section-to-be. Break up the large clods formed by the use of a garden spade when the deep-trench bed (*BED/1*) was installed and completed during the previous Autumn, and

TIP 18
➜ **For variety, more diverse colour at blossom time and to help to draw in the pollinators, mix two or three climbing-french-bean plantlets and/or seeds into the planting up of the runner-bean wigwam. The two bean types make similar demands on soil and gardener. See *BEAN: climbing french*.**

which have thwarted Winter's attempts to reduce their size

23 follow the forking with a raking. De-earth the rake frequently, to keep its tines unblocked

24 remove the stones that are trapped by the rake's unblocked tines. Store these for use in connection with other projects in the garden. [*Considerations:* **1** *— cost-conscious gardening aims always to conserve useful resources that may be difficult to obtain at some point in the future. Sometimes, stones are an irreplaceable ingredient in garden projects, and merit the small amount of storage space that they occupy when conserved;* **2** *— the stones that slip through the rake's unblocked tines are of the size that is required by the soil. They are an aid to drainage. They act as a moisture-retaining mulch. At all times, but especially in Summer, they release during the night the heat that they absorb during the day, relatively warming the section and its contents;* **3** *— the stones that are gathered by the rake's regularly de-earthed tines are likely to be too large to be wanted in the soil;* **4** *— generally, if no stone removal is desired, use a hoe when a bed's surface is being turned. The hoe's shape prevents it from gathering stones of any size*]

25 still at **the start of the April moon's fourth quarter**, dress the raked-level surface of the runner-bean section-to-be with 115g

to the square metre of fish-blood-and-bone fertiliser. Work it in lightly. Use a rake

26 achieve a less coarse tilth on the surface of the runner-bean section-to-be. Do so by re-applying the rake if no other tool is available. Move its head in all directions methodically. Seek a greater breaking down of the coarse particles of surface earth

27 for a better, more easily achieved breaking down of the surface particles, use R J Harris's preferred four-tined cultivator. Do so as if it were a rake. Reduce the coarse crumbs of the soil to crumbs which are as fine as the four-tined cultivator is capable of producing. Whether a rake or a cultivator is applied, penetrate the surface with it as deeply as its tines permit. [*Consideration:* of the many manually-operated cultivators that are available for this purpose, the head gardener uses the long-handled tool that has three, four or five long, curved tines. In the hands of a practised operator, the three-tined cultivator provides a coarse tilth, the four-tined a less coarse tilth, and the five-tined a fine tilth. Also, being*

TIP 19
➔ **Grow buckwheat or poached egg plant alongside the runner-bean wigwam. It attracts the hover fly. This predator feeds on black fly, the scourge of all beans and peas. Grow borage, also. It brings in the bees and other pollinators, which are attracted to the runner bean.**

much less prone to clogging and having far fewer and more widely-spaced tines than the rake, all three cultivators ignore the essential small stones that the initial raking leaves in situ]

28 whilst treating and preparing the surface of the earmarked runner-bean section of the deep-trench bed (*BED/1*), maintain as far as possible the rain-collecting depression that is a feature of this type of bed.
[***Consideration:*** *the depression is caused by bed settlement during the Winter months. Retaining it enhances the bed's ability to remain moisture-charged in the least rainy of weather conditions*]

29 **at the start of the May moon's second quarter**, transfer the pots to an earth surface. Gently water them thoroughly. Use a can with a fine rose. Ensure that the surplus water drains wholly onto the earth, not also onto hard standing.
[***Considerations:*** **1** — *thoroughly moistened compost playing host to a plantlet's roots slides effortlessly and without breakage from the pot containing it. This makes for a successful transplantation from pot to garden soil*; **2** —

11

The head gardener is one of the few horticulturists who take advantage of the seldom-considered fact that the runner bean is a perennial plant.

At the end of each season, after harvesting, he cuts a selection of the beans' stems at ground level and carefully digs out the stemless roots.

From these he chooses a few of the most robust-looking, washes them clean, dries them, and stores them through the Winter in trays in a dry place. He covers them with hessian sacks to protect them from the frost.

In March, he places each in a large-enough pot filled with anything from garden soil to moss to any John Innes compost, waters it correctly, and stations it in a cold greenhouse in full light. Once shoots have developed, it goes into a cold frame to be fully developed and fully hardened off.

After this, the weather being reliably frost-free (and acting at the start of the appropriate moon's second quarter) Mr Harris inserts the sprouting roots in their undisturbed compost into a deep-trench bed at the feet of the uprights of a cane rig.

"Do this," he says, "and you pick your runner beans at least one month sooner than when starting from seeds."

---

potentially, water drained onto a hard surface in the garden, whether deliberately or accidentally, creates habitat for diseases and/or

---

TIP 20
➜ **A runner bean's vine climbs up its supportive cane or string in an anti-clockwise direction. Be sure to emulate this performance when re-winding an errant stem or branch. Or when introducing a runner-bean plantlet to its supportive cane or string.**

pests. Drained onto and absorbed by earth, it does not]

30 park the drained, watered pots for a few hours in a sheltered, protected place for their compost to become comprehensively moistened

31 whilst waiting for this process to complete, erect an eight-cane wigwam of 300-cm long garden canes above the earmarked, prepared, 1m-square runner-bean section. Do so as follows

— insert one cane a few centimetres into the earth just outside each of the four corners of the section

— angle each cane inwards as it is inserted, so that the four canes' tops meet and cross each other

— fill in each of the four sides of the resultant wigwam with a single cane. The cane is equidistant from the two adjacent corner canes. Insert it into the earth just outside the section's side. Angle it inwards as it is inserted, so that the four canes' tops meet and cross and touch the tops of the corner canes

— thrust the eight canes fully into the earth. Tie them securely at their tops with garden string. Do so, preferably, with the help of a step ladder and another person to steady the ladder as it is used

32 still at **the start of the May moon's second quarter**, select the eight strongest-looking runner-bean plantlets. Earmark the unselected balance for further plantings or as presentations to friends, neighbours or relatives

33 insert one plantlet into the ground on the inside of each of the wigwam's eight canes. To do so, in each case

— trowel an approximately pot-sized, pot-shaped hole in the appropriate place

— place an empty 8cm pot in the hole (or an empty pot that is the same size as the pots in which the plantlets grow). Adjust the depth of the hole so that the rim of the empty pot's top levels with the surrounding ground surface

— firm gathered-in earth around the empty pot

TIP 21
➔ **If slug/snail attack removes the runner-bean plantlet's leaves, do not uproot the bared stem from the ground and re-sow or replant. In due course, provided that all proper management and maintenance measures continue to be taken, the stem produces new leaves and suffers only a check to its development. Use the head gardener's copper wire/tube way of keeping the slugs/snails at bay. See Tip 122.**

12

South America can lay claim to the runner bean. This explains why it is a tender plant, like the dwarf and climbing french beans. It arrived in Britain in the mid 1500s, and was one of the many benefits to Europe of the advent of the Europeans in that hapless part of the world.

R J Harris's favourite variety may or may not hail from those days. It is *Painted Lady*, a name which began to be mentioned in the UK half way through the 1800s. This variety was also known to the Victorians as *York and Lancaster*, because of its very attractive scarlet and white blossom. Such a bean was recorded in the early 1600s and could well have been *Painted Lady*'s predecessor.

It was the runner beans' blossom that first made the legume popular. Not until later did its seed pods arrive on the meal table.

— remove the empty pot, with care. Leave a pot-shaped, pot-sized hollow in the surface of the runner-bean section

— loosen the earth at the base of the hollow. Use a hand fork. [*Consideration: this prevents poor drainage. Poor drainage results in accumulated water, which is anathema to the developing plantlets' roots*]

— working as close as possible to the waiting hollow, place a potted plantlet upright in the palm of one hand

— place the fingers of the other hand over the top of the pot. Spread the fingers, so that they pass around the stem of the plantlet. By this means avoid touching and possibly damaging what is the plant's most sensitive feature — which, if harmed, will incur death for the plantlet

— grip the top of the pot with the tips of the spread fingers. Turn the pot upside down

— supporting the surface of the compost, still with the fingers spread out to avoid touching the plantlet's stem, permit the pot's contents to slide out slowly. If necessary, initiate this and encourage it to happen by first tapping the upturned base of the pot gently once or twice

— hold and support the pot-shaped glistening compost root ball upside

TIP 22
➔ **Stop mice from digging up sown dwarf-french-bean seeds (and pea seeds) in two ways: 1) bathe the seeds in a small bowl of paraffin just before sowing them; 2) place short lengths of the plant catnip in the seed channels as the seeds are sown and cover them as the seeds are covered. The plant's smell attracts cats. In turn, these — or their smell — keep the mice at bay. Another explanation is that mice associate the catnip aroma with cats, and, thus, are repelled.**

down in the palm of the hand. Place the empty pot to one side with the other hand

— using both hands, turn the compost root ball upright. Do so with utmost gentleness and without compressing it. Immediately slip the root ball into the waiting hollow. It fits the hollow perfectly

— gently firm in the compost root ball, depressing its surface slightly below that of the surrounding ground in order to create a rain-collecting depression

34 immediately insert a runner-bean seed 3cm into the soil alongside each transplanted plantlet. Site it at the edge of the compost root ball, as close as possible to the adjacent cane. Close the soil over the seed.
[**Consideration:** *the reward, in the event of successful germination and the development of plantlet to mature, producing plant, is a runner-bean season that is doubled in length and a wigwam that doubles its productivity*]

35 if frost threatens, protect each inserted runner-bean plantlet with fleece. Tuck the fleece around the plantlet with care to avoid damage to the plantlet's stem. Place weights on the fleece's edges — or pin it down — to hold it in situ in windy conditions. Remove the fleece the moment the day-time weather improves. Continue to have it in

readiness against the onset of night-time frost

36 mark the wigwam with a durable label stating what has been planted/sown and when

37 within the perimeter of the base of the wigwam place lengths of heavy-duty, bared copper wire or redundant copper tubing close to the plantlets' stems to ward off the slugs and the snails. Clean the empty pots and return them to store

38 at the start of **the June moon's fourth quarter**, dress the surface of the runner-bean bed with 60g of fish-blood-and-bone fertiliser. Use a hoe, if possible — lightly and with care. Otherwise, use a fork

39 harvest the runner beans when they are young and not yet fully-formed. Harvest them every other day whether or not they are required in the kitchen. Pick from ground level up.
[**Considerations: 1** — *the runner bean's cropping season is six weeks or so in*

TIP 23
➜ **The deep-trench bed needs no watering except in the very driest of dry conditions. At such times, use 1:80 strength comfrey solution once or twice per week. Apply it in the coolness of the day's end. The shallow-trench bed is more likely than the deep-trench bed to require water in an abnormally dry Summer — but also, for best results, with comfrey solution. See COMFREY/1 to -/3.**

length. This is from when the first young pod is ready to be picked. The seeds within the pods develop rapidly. As they do so, the plant devotes most of its energies to them. This induces a general reduction in the plant's ability to bear pods. At the same time, its quickly over-maturing pods are of reducing interest to the kitchen. Harvesting aims never to permit the pea- or bean-bearing plant to bring its seeds to the stage of fulfilment; 2 — try using the very young beans raw and chopped into short pieces, as a salad ingredient. Equally, raw, they are excellent as an occasional 'nibble']

40 give away, freeze or compost-bin the unwanted surplus of runner beans. Or place it in the bottom of the trench that awaits conversion into a deep-trench bed (*BED/1*) or shallow-trench bed (*BED/2*), if there is one in the garden

41 keep the ground surface at the base of the wigwam turned on a weekly basis. Use a hoe, if possible. Or use a hand fork. [***Considerations: 1*** *— this prevents weed-seed germination. As a result, it makes nutrients available to the bean plants alone. It deprives the slugs and the snails of food. Additionally, the turning raises extra moisture to the surface, where the developing plants' roots await it; **2** — weed growth is prevented, in the main, by the developing runner-bean vines as they mount to the top of the wigwam and prevent light*

from reaching the bed surface upon which the laden wigwam stands]

42 as the harvesting progresses, leave a few beans on the vines to mature fully so that their seeds may be collected for sowing in the following season. Mark them with ties of garden string, to avoid accidental removal. Pluck them when the pods have turned brown and have become paperlike in texture

43 complete the drying of the pods by placing them between sheets of brown paper and storing them in a dry, cool, airy place

44 de-pod the seeds. Place the seeds in a metal container. Shake the container. If the seeds rattle with a metallic sound, they are dry. If they do not, continue to dry them between sheets of brown paper and test them again

45 store the fully-dried seeds in a paper bag in a cool, dry, dark place. Do so until the next planting season. (***Consideration:*** *this presumes that cross-*

TIP 24
➔ **The bumble bee willingly pollinates the runner bean. The household bee does so reluctantly. Avoid the risk of non-pollination (bumble bees are getting scarcer and scarcer) by planting sweet peas alongside or among the runner beans. Their scent brings in the household bee, which then does not differentiate between the two kinds of blossom.**

13

If runner-bean production is desired in stages until the season ends, instead of a once-only harvest as the product of a May wigwam, prepare for, construct and plant up/sow a June wigwam, suggests the head gardener. Do almost the same in respect of a July wigwam, he goes on to advise, but — unlike as with the May and June wigwams — do not sow it with seeds in addition to equipping it with plants.

In short, for a June wigwam

- sow seeds in pots in early May

- prepare a previously earmarked section of the deep-trench bed's surface and feed it with 115g to the square metre of fish-blood-and-bone fertiliser at the start of the May moon's fourth quarter

- build an eight-cane wigwam on the section and plant it up/sow it at the start of the June moon's second quarter

- boost feed the section's surface with 60g to the square metre of fish-blood-and-bone fertiliser at the start of the July moon's fourth quarter

For a July wigwam

- sow seeds in pots in early June

- prepare a previously earmarked section of the deep-trench bed's surface and feed it with 115g to the square metre of fish-blood-and-bone fertiliser at the start of the June moon's fourth quarter

- build an eight-cane wigwam on the section and plant it up at the start of the July moon's second quarter. Do not seed sow it

- boost feed the section's surface with 60g to the square metre of fish-blood-and-bone fertiliser at the start of the August moon's fourth quarter

Note that, in the North of the British Isles and where very cold conditions are experienced at the close of the season, a July wigwam probably requires anti-frost protection with all-over fleece as it bears harvestable pods in September and October.

---

pollination with a different runner bean has not taken place. If it has, the outcome is a type that is other than the type the beans of which are saved. Only the responsible gardener can judge whether or not this matters)

vines at ground level. Use secateurs or garden shears. Leave their roots in the

TIP 25
➔ **A large jam jar filled with water keeps surplus runner-bean pods — and any other bean or pea pods — fresh for days. Put the pods into the water stalks first.**

46 when the wigwam is denuded of beans, cut the

ground, so that their nitrogen secretions remain in the soil

47 dismantle the wigwam. Clean the canes and return them to store

48 either

— permit the vines to dry thoroughly on an empty bed and burn them, and then turn their cold ashes into the bed's surface

or

— destroy the vines off site

or

— place the vines in a trench that awaits development into a deep-trench bed (*BED/1*) or shallow-trench bed (*BED/2*).
[**Consideration:** *the standard practice is to compost this kind of redundant vegetable matter. The head gardener does not do so. He believes that the material almost certainly harbours pests. Also, it may carry the beginnings of disease — and not only disease which is related to the original plant. These conditions may not be destroyed by the composting process. Better and safer, he is certain, to burn it, or to bury it and all that it may harbour beneath either bed's dense filling*]

49 at **the start of the soonest moon's third quarter** (in September or October or November), give the surface of the unemployed runner-bean section its pre-Winter

dig. Use a sharpened garden spade. Dig to the full length of the spade's blade. If the runner beans' roots are lifted by this process, turn them back into the depths of the soil.

50 make this a part of the total deep-trench bed (*BED/1*) end-of-year, pre-Winter dig. Aim for the surface finish that resembles the surface finish of a ploughed field. Aim to complete the dig by **the start of the moon's fourth quarter**

51 permit the section's highly broken surface — along with the other, now unemployed, highly broken surfaces of the deep-trench bed (*BED/1*) — to Winter unused and exposed to the elements in preparation for its second year's work. In R J Harris's crop rotation programme, this is the development and production of the harvest of annual flowers. In this it is joined by the similarly-treated shallow-trench beds (*BED/2*) and single-dug beds (*BED/3*) that have been installed as elements of the Tresillian rotation programme.

for background information, see
COMPOST: John Innes/1 & -/2, FERTILISER, MOON, ROTATION.

BED/1 — R J Harris's deep-trench bed. When newly created in the Autumn in an earmarked area of Tresillian's walled kitchen garden, three types of bed commence a new four-year, crop-rotation programme for head gardener R J Harris. The deep-trench bed is one of these three types. The other two are the shallow-

REQUIRED FOR *BED/1*

- A part of one of the four areas of the garden that are designated for management according to R J Harris's four-area, four-year, crop-rotation system.

- A 1m-wide-by-1m-deep trench of desired length dug in the chosen part. It is completed by **the end of the September, October or November moon's third quarter.**

- Layers of vegetable-waste compost, top soil, old or new straw, manure and leaf mould — placed in the trench at **the start of the chosen moon's fourth quarter.**

- A garden fork, a garden spade, a garden shovel (optional), a wheelbarrow, two garden lines.

- A storage/disposal point for excavated sub soil

For an overview of R J Harris's bed styles, see *BED/1* to *-/3*.

trench bed (*BED/2*) and the single-dug bed (*BED/3*). The shallow-trench bed (*BED/2*) is an alternative to the deep-trench bed. It is for those to whom digging a metre-deep trench, an important feature of the latter, does not come easily.

Singly or together, the three beds bear a different suite of compatible crops in each of the four years of their life cycle. In the Autumn of their fourth year they are exhausted and are renewed, and the four-year cycle begins again.

Use the deep-trench bed (*BED/1*) in its first year for the production of superlative runner beans, climbing french beans, sweet peas, marrows, courgettes and pumpkins.

Use it in its second year, together

with the shallow-trench bed (*BED/2*) and the single-dug bed (*BED/3*), for the production of annual flowers and flowers the tubers and corms of which are lifted annually.

Use it in its third year, together with the other two beds, for very fine potato production, and in its fourth year — again together with with the other two beds — for the production of splendid root crops such as beetroot, carrot and parsnip, and for celery and parsley.

To create the head gardener's deep-trench bed (*BED/1*)

1 choose one of the four areas in the garden that are to be committed to the R J Harris style of four-year, crop-rotation programme.
[***Consideration:*** *view this one area as the programme's launch area. It is to contain both the garden's and the rotation system's first crop-rotation beds: the deep-trench bed* (BED/1); *the shallow-trench bed* (BED/2); *the single-dug bed* (BED/3)]

2 choose within the launch area the site for a deep-trench bed (*BED/1*).
[***Consideration:*** *the bed's size is dictated by the space required by the most space-consuming crop to be*

TIP 26
➜ **The head gardener's three styles of bed may be completed in September or October or November by the start of the moon's fourth quarter. October is recommended, because it is the month, usually, of friendly conditions in the garden. It is also when — in the main — the ground has been emptied of crop bearing and, hence, is available to be worked on.**

14

The Autumn months are notable in the Victorian walled kitchen garden at Tresillian for the presence of men digging trenches of daunting size in readiness for deep-trench bed formation. Each trench is excavated with fork and shovel, prodigious physical effort being required as well as the rare skill that comes from years of practice following rigorous apprenticeship training. Head gardener R J Harris acknowledges that this is not gardening for most weekend gardeners, and offers an alternative, less demanding design of bed — his shallow-trench bed. It is described in *BED/2*.

produced in the launch area during its four-year life span. This, almost certainly, is the combination of first-early, second-early and maincrop potatoes. The potatoes are grown in the whole of the launch area in all three of the beds in their third year. The area of the deep-trench bed (BED/1) *at most, therefore, equals the area required by the total potato crop minus the area of the shallow-trench bed* (BED/2) *and the area of the single-dug bed* (BED/3). *A 'given' is that the deep-trench bed and the shallow-trench bed are each 1m in width*]

3 ensure that *BED/1* is positioned so that there is access to its sides for easy management and harvesting as it grows crops other than the potato crop. This takes account of the future presence alongside or

If further explanation is required, e-mail R J Harris on
rjh@moongardening.fsnet.co.uk

nearby within the launch area of newly-installed *BED/2* and *BED/3*

4 when standing in the garden to plan *BED/1* and its location, ensure that the site offers sufficient space for

— a trench that is 1m wide and as long as is required. This calls for an accurate forecast of the crops to be produced in the new *BED/1*

— an adjacent area for the temporary heaping of excavated top soil

— another adjacent area for the parking and manoeuvring of a wheelbarrow

5 decide where to store, or what to do with, excavated and removed-from-site sub soil and other valueless, excavated materials

6 at **the start of the October moon's third quarter**, position two garden lines on

TIP 27
➜ **The head gardener counsels: "Do not try to fight Nature when excavating the trench for the deep-trench bed. If, when the top soil has been removed, only compacted industrial deposits or sheer clay or rock is found, make do with the shallow-trench bed. Its results are no match for the other bed's results, but they are much better than when no preparation at all is done."**

the surface where the deep trench that gives the bed its name is to be dug. The lines are 1m apart, parallel to each other and the required length of the trench.

[**Consideration:** *the moon starting point is specified presuming that the trench-making work that follows is completed within two or three days' time. If more time than this is required, the trench making begins earlier. Overall, the aim is to have the required trench fully open by no later than* **the end of the October moon's third quarter**]

7 remove the top soil between the two garden lines. Use a garden fork to loosen the soil. Use a garden spade to lift the soil and transfer it to the pre-designated site for temporarily removed top soil. From here it can be recovered with minimum difficulty when the trench is reinstated. Better, use R J Harris's preferred shovel. It shifts soil from point to point more effectively than does the garden spade.

[**Considerations: 1** — *top soil is darker in colour than, and clearly of different structure from, the sub soil beneath it. In most gardens, top soil is at least one spade blade's length in depth;* **2** — *R J Harris's shovel possesses an unusually long, almost straight handle — the length of which is tailored to his height — and a pointed blade. The long handle calls for less stooping than does the handle of the garden spade. It also affords leverage with reduced effort. Also, its pointed blade*

15

Mr Harris places a new *BED/1* at least 2m away from any other bed should it be decided to have two or more adjacent beds of tall plants. Thus, the one tall development does not block out the sun from the other.

Routinely, the R J Harris *BED/1* — his deep-trench bed — is 15m in length. This is dictated by the 15m width of each of Tresillian's walled garden's four centrally-located, adjacent, 34m-long beds.

The head gardener bases his four-year vegetable/annual-flower rotation system on these four beds.

penetrates heaped or loosened earth with less effort on the gardener's part than does the squared-off blade of the more familiar, short-handled garden spade]

8 as the top soil is removed, separate out from it grass turfs and annual weeds that are not in seed. Place these to one side for use in the trench at a later stage

TIP 28

➔ **Making the deep- and shallow-trench beds (*BEDS/1 and -/2*) almost always creates a surplus of top soil. Recycle this valuable resource into the garden by scattering it over the widest possible area of garden-bed surface. Thus, it is applied as thinly as possible and — which matters to the established plants — increases hardly at all the thickness of top soil above the established root systems.**

16

The power house of the R J Harris deep-trench bed — the element that generates its magnificent results — is the sponge that is formed by the bed's layered content of soil and composted vegetable-matter. This not only provides nutrients. It also catches and retains the moisture that is directed to it from above by the bed's sunken surface and from below by the moon-raised water table.

This is a bed which requires no watering, even in severe drought conditions (although adding water to it harms neither it nor the plants for which it plays host).

9 separate out the annual and perennial weeds that are in seed, with their roots, and rubbish. Remove this material from site and dispose of it securely

10 separate out, also, the large stones and hard matter. Segregate and store this material for use in connection with other garden projects. [**Consideration:** in cost-conscious gardening, everything is a resource, and is retained to meet unforeseen needs. Often, large stones and hard materials are hard to come by when nothing else suffices]

11 loosen the revealed sub soil. Use a garden fork. Then use a garden spade or, better, a long-handled shovel to transfer the sub soil to the wheelbarrow. Separate out the large stones and other hard, large materials.

Segregate and store this material for use in connection with other projects. Empty the wheelbarrow each time it is full at the pre-designated storage/disposal point for sub soil and rubbish

12 continue until the trench is 1m wide, 1m deep and of the desired length

13 loosen the bottom of the trench with a garden fork. [**Consideration:** a hard pan at the bottom of the deep-trench bed (BED/1) reduces drainage and thus creates a collection point for water. Plants cannot thrive when their roots encounter such conditions. The loosening creates drainage]

14 noting that the aim is to be at this stage by **the end of the October moon's third quarter** at the latest, immediately cover the bottom of the deep trench with the earmarked seedless annual weeds and any other seedless vegetation that has arisen. Position the grass turfs upside down

15 place over the added waste vegetation a 17cm-to-18cm

TIP 29
➜ **Take care not to trample on the surface of a bed once it is complete, advises Mr Harris. Footprints not only look unsightly and cry aloud: 'Poor husbandry!'. Their compaction of the soil keeps out air — the plants' life blood — and rain. It also permits water to collect and remain upon the surface. That provides habitat for disease and unwelcome insects.**

thickness of thoroughly-rotted vegetable compost. If this is not available, use whatever material is in the compost bin being composted, no matter what stage of composting it has reached

16 follow this with a 17cm-to-18cm thickness of the top soil

17 follow this with a 17cm-to-18cm thickness of old straw. Failing old straw, use fresh straw. If straw of any kind is not available, omit it. Increase slightly the thickness of each of the other materials.
[**Consideration:** *old straw is best. This is the straw that the animals have lain on, but which has not been turned into farmyard manure. Being old and once-used, it has lost the traces of the farmer's chemicals that most probably once contaminated it. The head gardener is adamant that the chemicals that the farmer uses must be kept out of the garden's soil*]

18 follow the straw with a 17cm-to-18cm thickness of fully-composted — ie, at least two-years-old — farmyard manure

19 follow this with a 17cm-to-18cm thickness of the top-soil

20 follow this with a 17cm-to-18cm thickness of fully-composted — ie, at least two-years-old — leaf mould

21 finish off — using a sharpened garden spade, not a fork — with a 17cm-to-18cm thickness of the top

soil. This creates a bed surface that is raised above the surrounding ground level by some 20cm. The surface, being spade-created, has the appearance and texture of a ploughed field. Flatten and thus tidy its four edges with the flat of the spade's blade

22 ideally, complete the filling, and place the top layer of top-soil in position, as **the moon's third quarter merges into its fourth quarter**

23 permit the bed to over-Winter unused. As the Winter months pass, its surface sinks and creates a rain-collecting depression

24 permit the bed's surface to develop weeds through Winter. Using a spade, uproot them before they set seeds. Compost the annual weeds and their roots. Destroy the perennial weeds and their roots.
[**Consideration:** *by using this time-honoured method, greatly reduce the potential weed population of the bed's surface throughout its four-year, crop-bearing life. A reward is reduced competition for moisture and nutrients. Another is a reduced demand for especially difficult weeding around the stems of the plants growing in the bed*]

25 in the Spring, clean the bed's surface finally and thoroughly of weed growth before sowing/planting up with the seeds/plants for which it is intended in its first year. Use a garden fork. In the process, break down

the large earth clods created by the Autumn/Winter spade work. Thus, begin the surface preparation that is the forerunner of feeding at the correct moon time and, after that, sowing/planting out at the correct moon time. Dispose of the removed vegetable matter as above

26 at the beginning of each of the deep-trench bed's next three winters its current crop is harvested and it is stripped of all growth. Its surface is deep-dug with a sharpened, square-ended garden spade. This restores the required Winter-time appearance and texture of a ploughed field. It is left in that condition for Winter's rains and frosts to work upon and to encourage the process that results in enhanced soil fertility

27 at its fifth winter, the deep-trench bed (*BED/1*) is renewed. It is then ready to begin a fresh four-year, crop-rotation cycle.

for background information, see
COMPOST: vegetable waste, MANURE, MOON, ROTATION.

BED/2 — R J Harris's shallow-trench bed. When newly created in the Autumn in an earmarked area of Tresillian's walled kitchen garden, three types of bed commence a new four-year, crop-rotation programme for head gardener R J Harris. The shallow-trench bed is one of these three types. The other two are the single-dug bed (*BED/3*) and the deep-trench bed (*BED/1*). The shallow-trench bed is an alternative to the deep-trench bed. It is for those to whom digging a metre-deep trench, an important feature of the

REQUIRED FOR *BED/2*

- A part of one of the four areas of the garden that are designated for management according to R J Harris's four-area, four-year crop-rotation system.

- A 1m-wide-by-50cm-deep trench of desired length dug in the chosen part. It is completed by **the end of the September, October or November moon's third quarter**.

- Layers of vegetable-waste compost, top soil, old or new straw, manure and leaf mould — placed in the trench at **the start of the October moon's fourth quarter**.

- Or, instead, layers of vegetable-waste compost and top soil followed by a 'sponge' of uncontaminated lawn mowings or uncontaminated lawn mowings mixed with shredded fresh leaves — placed in the trench at the same moon time.

- A garden fork, a garden spade, a garden shovel (optional), a wheelbarrow, two garden lines.

- A storage/disposal point for excavated sub soil

For an overview of R J Harris's bed styles, see *BED/1* to *-/3*.

latter, does not come easily.

Singly or together, the three beds bear a different suite of compatible crops in each of the four years of their life cycle. In the Autumn of their fourth year they are exhausted and are renewed, and the four-year cycle begins again.

Use the shallow-trench bed

(*BED/2*) in its first year for runner beans, climbing french beans, sweet peas, marrows, courgettes and pumpkins which rank among the no more than ordinary.

Use it in its second year, together with the single-dug bed (*BED/3*) and the deep-trench bed (*BED/1*), for the production of all annual flowers and flowers the tubers and corms of which are lifted annually.

Use it in its third year, together with the other two types of bed, for, in its case, only adequate potato production, and in its fourth year — again together with the single-dug bed (*BED/3*) and the deep-trench bed (*BED/1*) — for beetroots, carrots, celery, parsley and parsnips which, certainly, are better than can be collected from the supermarket fruit and veg display.

To produce this compromise bed

1   carry out *BED/1*'s instructions in their entirety, except

   — make the trench 50cm deep, not one metre

   — make the layers of vegetable matter, manure and top soil in the trench 7cm-to-8cm in thickness, not 17cm-to-18cm

2   if the prescribed range of vegetable materials is not available

   — line the bottom of the half-metre-deep

💻 Visit *R J Harris's Moon Gardening's* companion web site
    www.moongardening.fsnet.co.uk
to keep in touch with the results of the head gardener's latest experimental archaeological projects and developmental work in the walled kitchen garden at Tresillian in Cornwall.

trench with a 10cm thickness of waste-vegetable compost

— follow this with a 10cm thickness of the edited top soil

— follow this with a 20cm-thick 'sponge' made of

   — a compacted layer of weed-killer/poison-free lawn mowings of any age from fresh to blackened

   or

   — a compacted layer of weed-killer/poison-free lawn mowings of any age from fresh to blackened, mixed with fresh leaves shredded by a shredder or by having been worked over thoroughly with a lawn mower

3   fill the trench to the level of the surrounding ground with the edited top soil

4   cap the filled trench with a layer of top soil. The layer raises the level of the bed's surface 17cm-to-18cm above that of the surrounding surface

---

TIP 30
➜   "Remember," says the head gardener, "if straw or manure or leaf mould *is* layered into either the shallow trench or the deep trench — any one or two or all three of the materials — it *must* be separated from the waste-vegetable compost at the bottom of the trench by a thickness of the edited top soil."

5 permit the bed, however it is filled, to Winter unused. Manage it in all respects, until it is sown/planted up, as *BED/1* is managed.

Related sections
COMPOST: vegetable waste, MANURE, MOON, ROTATION, SOIL.

BED/3 — **R J Harris's single-dug bed.** When newly created in the Autumn in an earmarked area of Tresillian's walled kitchen garden, three types of bed commence a new four-year, crop-rotation programme for head gardener R J Harris. The single-dug bed is one of these three types. The other two are the deep-trench bed (*BED/1*) and the shallow-trench bed (*BED/2*). The shallow-trench bed is an alternative to the deep-trench bed. It is for those to whom digging metre-deep trenches does not come easily.

Singly or together, the three beds bear a different suite of compatible crops in each of the four years of their life cycle. In the Autumn of their fourth year they are exhausted and are renewed, and the four-year cycle begins again.

Use the single-dug bed (*BED/3*) in its first year to grow superlative broad beans, broccoli, cabbages, cauliflowers, dwarf french beans, kale, kohlrabi, onions, peas, savoys, spinach, swedes and turnips.

Use it in its second year, together with the deep-trench bed (*BED/1*) and the shallow-trench bed (*BED/2*), for the production of all annual flowers and flowers the tubers and corms of which are lifted annually.

Use it in its third year, together with the other two types of bed, for potato production, and in its fourth year — again together with the deep-trench bed (*BED/1*) and the shallow-trench bed (*BED/2*) — for beetroot, carrot, celery, parsley and

REQUIRED FOR *BED/3*

• A part of one of the four areas of the garden that are designated for management according to R J Harris's four-area, four-year crop-rotation system.

• A series of side-by-side trenches dug in the chosen part. Each is as deep and wide as the length and width of the employed spade's blade. The work commences at **the start of the September, October or November moon's third quarter**. The bed is fully installed by **the start of the chosen moon's fourth quarter**.

• Fully-composted farmyard manure to fill the trenches.

• A garden spade, a garden fork, a garden shovel (optional), a wheelbarrow, four garden lines.

For an overview of R J Harris's bed styles, see *BED/1 to -/3.*

parsnip production.

Create and manage the single-dug bed (*BED/3)* as follows

1 choose one of the four areas in the garden that are seen as committed to the R J Harris style of four-year, crop-rotation programme. [***Consideration:*** *view this one area as the programme's launch area. It is to contain both the garden's and the rotation system's first crop-rotation beds: the single-dug bed (*BED/3)*, the deep-trench bed (*BED/1)* and the shallow-trench bed (*BED/2)*]*

2 choose within the launch area the site for the single-

17

Bed making, like all of the works carried out in Tresillian's walled kitchen garden in Cornwall, closes with a return of tools and materials to their permanent homes. For head gardener R J Harris, a never-neglected element of this is the removal of earth from all aids, followed by a thorough washing and drying of the tools. Their metal parts are then oiled, and they are returned to their appointed places in the display on the wall of the garden's potting shed.

dug bed (BED/3).
[*Consideration: the bed's size is dictated by the space required by the most space-consuming crop to be produced in the launch area during its four-year life span. This, almost certainly, is the combination of first-early, second-early and maincrop potatoes. The potatoes are grown in the whole of the launch area in all three of the beds in their third year. The area of the deep-trench bed (BED/1) at most, therefore, equals the area required by the total potato crop minus the area of the shallow-trench bed (BED/2) and the area of the single-dug bed (BED/3). A 'given' is that both the deep-trench bed and the shallow-trench bed are one metre in width*]

3 ensure that the single-dug bed (*BED/3*) is positioned so that there is access to its sides for easy management. This takes account of the future presence alongside or nearby within the launch

area of the other two types of bed

4 at **the start of the September, October or November moon's third quarter**, mark out the width of *BED/3* with two parallel garden lines. Each line is as long as the required length of the bed.
[*Consideration: the moon-quarter starting point is recommended assuming that the bed-making work is completed within a week or so. If more time is required, the installation work begins earlier. Overall, the aim is to complete the bed by no later than **the end of the chosen moon's third quarter**. This*

TIP 31
➔   **Four Autumns are required in order to achieve the vegetable garden that is organised according to the R J Harris four-area, four-year, crop-rotation system. Autumn One sees the installation in a selected area of one or more of his deep-trench bed and/or shallow-trench bed and of his single-dug bed. Autumn Two sees the installation of these beds in another selected area, Autumn Three in another, and Autumn Four in another. In Autumn Five, the beds installed during Autumn One are exhausted and are replaced by new beds. With these, the four-year programme begins anew. The beds installed in Autumn Two are renewed in Autumn Six, those installed in Autumn Three are renewed in Autumn Seven, and those installed in Autumn Four are renewed in Autumn Eight. Each of the four areas is always in the same position in the garden.**

18

'Reject hay, if that is suggested in place of straw for either the deep- or the shallow-trench bed," warns R J Harris.

"When hay is cut by the farmer, its seed content is ripe and at its maximum volume.

"That is what makes it of value as animal feed.

"Incorporated into the garden soil it introduces a terrific amount of grass seed, which is what neither garden nor gardener wants."

Do not buy straw from pet shops, the head gardener advises. There is likely to be chemical contamination

"Or seed contamination," says Mr Harris, "as a result of the straw possibly being stored in the shop next to the hay.

"And going to a pet shop," he points out, "is the most expensive way to buy straw."

is the optimum time for manure (and any other kind of feed) to be newly present in the ground. It is at this time — with the water table fallen and still falling — that the ground is at its most receptive to added nutrients and composted vegetable matter]

5 mark out one end of the planned bed with a third garden line. Position this line between the ends of the two parallel garden lines

6 mark out the other end of the planned bed with a

For the starting dates of each month's moon quarters see almost any diary — but it is essential to consult *MOON* first of all.

fourth garden line. Position this line between the other ends of the two parallel garden lines

7 dig Trench 1. Use a sharpened, clean, garden spade. Trench 1 is as long as the planned bed's width. It follows, and is on the inside of, the garden line marking out one end of the planned bed. In depth, and in width, the trench equals the length and the width of the garden spade that is used

8 place the top soil removed from Trench 1 into a wheelbarrow. Fill and empty the wheelbarrow as often as is necessary as Trench 1 is dug.
[*Consideration: the wheelbarrow is stationed as close as possible to the point of digging, for convenience*]

TIP 32
➔ **An alternative 'sponge' material for the shallow-trench bed (*BED/2*)is a 5cm thickness (at least) of newspapers. It is for use when only composted waste-vegetable matter is available. It is placed at the bottom of the trench, to keep it as far as possible from the surface. It is followed by a waste-vegetable-compost layer (a 10cm thickness, or thereabouts) and then by the top soil that completes the filling of the trench plus the raising of its surface level above that of the surrounding ground by some 17cm. Expect no more than ordinary results from this bed — which are likely, in any event, to be superior to the produce on offer at the retail outlets.**

9 as the top soil is removed to create Trench 1, separate out from it

— the uprooted annual weeds that are not in seed and their roots, and grass turfs. Place these nearby for use in the trench at a later stage

— the annual weeds that are in seed and their roots, the perennial weeds and their roots and rubbish. Remove this material from site and dispose of it

— the large stones and other hard, large materials that arise. Store these for specific uses in connection with other garden projects. [*Consideration: in cost-conscious gardening, everything is a resource, and is retained to meet unforeseen needs. Often, large stones and hard materials are hard to come by when nothing else suffices*]

10 each time the wheelbarrow is filled with the top soil from Trench 1, wheel it to the planned other end of the designated bed area and empty it just beyond the fourth garden line, outside the designated area. Do not create a single, increasingly large heap of top soil. Space out the deposited barrow loads along the length of the fourth line. [*Consideration: by this means, the discharged earth is positioned conveniently in small heaps where it can be recovered with least effort when the final trench is reinstated*]

11 loosen the earth at the bottom of completed Trench 1 with a garden fork. [*Consideration: this aids drainage when the bed is complete*]

12 place in the bottom of Trench 1 the segregated grass turfs, turned upside down, and the segregated annual weeds that are not in seed, plus their roots

13 fill Trench 1 with fully-composted (ie, at least two-year-old), farmyard manure

14 dig Trench 2. Make it exactly like Trench 1. Position it immediately alongside manure-filled Trench 1, moving into the bed's designated area. Deposit the dug-out earth from Trench 2 on top of the farmyard manure in Trench 1. [*Consideration: do this as precisely as possible. The earth above manure-filled Trench 1 delineates one end*]

TIP 33
➔ **Hoe the surfaces of the three beds regularly throughout the year, weather permitting, no matter what kind of crops they bear and even when, apparently, there is no reason to do so. An enormous benefit (although there are others) is that the weed seeds are prevented from germinating. Hence, there are no weeds. This renders the hoe one of the most-used of the garden tools. For that reason, acquire the best quality of hoe that can be afforded. Keep it in spic-and-span condition, with an always-sharp edge to its blade.**

19

'The surface of the newly-completed, single-dug bed," points out R J Harris, "is in a highly broken-up state, just as when a farmer ploughs a field.

"This is thanks to its being prepared with a spade, not a fork."

The bed goes through Winter in that condition. The frost and the elements get down into its surface, break it up, moisten it, introduce air into it and generally increase fertility. They also kill off many of the undesirables that have been exposed by the digging.

"Those, that is, that have been missed by the robin that will have been working alongside you from the moment you struck spade into soil," comments the Cornish head gardener.

A year after completion, in September, October or November — and having produced its first crops — the single-dug bed (*BED/3*) is cleaned of all growth and then turned over with a spade and left in a rough condition for Winter and the birds to do their work once again.

"Note," says Mr Harris, "dug with a spade, not a fork. And to the full length of the spade's blade. The aim, once again, is a surface with the finish of a ploughed field."

The cleaning and the spade turning are repeated at the end of each of the bed's next two years. At the end of the following year, the fourth and final year, the bed is renewed and receives its ploughed-field finish as a part of that process.

20

If head gardener R J Harris is fortunate, the location of any of his three basic beds — decided by his four-year, crop-rotation system — receives day-long sunshine.

If he is not, the shadow from one of the kitchen garden's four, 4m-high walls falls upon it for a part of the day.

"I take what comes and make the best of it," he comments. "After all, reduced sunshine can offer the opportunity of a slightly later crop, depending upon what kind of crop it is, of course.

"Overall, this can bring a usefully extended cropping period.

"The one location I say 'No' to, whatever the overall plan dictates, is situated immediately beneath the north-facing wall.

"That is an almost entirely sunless area."

of what is to be a bed with a surface raised some 17cm above the level of the surrounding ground.]

Conserve or dispose of the weed, grass, stones and other hard material as when digging Trench 1

15 place the edited weeds and grass in Trench 2, as before. Fill Trench 2 with composted farmyard manure

16 cover the manure with the soil that results from digging Trench 3 immediately alongside Trench 2. Again,

conserve or dispose of the weed, grass and stone

17 complete in this way as many manure-filled, covered trenches as are required to create a bed of the desired size

18 place the heaped soil from Trench 1 on top of the last of the manure-filled trenches. This completes the bed. The bed has a very rough, broken, spade-created surface which is raised some 17cm above the level of the surrounding ground.

[*Consideration: if possible, use R J Harris's preferred tool for earth moving when undertaking the final trench-filling operation. It is the shovel with the unusually long, almost straight handle — the length of which is tailored to the gardener's height — and the pointed blade. The long handle calls for less stooping than does the handle of the garden spade. It also affords leverage with reduced effort. As well, its pointed blade penetrates heaped or loosened earth with less effort on the gardener's part than does the squared-off blade of the garden spade*]

19 ideally, complete the single-dug bed (BED/3) by **the start of the chosen moon's fourth quarter**. Remove the four garden lines. Neatly 'angle' the four edges of the bed's raised surface with the flat of the spade's blade

20 during its first Winter, BED/3 is used or not used according to the demands of the crop-rotation programme

21 at the beginning of each of its next three winters its current crop is harvested and it is stripped of all growth. Its surface is deep-dug with a spade. This gives it the appearance and texture of a ploughed field. It

is left in that condition until the following Spring

22 during each of its winters the single-dug bed (BED/3) is permitted to grow weeds. These are uprooted at seedling/plantlet stage by hoeing, with the result that they never set seed. They are removed from the bed's surface and disposed off securely off site.

[*Consideration: the reward for this painstaking effort with long-term aims is top soil in which the weed population steadily — if slowly — reduces*]

23 at its fifth winter, the single-dug bed (BED/3) is exhausted. It is renewed at **the start of the September, October or November moon's third quarter**. It is then ready to begin a fresh four-year, crop-rotation cycle.

for background information, see
MANURE/1 & -/2, MOON, ROTATION, SOIL.

BEETROOT — **preparation, sowing, management, harvesting, storage.** The head gardener produces beetroot throughout the growing season — the end of June to October — in its own section of his single-dug bed (BED/3), deep-trench bed (BED/1) or shallow-trench bed (BED/2) during the fourth and final year of the three beds' four-year life span of employment according to the R J Harris crop-rotation system. The beds have borne crops during each of the previous three years. Their top soil has received major loosenings and, hence, fertility-enhancing aerations at least three times with spade and fork. Their manure

REQUIRED FOR *BEETROOT*

- A section of a fourth-year *BED/1*, *BED/2* or *BED/3* for use as a beetroot producer.

- 115g to the square metre of fish-blood-and-bone fertiliser, applied to the beetroot-section-to-be at **the start of the April moon's fourth quarter**.

- Beetroot seeds, sown in the beetroot section at **the start of the first quarter of the May moon, the June moon and the July moon**.

- A hoe, a garden fork, a rake, a garden line, a seeds dispenser, garden labels, bushy twigs, a compost bin or heap, boxes for root storage, dry sand or dry peat, a place to house boxes containing stored roots, a trench for a deep- or shallow-trench bed (optional), end-of-row marker sticks, a 6mm sieve.

content is more than three years old and, hence, almost fully dissipated. The well-worked top soil and the dissipated manure render the fourth-year *BED/1*, *BED/2* and *BED/3* ideal for the growing of root crops.

Accompanying the beetroot in the fourth-year *BED/1*, *BED/2* and *BED/3* are this manual's highlighted carrot and parsnip, each in its own section.

To achieve the results with beetroots that are obtained in the kitchen garden at Tresillian

1 at the earliest moment in the new season, acquire the seeds of the selected variety of beetroot

2 at **the start of the April moon's fourth quarter**, earmark for beetroot

development a section of a fourth-year *BED/1*, *BED/2* or *BED/3*

3 make the beetroot-section-to-be large enough, and appropriately positioned, so as to

— house the required number of beetroot rows spaced 30cm-to-45cm apart. Each row contains fully-grown beetroots spaced 15cm-to-20cm from each other. [***Consideration:*** *in ideal weather/soil conditions, three monthly sowings in the one season are expected. Hence, the single monthly sowing is not excessive. Probably, a drill per month which is two metres in length provides a large enough total crop*]

— ensure that the section provides for access to each of its four sides for easy management and harvesting. The access acknowledges that adjacent sections for other crop production exist, or are to exist, within *BED/1*, *BED/2 or BED/3*

4 de-weed the beetroot-section-to-be. Use a garden fork

5 compost the annual weeds that have not set seeds.

TIP 34
➔ **The beetroot hates clayey, cold soil and poor drainage. Lighten such soil by digging in finely-sifted coal ash or peat or fully-composted leaf mould.**

Include their roots. Or place them in the trench that awaits development into a deep-trench bed (*BED/1*) or shallow-trench bed (*BED/2*), if there is one in the garden

6 off site, destroy or dispose of the annual weeds that have set seeds, together with their roots. Do the same with the perennial weeds and their roots, and the grass growth and its roots

7 at the same time as de-weeding the beetroot section-to-be, use the garden fork to level its surface. Break up the large clods formed by the use of a garden spade when the bed was Autumn-dug, and that have thwarted Winter's attempts to reduce them in size

8 follow by using a rake. Move the surface of the ground backwards and forwards with the rake's tines. Criss-cross it in the process. Use the full length of the rake's handle. Aim for a rake-tine depth of very coarse earth crumbs, evenly laid out

9 de-earth the rake frequently, to keep its tines unblocked

10 remove the stones that are trapped by the rake's unblocked tines. Store these for use in connection with other projects in the garden. [*Considerations:* 1 — *cost-conscious gardening*

-21
'Useful' is the word that head gardener R J Harris applies to the beetroot. Certainly, that has been the common view in Britain since the 1600s, when its cultivation was mentioned in written records for the first time. It was an immigrant, arriving from southern Europe, where it had been grown for centuries. As with so much of today's vegetable produce, it was around when the ancient Greeks were doing and writing about their gardening.

Its 17th-century migration deprived it of one advantage: it was no longer able to remain in the ground and — like the parsnip — to be lifted for the kitchen through Winter, as when in its native habitat. The cold and the damp of the British Winter proved to be too much for it.

Like its fellows the carrot and the parsnip, it is, truly, a biennial plant.

"It makes a fleshy root from a seed during its first year, in which it stores all of the necessary food to enable it to produce a strong, flowering stem and an abundant crop of seeds during the following year," explains Mr Harris.

"This," he points out, "is how the seed merchants are able to keep on supplying. They grow it from seed to death, harvesting the seeds at the end of its second season.

"We catch it at its fleshy root stage in its first season, and get the benefit of all that goodness accumulated for another purpose."

Also like the carrot, it stores well through Winter provided that the storage conditions are right for it.

Almost every variety available in Britain has been grown in the kitchen garden at Tresillian during the head gardener's term of office "and not one of them has been other than very, very useful, indeed," he comments.

aims always to conserve useful resources that may be difficult to obtain at some point in the future. Sometimes, stones are an irreplaceable ingredient in garden projects, and merit the small amount of storage space that they occupy when conserved; **2** *— the stones that slip through the rake's unblocked tines are of the size that is required by the soil. They are an aid to drainage. They act as a moisture-retaining mulch. At all times, but especially in Summer, they release during the night the heat that they absorb during the day, relatively warming the section and its contents;* **3** *— the stones that are gathered by the rake's regularly de-earthed tines are likely to be too large to be wanted in the soil;* **4** *— generally, if no stone removal is desired, use a hoe when a bed's surface is being turned. The hoe's shape prevents it from gathering stones of any size*]

11 still at **the start of the April moon's fourth quarter**, dress the surface of the rake-levelled beetroot-section-to-be with 115g to the square metre of fish-blood-and-bone fertiliser. Lightly rake it into the surface. Restore the level surface

12 achieve a less coarse tilth on the beetroot section's surface. Do so by re-applying the rake if no other tool is available. Move its head in all directions

---

If further explanation is required, e-mail
R J Harris on
rjh@moongardening.fsnet.co.uk

methodically. Seek a greater breaking down of the coarse particles of surface earth

13 for a better, more easily achieved breaking down of the surface particles, use R J Harris's preferred five-tined cultivator. Do so as if it were a rake. Reduce the coarse crumbs of the soil to crumbs which are as fine as the five-tined cultivator is capable of producing. Whether a rake or a cultivator is applied, penetrate the surface with it as deeply as its tines permit. [***Consideration:*** *of the many manually-operated cultivators that are available for this purpose, the head gardener uses the long-handled tool that has three, four or five long, curved tines. In the hands of a practised operator, the three-tined cultivator provides a coarse tilth, the four-tined a less coarse tilth, and the five-tined a fine tilth. Also, being much less prone to clogging*

TIP 35
➔ **For exhibition-quality beetroots, sow seed into the unmanured soil in the base of a cold frame in March at the start of the moon's first quarter. First of all, feed the soil with a very light dusting of fish-blood-and-bone fertiliser. Do this at the start of the fourth quarter of the February moon. With the seeds sown, ventilate the frame regularly by day. Close it by night whilst cold conditions obtain. By this means achieve a protected, earlier start, a longer growing season and, hence, globes of a size that merits competitive showing.**

and having far fewer and more widely-spaced tines than the rake, all three cultivators ignore the essential small stones that the initial raking leaves in situ]

14 at **the start of the May moon's first quarter**, position a garden line at one edge of the beetroot-section-to-be. It is as long as the intended first beetroot row is long. Do so on the morning of what promises to be a fine, dry day

15 excavate a 25mm-deep drill, following the garden line. Do so with the edge of a hoe or with a suitable stick

16 insert a 30cm-long marker stick into the ground at each end of the drill. Leave half of the stick showing above the surface. Later, place lines between the sticks over the sown seeds to mark where not to ply the hoe if wanted seeds are not to be disturbed

17 leave the drill open and unsown from morning until late afternoon. *[Consideration: the beetroot seed gets its best start in comparatively warm soil. The exposure of the open drill to the sun and the air throughout the day helps to achieve this]*

18 still at **the start of the May moon's first quarter**, and in the late afternoon, station single beetroot seeds 25mm-to-35mm apart in the drill. Do not sow by hand. Use a dispenser obtained from a garden centre. Fill it from the packet without touching the seeds. *[Consideration: seeds — even the very large seeds of the beetroot — sown by hand are in risk of being crushed by the fingers. Crushed seeds are unlikely to germinate]*

19 fill in the drill by hand with finely sieved earth

20 if more than one row of beetroot seeds is sown, position them so that they are parallel to each other and spaced at 30cm-to-45cm distance from each other

21 mark one end of each row with a durable label. Note on it what has been sown and when

22 cover the row with a carefully-placed, loose layer of small, bushy twigs. *[Consideration: the birds are attracted to the vivid red of the beetroot seedling, and cannot resist extracting it from the ground. The twigs provide protection against this]*

23 repeat the May beetroot sowing in its entirety at **the start of the June and July moons' first quarters**

TIP 36
➔ **Ideally, thin the beetroot seedlings in dull, damp weather conditions as the season progresses. If that is not possible, thin in the evening, when the heat of the sun has reduced. This is a root which dislikes disturbance under the full heat of daytime sunshine. When it is so disturbed, it is a root of diminished quality.**

24 when, as the season progresses, germination of the beetroot seeds takes place and there is visible growth above ground

— maintain the protective, bushy, anti-bird twigs until the seedlings are about 5cm high. Then remove them

— examine the beetroot section daily as the roots' green tops begin to appear. As the swelling roots become crowded, extract every other one

— thin in this way with minimum disturbance to the soil and to the plants. Continue until a final spacing of 15cm to 20cm between the maturing beetroots has been achieved. As the extracted young beetroots become finger-thick, use them in the kitchen

25 maintain hoeing throughout the season to prevent weed development and to raise residual moisture to where the developing roots await it

26 as the season progresses, harvest and consume the beetroots before they reach full maturity.
[*Consideration: this timing ensures roots of the best flavour and texture. Frequent test checks to ascertain root development are well worth the time spent making them*]

27 use a garden fork to loosen the soil before removing the beetroots. This helps to secure unbroken, unbruised specimens

28 at no later than **the start of the October moon's fourth quarter**, lift the whole of the beetroot crop. Do so without root bruising or breakage, as far as possible
[*Consideration: this moon quarter is when roots and tubers contain the least amount of moisture and, hence, are at their driest. This increases the length of their life during storage. The reduced moisture is caused by the falling water table. This falls during the moon's third and fourth quarters, reducing the moisture content of the top soil and of all that is in it*]

29 clean the roots, after a fashion, by lightly brushing the earth from them. Do not wash them

30 twist off the tops of the lifted beetroots. Do not cut them off. In each case, leave some 5cm of the top growth

---

TIP 37
➔ **When it receives a sudden check in its growth, the beetroot panics and sets seed in the year of sowing instead of waiting, as it should, until the following year. Thus, it becomes useless as an edible root. Too early sowing or placing the seedlings in cold or draughty conditions can produce the same result. A May sowing helps to avert this. So does regular hoeing of the beetroot bed, to raise moisture to the depth at which the roots quest for it. Do not counter possible drought by watering. Trust, instead, to the hoeing and to the correct observation of the moon quarters when preparing, feeding and sowing.**

attached to the parent root. [**Consideration:** *twisting off, not cutting off, eliminates bleeding and consequent loss of sap from the beetroot. Bleeding results in loss of flavour*]

31 consign the removed tops to the trench that awaits completion as a deep-trench bed (*BED/1*) or a shallow-trench bed (*BED/2*). [**Consideration:** *the standard practice is to compost the beetroots' redundant vegetation. The head gardener does not do so. He believes that the material almost certainly harbours pest. Also, it may carry the beginnings of disease — and not only disease related to the beetroot. These conditions may not be destroyed by the composting process. Better and safer, he is certain, to burn it, or to bury it and all that it may harbour, beneath either bed's dense filling*]

32 send the damaged roots to the kitchen for use or dispose of them securely

33 as soon as possible after lifting, pack the perfect beetroots for storage in layers in boxes. Place a thickness of dry peat or dry sand between the layers. It does not matter if the roots touch each other within the layers

34 lodge the filled boxes in a cold, dry, frost-free place. Expect the beetroots to store perfectly throughout the Winter and into the next Spring until March or April. Consume them as from the moment their storage begins

to reduce the risk of loss due to deterioration

35 as soon as the beetroots are out of the ground, fork over the empty beetroot section. Leave it thus for a day or two, so that the birds can investigate its insect life

36 by the time the October moon's third quarter ends, install in the defunct beetroot section and the associated other defunct sections fresh, single-dug (*BED/3*), shallow-trench (*BED/2*) or deep-trench (*BED/1*) beds. These are in readiness for the commencement of a new, four-year rotation cycle in accordance with the head gardener's crop-rotation programme.

for background information, see *FERTILISER, ROTATION, SOIL.*

CARROT — **preparation, sowing, management, harvesting, storage.** The head gardener produces the early carrot and the maincrop carrot for the duration of the growing season — March/April to August/ September — in its own section of his single-dug bed (*BED/3*), his deep-trench bed (*BED/1*) or his shallow-trench bed (*BED/1*) during the fourth and final year of these three bed's four-year life span of employment according to the R J Harris crop-rotation programme. The beds have borne crops during each of the previous three years. Their top soil has received major loosenings and, hence, fertility-enhancing aerations at least three times with spade and fork. Their manure content is more than three years old and, hence, almost fully dissipated. The well-worked top soil and the dissipated

REQUIRED FOR *CARROT*

- A section of a fourth-year *BED/1*, *BED/2* or *BED/3* for use as a carrot producer.

- 115g to the square metre of fish-blood-and-bone fertiliser, applied to the carrot section at **the start of the moon's fourth quarter** in the month preceding the month of carrot-seeds sowing.

- Early and maincrop carrot seeds, sown in the carrot section at **the start of the moon's first quarter in March, April, May, June and July**.

- *Orange King* or *Scotch Prize Calendula* pot marigold and spring onion seeds, sown in the carrot section as a carrot-fly preventative at **the start of the moon's second quarter** in the month of the carrot-seeds sowing.

- A hoe, leaf mould (if possible), a garden fork, a rake, a garden line, mint or thyme (if possible), a pressure spray, a filter, a 6mm garden sieve, a seeds dispenser, wood ash (if possible), garden labels, small bushy twigs, a compost bin or heap, a hand fork, boxes for root storage, dry sand or peat, a place to house boxes containing stored roots, a trench for a deep- or shallow-trench bed (if possible), end-of-row marker sticks.

manure render the fourth-year *BED/1*, *BED/2* and *BED/3* ideal for the growing of root crops.

Accompanying the carrot in the fourth-year *BED/1*, *BED/2* and *BED/3* are this manual's highlighted beetroot and parsnip, each in its own section.

Seeking the results with carrots that the head gardener achieves in the walled kitchen garden at Tresillian

1 at the earliest moment in the new season, acquire

— the seeds of the selected variety of early and maincrop carrots

— the seeds of any variety of spring onion

— the seeds of *Orange King* or *Scotch Prize* pot marigold, the packets of which are marked, usually, *Calendula*. If these varieties are not available, procure the seeds of any old-fashioned pot marigold

2 at **the start of the February moon's fourth quarter**, earmark for carrot development a section of one of the three fourth-year beds

3 make the carrot-section-to-be large enough, and appropriately positioned,

— to house the required number of carrot rows spaced 30cm from each other.
[***Consideration:*** *in ideal*

TIP 38

➔ **Lose the least possible time between carefully lifting the carrot crop and placing it between layers of material such as bone-dry sand or bone-dry peat in closed, stout boxes for storage. The aim is to give the roots no opportunity to suffer moisture evaporation and, hence, reduced flavour. Store dirty (but not earth-encrusted) roots, for best keepability.**

*weather/soil conditions,
five monthly carrot-seed
sowings in the one season
are expected. Hence, the
single monthly sowing is
not excessive. Probably, a
2m-long drill per month
provides a large enough
total crop* — or pro rata *if
the growing season starts
late due to adverse
weather/soil conditions*]

— to accept a four-sided,
right-angled border of a
single line of pot marigold
flowers around each
month's sowing of carrot
seeds. Each side of the
marigold-flower border
keeps a 50cm distance
from the nearest row of
carrots or nearest carrot-
row end

— to ensure that the section
provides easy access to
each of its four sides for
management and
harvesting. The access
acknowledges that
adjacent sections for
other crop production
exist, or are to exist,
within *BED/1, BED/2* or
BED/3

4 the February-initiated
carrot-section-to-be almost
certainly bears few Winter-
grown weeds. Remove these.
Use a garden fork. Dispose
of all of them off site.
[**Consideration:** *it could be
considered that these weeds
are too few in number to
merit the time that has to be
given to separation into
matter for composting and
matter for destruction.
However, if every available
scrap of vegetable matter is
prized for composting or
other re-use, find the time to*

22

The carrot fly and the parsnip fly are foes to be taken seriously. In the face of successful onslaughts of the grubs of these pests, many a gardener has given up trying to produce these two root crops.

Sending as many different signals as possible at the one time is the key to confusing and thus deterring the questing flies.

In addition to acting upon this section's suggestions, alternate carrot and parsnip rows in the one sowing. Their soil/nutritional/ management needs are almost identical. See *PARSNIP*.

*separate them and
apply/dispose of them
appropriately*]

5 a March- or April-initiated
carrot-section-to-be
(unfriendly weather/soil
conditions having enforced a
postponement of gardening)
almost certainly bears weeds
which have potential as
vegetation for re-use or
destruction. If so, remove
them. Use a garden fork to
do so

6 compost the annual weeds
that have not set seeds,
together with their roots. Or
place them in the trench
that awaits development into
a deep-trench bed (*BED/1*)
or shallow-trench bed
(*BED/2*), if there is one in
the garden

7 off site, destroy or dispose of
the annual weeds that have
set seeds, together with their
roots, the perennial weeds
and their roots, and the
grass growth and its roots

8 at the same time as de-weeding the carrot section-to-be, use the garden fork to level its surface. Break up the large clods formed by the use of a garden spade when the bed was Autumn-dug, and that have thwarted Winter's attempts to reduce them in size

9 ideally, dress the surface of the carrot-section-to-be with a thickness of fully-composted leaf mould. Turn it in to the depth of the garden fork. [**Consideration:** omit this if leaf mould is not available. With leaf mould, the resultant crop is a superior one]

10 follow by using a rake. Move the surface of the ground backwards and forwards with the rake's tines. Criss-cross it in the process. Use the full length of the rake's handle. Aim for a rake-tine depth of very coarse earth crumbs, evenly laid out

11 de-earth the rake frequently, to keep its tines unblocked

12 remove the stones that are trapped by the rake's unblocked tines. Store these for use in connection with other projects in the garden. [**Considerations: 1** — cost-conscious gardening aims always to conserve useful resources that may be difficult to obtain at some point in the future. Sometimes, stones are an irreplaceable ingredient in

23

The old-fashioned pot marigold (known as *Calendula*) furnishes more than protection against the carrot fly and a decorative, dark-eyed, deep-orange flower standing some 45cm high.

The petals of this hardy and extremely easily-grown plant decorate green salads beautifully (scatter them over — they are edible) and add a subtle orange-yellow tint to the baked rice pudding.

The Elizabethan gardeners were fond of it. So were the surgeons of their day. They used poltices of it to help to heal wounds.

The farmers' wives of the time coloured their cheeses with it.

garden projects, and merit the small amount of storage space that they occupy when conserved; **2** — the stones that slip through the rake's unblocked tines are of the size that is required by the soil. They are an aid to drainage. They act as a moisture-retaining mulch. At all times, but especially in Summer, they release during the night the heat that they absorb during the day, relatively warming the section and its contents; **3** — the stones that are gathered by the rake's regularly de-earthed tines are likely to be too large to be wanted in the soil; **4** — generally, if no stone removal is desired, use a hoe when a bed's surface is turned. The hoe's shape prevents it from gathering stones of any size]

13 still at **the start of the February moon's fourth quarter**, dress the surface of the rake-levelled carrot section with 115g to the square metre of fish-blood-and-bone fertiliser. Lightly rake it into the surface. Restore the level surface

14 achieve a less coarse tilth on the carrot section's surface. Do so on the morning of what promises to be a fine, dry day. Do so, also, by re-applying the rake if no other tool is available. Move its head in all directions methodically. Seek a greater breaking down of the coarse particles of surface earth

15 for a better, more easily achieved breaking down of the surface particles, use R J Harris's preferred five-tined cultivator. Do so as if it were a rake. Reduce the coarse crumbs of the soil to crumbs which are as fine as the five-tined cultivator is capable of producing. Whether a rake or a cultivator is applied, penetrate the surface with it as deeply as its tines permit. [*Consideration: of the many manually-operated cultivators that are available for this purpose, the head gardener uses the long-handled tool that has three, four or five long, curved tines. In the hands of a practised operator, the three-tined cultivator provides a coarse tilth, the four-tined a less coarse tilth, and the five-tined a fine tilth. Also, being much less prone to clogging and having far fewer and more widely-spaced tines than the rake, all three cultivators ignore the essential small stones that the initial raking leaves in situ*]

16 at **the start of the March moon's first quarter**, at a spot which is 50cm away

from — and parallel to — one edge of the carrot-section-to-be, position a garden line. It is as long as the intended first carrot row is long. Do so in the morning.
[*Consideration: the carrot seed gets its best start in comparatively warm soil. A drill opened in the morning and exposed to the sun and the air throughout the day becomes relatively warmed, helping to achieve the desired warm start*]

17 excavate a 12mm-deep drill, following the garden line. Do so with the edge of a hoe or with a suitable stick.
[*Consideration: achieving a drill that is 12mm (half an imperial inch) deep is not*

TIP 39
➔ **Monthly, from September to January, correctly fill two or three 25cm pots with John Innes No 2 potting compost. Moisten the compost correctly. Scatter the seeds of an early short (not long) carrot very thinly on its surface. Use a seed dispenser.** *Early Shorthorn* **is one of the head gardener's favourites for this purpose. Cover the seeds with a dusting of the compost, obtained by passing the compost through a 6mm-mesh sieve. Lodge the pots in a cold frame, a cold greenhouse or a conservatory. Protect the cold frame and the very small greenhouse against frost by day and/or by night. Keep the compost moist. Make a monthly chore of this and harvest finger-thick roots in time for and as from Christmas. Use them scrubbed clean and unscraped.**

24

The carrot has been known in Britain since the 1500s. It arrived from Afghanistan via Europe. Viewed by many as an annual plant, it is, strictly speaking, biennial. It belongs to the vast family of vegetables and flowers that begins as seeds in a given Spring and sets seeds in the following Spring.

It is with us in heavy disguise. The greengrocers of before the 1600s would not recognise today's roots; for them, the humble carrot was coloured purple, white or yellow. It was those master horticulturists, the Dutch, who recognised and seized the marketing opportunity presented by the colour that we know today. They were guided to it by the clog-shod gardener who espied and conserved an offspring of the purple root that had changed its complexion to deep orange.

The purples, the whites and the yellows have disappeared from the shops, and only where gardeners sow the seeds of these ancient roots is the secret of the coloured carrots preserved. These are the gardeners who know about Tuckers of Newton Abbot, one of Mr Harris's seed suppliers.

easy. The aim, for best results, is too shallow a drill rather than too deep a drill]

18 leave the drill open and unsown from morning until late afternoon.

19 ideally, just before sowing, spray the drill with a mint or thyme solution to help to deter the carrot fly. Make the solution by boiling a handful of chopped mint or thyme in a litre of water. Filter the resultant liquid when it is cold to remove the herb particles. Spray as a fine mist with a pressure spray.

*[**Considerations: 1** — omit this stage if neither herb is available; **2** — do not filter the solution if time presses or a pressure spray is not available. Fill a cup with the solution and gently discharge it along the length of the drill. Keep back as much as possible of the herb particles. If a few of these escape into the drill, no harm is done]*

20 still at **the start of the March moon's first quarter**, sow early carrot seeds into the drill in the late afternoon. Do so as sparsely as possible. Do not sow the seeds by hand. Use a dispenser obtained from a garden centre. Fill it from the packet without touching the seeds.

*[**Consideration:** fine seeds sown by hand are in risk of being crushed by the fingers.*

TIP 40
➔ **When a seed drill has been opened in readiness for sowing: 1) remove the garden line along which the drill has been traced; 2) insert a 30cm-long stick into the ground at each end of the open drill; 3) leave half of the stick showing above the surface; 4) sow the drill, 5) reinstate the drill. Later, place lines between the sticks over the invisible, sown seeds so as to know where not to ply the hoe if wanted seeds are not to be disturbed. Use the same technique when sowing seeds into dibbered holes.**

Crushed seeds are unlikely to germinate]

21 fill in the drill by hand with finely sieved earth. Ideally, do so with sieved earth in which one part of wood ash has been added to four parts of earth. Use a 6mm-mesh garden sieve.
[*Considerations:* **1** — *omit the wood ash if it is not available. With wood ash, the resultant crop is a superior one;* **2** — *omit the sieved earth, if time presses. Instead, move the in-situ soil back into the seed drill. Use a rake, with care*]

22 if more than one row of carrot seeds is sown, position them so that they are parallel to each other and spaced 30cm apart

23 mark one end of each row with a durable label. Note on it what has been sown and when. Mark both ends with a row-position marker stick

24 cover the row with a carefully-placed, loose layer of small, bushy twigs.
[*Consideration: the top growth of this early sowing is vulnerable to the early season's uncertain weather conditions. The twigs provide protection*]

25 at **the start of the March moon's second quarter**, position four garden lines around the March first-moon-quarter sowing. The lines form a right-angled box. The box's four sides are 50cm away from the nearest carrot row or carrot-row end. Site one of the two long sides of the box at the edge of the carrot section. Thus,

position it 50cm away from the established first carrot-seeds row

26 excavate a 12mm-deep drill, following the four garden lines. Do so with the edge of a hoe or with a suitable stick

27 station two pot marigold seeds in the drill at 15cm intervals. Use the finger tips to do so, with care. Touch these very large seeds as little as possible in order not to inhibit germination

28 when germination is achieved, do not thin the marigolds. Permit both seeds at each posting to reach maturity .
[*Consideration:* **1** — *these marigolds are very vigorous in germination and in growth. For this reason, the thinnest of sowings is required;* **2** — *the aroma of the marigolds helps to confuse and, thus, deter the carrot fly as it quests for egg-laying territory;* **3** — *ensure that the 50cm spacing from the nearest carrots is observed. This makes it unlikely that the fully-grown pot marigolds deprive the carrots of sunlight. Also, if*

TIP 41
➔ **Leaving mature carrots in the ground with the intention of lifting them as Autumn ends and Winter progresses is bad practice. Once September ends, the feathery, green carrot tops deteriorate rapidly and the roots cease to increase in size. They then split and are attacked by the hungry creatures of the soil and the garden.**

the marigolds flop, they do not damage the carrots' tops]

29 repeat the March carrot sowing in its entirety at **the start of the April moon's first quarter**. Use early carrot seeds

30 repeat the March marigold sowing at **the start of the April moon's second quarter**

31 relate the April carrot and marigold sowings to each other as when making the March carrot and marigold sowings

32 position and align the total April carrot-plus-marigold development so that it accompanies the March development in the carrot section and is located 10cm away from it.
[***Considerations: 1*** *— an important result of this is that, in due course, a double row of marigolds stands between the March sowing and the April sowing of early carrot seeds;* **2** *— the 10cm spacing between the two developments enables the double row of marigolds to reach maturity without undue crowding*]

33 comprehensively repeat the March and April developments in May, June and July

34 use maincrop carrot seeds for the May, June and July sowings. Do not protect the sowings with twigs. The protection is not necessary in these Summer months.
[***Consideration:*** *the overall end product of this at the height of the season is a*

visually attractive, fly-resistant single-row marigold perimeter encasing, at best, five monthly sowings of carrots divided one from the other by four double-row banks of marigolds. Abutting this overall development is an identical development of parsnips, if that crop is being grown]

35 from the earliest moment of sowing the carrot seeds, add a few spring onion and pot marigold seeds here and there to the surface of the empty ground between the carrot rows and between the carrot and marigold rows. Sow the spring onion seeds via a dispenser. Make these two sowings at **the start of each moon's second quarter**. Cover them with a dusting of soil first passed through a 6mm-mesh garden sieve.
[***Consideration:*** *this intermixed development helps to confuse further the carrot fly as it seeks egg-laying opportunities*]

TIP 42
➜ **If a February initiation of carrot development is not possible because of adverse weather or soil conditions, postpone activity until March or April. Overall, little is lost. In this event, be sure to observe:**
1) in the month of commencement, the start of the fourth moon quarter for feeding;
2) in the following month, the start of the first moon quarter for sowing the carrot seed;
3) the start of the second moon quarter for sowing marigolds and spring onions.

25

The head gardener counsels: "In the colder parts of the country, it pays to warm the area where the carrot seeds are to be sown. Do this as from the end of February."

Cloches can be used. Once the ground preparation has been completed, line them up over where the drills are to be made. Leave them in situ until the start of the March moon's first quarter. Then form the drills and sow.

"This is if soil and weather conditions permit," comments R J Harris.

Bad conditions may enforce a wait until March/April or even April/May.

"If a March sowing *is* achieved, leave the cloches on as the young plants grow. In this case, protective twigs over the drill are not necessary.

"Remove the cloches the moment warmer conditions arrive."

Cheaper (and safer, perhaps) than cloches incorporating glass panes is heavy-gauge, clear plastic sheet. Place a strip of this over each drill site. Use improvised, hooped wire supports to keep it from touching the earth's surface. This obviates condensation and, consequently, undesirable humidity between it and the earth's surface. Tuck the edges of the plastic strip into the soil to prevent wind lift.

Place the material over its hoops after sowing, until top growth insists that it be removed.

37 when, as the season progresses, germination of the carrot seeds takes place and there is visible growth above ground

— remove the now unnecessary protective, bushy twigs (the weather has improved), as these threaten to inhibit development

— examine the carrot section daily as the roots' green tops begin to appear. As the roots become crowded, extract every other one

— thin in this way with minimum disturbance to soil and to plants. Do so continuously throughout the season until a spacing between the maturing carrots of 5cm has been achieved. As the extracted young carrots become finger-thick, use them in the kitchen

— remove the carrot thinnings from site instantly, whether to the kitchen or to a secure disposal point. [**Consideration:** *the aroma created by the pulling of the young carrots attracts the carrot fly. So does the aroma of the thinnings when they are left lying on the ground. The less there is of this, the better. That is*

36 do not harvest the spring onions. Leave them in the section for as long as carrots are in situ and at risk, to retain the benefit of their anti-carrot-fly aroma

TIP 43
➜ **Decide at the outset whether to grow short or long carrots. Sow the seeds of the former in shallow soil, the seeds of the latter in deep soil.**

why, initially, sparse seed sowing is essential]

38 maintain hoeing throughout the season to prevent weed development and to raise residual moisture to where the developing roots await it

39 as the season progresses, harvest and consume the carrots before they reach full maturity. By this means completely clear and consume the early-carrot crop.
[*Consideration: this timing ensures roots of the best flavour and texture. Frequent test checks to ascertain root development are well worth the time spent making them. Also, the early, continuous removal of roots from the section reduces the impact of successful carrot-fly attack, and the severity of the attack*]

40 use a garden fork to loosen the soil before removing the carrots. This secures unbroken specimens and reduces carrot aroma

41 extract maincrop carrots for consumption as they approach maturity. Consume them when they are young rather than when they are fully grown

42 at **the start of the September moon's fourth quarter**, lift the whole of the carrot crop. Do so without root breakage, as far as possible. Use a garden fork.
[*Consideration: this moon quarter is when roots and tubers contain the least amount of moisture and, hence, are at their driest. This increases the length of*

their life during storage. The reduced moisture is caused by the falling water table. This falls during the moon's third and fourth quarters, reducing the moisture content of the top soil and of all that is in it]

43 clean the roots by lightly brushing the dried earth from them. Do not wash them

44 check that they show no tiny holes indicating the presence internally of carrot-fly grubs. Check, also, that there are no external traces of tunnelling by the grubs

45 withhold those that show these signs. Remove them and their tops from site and destroy them

46 de-leaf the retained, lifted carrots by cutting off or twisting off their tops. In each case, leave 5cm or so of the top growth attached to the parent root

47 consign the removed tops to the trench that awaits completion as a deep-trench bed (*BED/1*) or a shallow-trench bed (*BED/2*).
[*Considerations: 1 — at this time of the year — September/October — the carrot fly is no longer present*

TIP 44
➔ **Sow chives instead of pot marigolds as an anti-carrot-fly barrier, in the same defensive positions in relation to the drills of carrot seeds and at the second moon quarter. Hoe regularly, as advocated by R J Harris, to prevent the chives re-seeding themselves.**

*to be attracted. The
entrenched carrot tops are
buried beneath a depth of
other matter by the time the
pest re-appears in the
following late Spring; 2 —
the standard practice is to
compost the carrots'
redundant vegetation. The
head gardener does not do
so. He believes that the
material almost certainly
harbours pests. Also, it may
carry the beginnings of
disease — and not only
disease related to the carrot.
These conditions may not be
destroyed by the composting
process. Better and safer, he
is certain, to dispose of them
as suggested above]*

48 at the same time, uproot
and remove from the section
what is left of the marigold
and spring onion
developments. Compost
these or place them in the
trench that awaits
development into a deep-
trench bed (BED/1) or a
shallow-trench bed (BED/2)

49 send the damaged carrots to
the kitchen for use or for
secure disposal

50 pack the perfect, lightly de-
earthed carrots for storage
in layers in boxes. Place a
thickness of dry peat or dry
sand between the layers. It
does not matter if the roots
touch each other within the
layers

51 lodge the filled boxes in a
cold, dry, frost-free place.
Expect the carrots to store
perfectly throughout the
Winter and into the next
Spring until March or April.
Consume them as from the
moment their storage begins

to reduce the risk of loss of
roots due to deterioration

52 as soon as the carrots are
out of the ground, fork over
the empty carrot section.
Leave it thus for a day or
two, so that the birds can
investigate its insect life

53 by the time the September
or the October moon's fourth
quarter ends, install in the
defunct carrot section and
the associated other defunct
sections fresh, single-dug
(BED/3), shallow-trench
(BED/2) or deep-trench
(BED/1) beds. These are in
readiness for the
commencement of a new,
four-year rotation cycle in
accordance with the
requirements of R J Harris's
crop-rotation programme.

for background information, see
*BED/1 to -/3,
COMPOST: vegetable waste,
FERTILISER, MANURE, MOON,
ROTATION.*

COLD **FRAME.** In essence,
the cold frame — without
which R J Harris could not
function as a professional
horticulturist and could
not achieve the results
that he achieves on the Tresillian
estate — is an unheated, bottom-
less box made of timber or brick and
having a sloping, glazed lid which
can be raised fully to admit access to
the interior, or in stages to admit air.
The frame rests upon the earth in an
unshaded place and is angled so
that the slope of its lid faces south.
Usually, it is accompanied by an
immediately adjacent area of hard
standing for general working
purposes. This area can also
accommodate trayed, potted or
containerised plants when they are
removed from the frame in a planned

26

A sound, redundant, newly-puttied (if that is necessary) casement window can be the starting point in constructing a cost-cutting cold frame. Its size dictates the size of the area of the frame's top. That dictates the length of each of the cold frame's four sides.

If the window is equipped with its hinges, these are fastened to the rear of the frame's top. Otherwise, the cabin hooks and eyes noted in COLD FRAME are utilised.

sequence to accustom them to open-air conditions before they are planted out permanently.

In a cold frame 1) seeds sown in the earth base can be brought to seedling or plantlet stage prior to being planted out; 2) seeds sown in the earth base can be brought to maturity to provide a crop; 3) seeds sown in trays or pots can be brought to seedling or plantlet stage prior to being planted out in the open garden; 4) plants not native to the British Isles and removed from the open ground at the end of the season and potted can be protected from the elements during Winter.

A t Tresillian, in the walled kitchen garden, two cold frames are available to the head gardener and his staff.

Each is brick-built. It is about 10m long and about 1.5m wide. Its sloping, glass-glazed lid comprises twelve, 75cm-wide sections, each of which is hinged to the back of the frame and can be raised independently of the others for ventilation or access.

For the starting dates of each month's moon quarters see almost any diary — but it is essential to consult MOON first of all.

The interior of the cold frame offers an uninterrupted area of ground for seed sowing, planting out, the parking of pots and containers, and cultivation for specific purposes and plant developments "bearing in mind," the head gardener comments, "that when using the frames for the development of rooted plants, I observe the moon's quarters in the correct way."

The two Tresillian frames back onto the south-facing wall of the kitchen garden's heated greenhouse. In turn, this backs onto the south-facing, inner side of one of the garden's four perimeter walls.

T he head gardener recommends the following way to create a simple, low-cost, durable cold frame

1 construct a one-metre-square timber frame. Give it a 40cm high back and a 25cm high front. Use exterior-quality ply wood, planking or planed, tongued and grooved boards. Use timber strip positioned internally to join together the planks or boards and the four sides

2 for the cold frame's lid, use a sheet of translucent, rigid, plastic sheeting of a size to

TIP 45
➔ **The watering of the cold frame's contents is done first thing in the morning. Not at the end of the day (as is good practice in the open garden). Watered at the end of the day, the plants inside the frame endure a night of unrelieved wet and cold, especially when the lid is closed. It does them no good at all, advises the head gardener.**

27

The head gardener favours a simple refinement to the home-made cold frame.

"Build a deep frame," he suggests, "and fill it with a depth of 30cm-to-45cm of home-made compost to within about 30cm of its top at the front."

He makes the compost by mixing together three parts of top soil from the garden, one part of sand and two parts of fully-composted leaf mould. First, he removes the large stones, weed growth and rubbish from the top soil.

He stifles the weed-seed content of the garden soil by covering the mixture when it is in the deep frame with a 10cm layer of John Innes No 2 potting compost.

Seeds can be sown directly into the John Innes.

Such a frame, Mr Harris believes, is of benefit especially to the gardener whose bending and stooping days are in the past. A very wide range of plants can be developed (albeit it in limited numbers), thanks to the controlled protection that the lid makes possible. Another advantage, he finds, is that — easily and at low cost — the John Innes compost can be replaced with fresh compost when necessary.

"Sprinkle the removed, redundant compost as thinly as possible on the garden's beds," he advises.

more than cover the cold frame's top by 5cm all round

3 screw a 5cm-wide timber-strip edging to the perimeter of one face of the plastic sheet

4 join the timber-strip edging together at each of its four corners by affixing a galvanised or brass flat, metal, L piece

5 throughout, use galvanised or brass screws (preferably) or galvanised nails. Favour the Pozidrive screw with the Philips head over the old-fashioned, slotted-head screw. Use a powered screwdriver, if one is available

6 position the lid on the cold frame's top so that its timber-strip edging is underneath.
[*Consideration:* *thus, rain water runs off the plastic sheet without being impeded by — and, possibly, adversely affecting — the timber-strip edging. Also, the edging forms a seal around the top of the cold frame*]

7 'hinge' the lid to the cold frame's back with two galvanised or brass cabin hooks and eyes. Secure it at the front when it is fully closed by two more cabin hooks and eyes. Fasten the hooks to the timber edge of

TIP 46
➔ **Seen in a 'Yellow Book' garden: a timber-built cold frame made portable by the addition at its back and its front of carrying arms. These were two lengths of screwed-on timber strip the ends of which extended beyond the frame's sides by some 45cm. Thus, two people were provided with convenient handles. The owner claimed that a removable frame provided her with more scope in her very small garden.**

28

The head gardener's lifetime of horticulture has taught him, among many things, that the places where plants are developed and managed can be places of unexpected and, sometimes, alarming hazards. The home-made cold frame offers a case in point.

"Glass *can* be used instead of rigid plastic for the lid," he notes. "In some places it is more easily obtained.

"I do not recommend it.

"It complicates the construction method. More seriously, imagine anyone being unlucky enough to fall upon the lid and crashing through it."

The head gardener suggests that if only glass can be used its external face be covered with fine-mesh wire netting.

"Stretch it tautly in both directions," he recommends. "Wrap it around the lid's edges and fasten it securely to the underneath of the lid's timber frame.

"It prevents the glass from caving in in the event of the worst happening."

the lid. Screw the eyes into the timber body of the cold frame

8 before bringing lid and frame together, paint all of the timber surfaces with as many coats of exterior-quality, glossy white paint as patience and resources permit. [*Consideration: this is both to preserve the timber and to concentrate and reflect as much light as possible within and around the cold frame*]

9 position the completed cold frame in an unshaded place, with the downward slope of its glazed lid facing south

10 position it, also, adjacent to the garden's greenhouse, if there is one. Do so on the greenhouse's south side. [*Considerations: 1 — this obviates the taking of plants over a distance when they are transferred from cold frame to greenhouse, or from greenhouse to cold frame; 2 — it is more than solely a fatigue-relieving measure on behalf of the gardener, in that plants suffer when removed from one level of ambient temperature to another. This kind of changed condition must be experienced by them for the shortest possible time*]

11 ideally, but not essentially, establish the cold frame upon a metre square rectangle of bricks set into the earth, so that the bottom edges of the frame's four timber sides are not in contact with the earth. There is no need to mortar the bricks together. Line them up close together, so that as little draught as

TIP 47

➔ **Today's DIY materials, tools and skills render it possible for the cold frame to be made in any width, any length. Necessarily, the large structure must have a large lid requiring a stout timber frame. The lid is, as a result, heavy. When very large, it can be too heavy for one person to raise. Also, as a result, it may be unsafe. The limitation must be borne in mind at the design stage.**

possible is admitted into the frame's interior

12 also ideally, but not essentially, place a strip of damp-proof course material between the brick course and the lower edges of the cold frame's timber walls

13 provide props to support the frame's lid at its two front corners when it is raised. Cut them from strip timber. Make a range of props making possible air-admitting openings beginning at 2cm wide and advancing in 2cm stages to 30cm wide. Beyond this width, the lid is raised fully (or removed entirely) to facilitate access to the frame's interior.

‛This is the cold frame for the gardener whose skills do not include brick laying," comments Mr Harris.

"Most professional frames are of brick construction throughout. Brick provides the longer life and does not have timber's need for pre-use painting and sustained maintenance throughout the frame's life.

"Moreover, in most professional gardens, the greenhouse has a brick-wall base. That becomes the back wall of the brick-built cold frames when they are attached to it. So there is an economy as well."

IN the days when the greenhouse was heated by water pipes, the attached cold frames were converted into hot frames by switching them, at will, into the heating system. This was achieved, simply, by directing the run of the pipes through the heated greenhouse's wall into the frames at ground level and then back into the greenhouse.

The head gardener recommends

that when the home-made cold frame is in use — however it is constructed — the exterior of its body and both sides of its glazed lid be kept clean.

"Equally," he adds, "always have a couple of clean sacks or a piece of redundant carpet ready to drape over the frame to guard its contents against the frost.

"Keep these where they can be found rapidly and with ease," he advises.

"Many a plant has been lost to Jack Frost because improvising or searching for coverings takes too long. "

COMFREY/1 — growing comfrey and managing mature comfrey plants, beginning with bought, potted plantlets. For the annual feed needs of the average size of garden, suggests the head gardener

1 purchase five or six potted comfrey plantlets in any month that they are available. Ideally, acquire them as early in the year as possible, to give them the longest possible initial growing period prior to their first Winter in the ground

2 at **the start of the moon's second quarter —** immediately prior to planting out the comfrey plantlets — stand the pots in water for at least two hours. Do so towards the end of the day.
[*Consideration: this timing represents good practice when inserting any plant into the garden soil. The plant has the whole, cool night in front of it in which to recover from the trauma of transplantation. Moisture evaporation is at its least, so*

there is maximum moisture in the soil. This is enhanced by the chosen moon time, at which the moisture content of the soil is at its greatest volume]

3   decide to insert the comfrey plantlets either

— dotted haphazardly around the garden, using unoccupied or unusable corners in which they will not offer competition to existing developments

or

— 45cm apart in a single row in a 45cm-wide bed. Establish the bed where ground is used most economically — eg, at the foot of a between-gardens fence. The fence is low in height and of open structure in order not to reduce received sunlight and rain

4   overall, this order of site

— simplifies management

— provides the garden with a development of interesting foliage

— produces an associated, repeated show of wild-flower blossom. This helps to draw in the bees and the other plant pollinators

5   whether the young comfrey is in 'natural' or regimented formation, choose damp ground that is sunlit for most of the day and is well exposed to the rain. [*Considerations:* **1**— *if damp ground is not available, select places at*

REQUIRED FOR *COMFREY/1*

- Five or six bought, potted comfrey plantlets, inserted into damp, sunny, deep-soiled locations at **the start of the moon's second quarter** during the evening.

- Liquid manure, applied on or about the **start of the moon's fourth quarter** during the evening.

- Comfrey solution (1 part of comfrey stock to 40 parts of water).

- A trowel, a hand fork, a garden fork, a watering can with water, a seep hose (if possible), garden shears, commercial dried manure such as 6X (if possible), a wheelbarrow.

For the complete instruction, see *COMFREY/1* to -/3.

---

which routine watering is carried out easily. Being 95% water, comfrey repays handsomely when moistened regularly; **2** — *if a seep hose is in situ, extend it to the bed of the new plants and turn it on regularly by night for an*

TIP 48

➔   **Ideally, cut the comfrey for stock making early in the growing season, in early June or July and before the plants begin to flower. This ensures that young leaves and stems are put to work. Make a practice of this until sufficient stock is being 'brewed'. "The older leaves and stems** *can* **be converted, even when the plant is flowering," advises Mr Harris, "but you need young growth for the best quality of stock."**

29

Fully-established comfrey grows prolifically in one spot for twenty to thirty years. Its leaves begin to shoot in April. They die down in October. In between, they and their stems can be cut to ground level as often as they regenerate: three or four times annually. Thus, given a sufficient number of harvestable plants, three or four 'makes' of head gardener R J Harris's comfrey stock are possible each year.

Most garden centres offer young comfrey. Mail-order requests are met by an increasing number of specialist firms. These include Chase Organics and Suffolk Herbs (see SUPPLIERS).

"Garden fetes and charity plant sales almost always feature a representative or two," says R J Harris.

hour or two to create the constantly damp conditions in which comfrey thrives]

6 before planting, do not prepare the ground in any way. Merely divest it of weed growth and loosen its surface with a garden fork to the depth of the fork

7 to plant out, take each well-watered comfrey plantlet in its pot and

— excavate an approximately pot-size, pot-shape hole in the appropriate place. Use a trowel

— place one of the pots in the hole. Take care not to damage its occupant

— adjust the depth of the hole so that the pot's rim levels with the surrounding ground surface

— firm the earth around the pot

— remove the pot, with care and still safeguarding its plantlet. Leave a pot-shaped, pot-sized hollow in the ground

— loosen the earth at the base of the hollow. Use a hand fork. [*Consideration: this prevents poor drainage. Poor drainage results in accumulated water, which is anathema to the plantlets' roots*]

— working as close as possible to the waiting hollow, place a potted plantlet upright in the palm of one hand

— place the fingers of the other hand over the top of

TIP 49

➜ **The best comfrey stock 'brewer' is a plastic rain-water butt raised above ground level and equipped with a tap. The raised position facilitates the placing of a bucket on the ground beneath the tap to collect the drawn-off stock. When the tap is opened, a gauze filter affixed within the butt withholds the comfrey debris and the coarser particles of saturated plant matter. Usually, further filtering of the drawn liquid is necessary if watering-can-rose or pressure-spray blockage is to be avoided.**

30

THE herb that the Cornish head gardener converts into an organic nitrogen- and potash-rich plant food at no financial cost is at once easy and difficult to grow.

It is easy in that, being its own master — as well as one of Nature's almost incontestable survivors — it establishes itself, develops, thrives and creates an ever-extending family with help from nobody. Indeed, once arrived in a garden and having decided that it likes where it is, it stays, almost no matter what is done to see it on its way. Only the removal from the soil of every last scrap of its roots (not the least arduous of undertakings) brings an end to its life.

It is a difficult plant to grow in that, left to its own devices, it will offer its unmatchable endowments of cost-free nutrients only when the constantly damp and sun-drenched conditions that it prefers are there to provide it with habitat.

Its home from home is what R J Harris refers to as marginal land. This is land that fringes areas of water. The properties the head gardener manages horticulturally in Cornwall have a great deal of it, being endowed with lakes and ponds. By that token, they play host to a great deal of self-sown (as well as head-gardener-sown) comfrey. Additionally, the walled garden possesses a bed of some 25 mature plants. These cater for the needs of an acre of productive ground.

Few of today's gardens offer such potential. In these, usually — and for best results — the conditions have to be created and maintained. This calls for the simplest of procedures.

the pot. Spread the fingers, so that they pass around the stem of the plantlet. By this means avoid touching and possibly damaging what is the plant's most sensitive feature —
which, if harmed, will incur death for the plantlet

— grip the top of the pot with the tips of the spread fingers. Turn the pot upside down

— supporting the surface of the compost, still with the fingers spread out to avoid touching the comfrey plantlet's stem, permit the pot's contents to slide out slowly. If necessary, initiate this

and encourage it to happen by first tapping the upturned base of the pot gently once or twice

— hold and support the pot-shaped, glistening compost root ball upside down in the palm of one hand. Place the empty pot

TIP 50
➜ "Comfrey has a rough, ragged underneath to its leaves, rather like sand paper," notes R J Harris. "Wear gloves when handling the plant. And grow it where bare legs and arms will not brush against it, especially if children use the garden as a playground. Bear in mind, in this respect, that, when in flower, comfrey is regularly alive with bees."

to one side with the other

— using both hands, turn the compost root ball upright. Do so with utmost gentleness and without compressing it. Immediately slip the root ball into the waiting hollow. It fits the hollow perfectly

31

The bees love comfrey. Its misty-blue blossom draws them into the garden, with benefit to the other blossom that requires pollination.

"No walled garden is complete without bee hives and their busy workers, and I have two swarms, which have been here at Tresillian for many years," says head gardener R J Harris.

"Doing a useful job with them are the many wild bees, which live in the beech trees just outside the walled garden."

— gently firm in the compost root ball. Depress its surface slightly below that of the surrounding ground in order to create a rain-collecting depression

— use the emptied pot as a form when transplanting the remaining four or five plantlets

8 immediately after installation is complete, water the plantlets' sites thoroughly. Use a can with a medium rose

9 for the first two years of the plants' lives do not harvest their leaves and stems. Permit their root systems to become established without above-the-ground loss. Pluck off any blossom that develops during this initial period, to encourage maximum development

10 at the end of year one and of year two, permit the comfrey's top growth to die down and return to the soil

11 in year three, harvest for stock-making for the first time. Cut at ground level. Use garden shears

12 harvest annually thereafter as soon as the leaves and stems are sufficiently developed for stock making or for adding to the compost bin or heap or to the trench that awaits development into a deep-trench bed (BED/1) or a shallow-trench bed (BED/2)

13 for hastened leaf/stem development, give each plant a feed of liquid manure at the beginning of the season. Repeat this monthly, ideally during the evening at **the start of the moon's fourth quarter**

TIP 51
➔ **Place comfrey leaves and stems in a garden bucket and cut through them, repeatedly, with very sharp hedge shears. In a surprisingly short space of time, the bucket contains milled comfrey matter that is ideal for conversion into comfrey stock.**

14 make the liquid manure by mixing a cup or two of proprietary dried manure into a standard garden bucket of water. Allow the mixture to rest for an hour or two before use, to ensure the total absorption of the dried manure into the water. [*Consideration:* comfrey *prefers poultry manure. 6X, being the dried product of chicken runs, is ideal for this purpose (see SUPPLIERS). Before applying the liquid manure, water the plants' positions or bed well. Pre-water and feed in the cool of the end of the day*]

15 after year three of the plants' lives, when comfrey solution becomes available due to the availability of comfrey vegetable matter, either

— use comfrey-strengthened water each time the plants are watered. Produce this in the ratio of one part of comfrey stock to eighty parts of water.
[*Consideration:* watering *and feeding in this way is not moon-oriented. "Watering," comments R J Harris, "is an on-going process"*]

or

— if the watering is done via a seep hose, apply comfrey-strengthened water manually in the ratio 1:40. Do so monthly, at **the start of the moon's fourth quarter**

16 in October of year three, and each October thereafter, cut the plants at ground level. Transfer their season-weary

---

32

'Comfrey solution has advantages over and above the fundamental advantage that so many plants flourish when fed on it — especially, as example, tomato plants," says R J Harris. "It costs nothing to produce. It is organic. It is available, given the appropriate production programme, in unlimited supply. Made in volume, it is available on demand. Producing it requires little more than a modicum of the gardener's time, water and one or two readily-available utensils. "Its source, the herb comfrey, is of benefit to the garden as a whole."

---

leaves and stems to the compost bin or heap or to the trench for a *BED/1* or *BED/2*, if there is one in the vegetable garden

17 de-weed around the cut-down plants. Recycle or destroy the resultant annual and perennial weeds appropriately and correctly.

for background information, see
MOON, SUPPLIERS.

COMFREY/2 — **growing comfrey and managing mature comfrey plants, beginning with root cuttings.** For the annual needs of the average size of garden, R J Harris recommends

1 insert into the ground two purchased, potted, comfrey plantlets. Bring them to the third season of their adulthood as described in *COMFREY/1*

REQUIRED FOR *COMFREY/2*

● One or two bought, potted comfrey plantlets, to develop to season three maturity as described in *COMFREY/1*.

● Root cuttings, obtained from the bought plants at the end of season three at **the start of the moon's second quarter** at the end of the day — for immediate planting out.

● Liquid manure, water, a watering can, garden shears, hand fork, a sharp knife, a firm surface upon which to cut.

For the complete instruction, see *COMFREY/1* to *-/3*.

2 in their third season, do not take their leaves and stems. Permit them to grow to full height and to bear full blossom until they fade in October or November

3 harvest the top growth for the compost bin or heap or the trench that awaits development into a *BED/1* or a *BED/2*, if there is one in the garden. Cut at ground level with garden shears

4 dig up the roots of the two comfrey plants. Extract the whole root in each case, leaving nothing in the ground.
[***Consideration:*** *overlooked scraps of root are likely to become mature plants in the wrong place.*]

5 take this step, ideally

— at **the start of the moon's second quarter**

— in the cool of the end of the day

6 immediately divide the roots into sections. Use a very sharp knife. Cut on a firm surface. Make sure that each section carries a point which, clearly, is destined to produce new leaves. Expect to glean five or six usable sections in total

7 immediately, plant the root sections in their permanent home. Their growing points are uppermost and just beneath the surface of the ground. Water well

8 in deciding where to plant the root sections, and in managing them once they are planted, treat them as potted plantlets are treated when permanently inserted into the ground. This is explained in *COMFREY/1*.

for background information, see
MOON, SUPPLIERS.

C **OMFREY/3 — making comfrey stock, for dilution into comfrey solution.** For the annual feed needs of the average size of garden

1 ideally, harvest the ready comfrey leaves and stems at **the start of the moon's third quarter**.
[***Consideration:*** *this is when the leaves and the stems are most charged with sap, due to the water table being at its highest level and, hence, creating the greatest moisture content in the top soil and all that grows in it*]

2 cut the comfrey material at ground level with garden

REQUIRED FOR *COMFREY/3*

• Shredded comfrey, cold water, a non-metallic container, garden shears, a garden bucket, a wooden stick, a watering can, a means of filtering comfrey stock.

For the complete instruction, see *COMFREY/1* to *-/3*.

shears. Leave tidily decapitated plants. Do not pull off or break off the vegetable matter, for the affected plants' sake

3 shred the leaves and stems, or break or cut them up into small pieces

4 place one kilo weight of plant matter and eleven litres of cold rain or tap water in a non-metallic container. [*Considerations:* **1** — *a widely-available, suitable container is an 80-litre plastic dustbin with a lid. It retails for about £5;* **2** — *a plastic container is a 'must'. A metal container is adversely affected by the chemical content of the comfrey stock*]

5 repeat, until the container is filled with herb and water, or until the current supply of the herb comes to an end

6 put on the container's lid, to exclude the light and to prevent the accidental drowning of local fauna. Leave the contents to 'brew' for at least one calendar month

7 date the container, so that it is known when the calendar month has elapsed

8 stir the 'brew' occasionally, as the month passes. Use a wooden stick

9 to make comfrey solution, mix one part of the resultant stock to eighty parts of cold water. Strain the stock beforehand, to remove the comfrey debris

---

33

Comfrey feed is neither a plant drug nor a plant medicine. Neither is it a deficiency corrective. If used as such — that is, from time to time in large quantities of great strength — it is ill-used and, probably, the plants involved have been ill-planted and/or ill-managed.

Rather, the head gardener points out, his recommended 1:80 dosage is applied every time water is applied in response to a plant's declared need for moisture.

"So for all the time it drinks it gets a tiny supplement of diet-improving nutrients," he says. "Your reward is plants that are fully healthy throughout their lifespan and, thus, have the maximum opportunity to fulfil their potential."

Sometimes, the rewards can be greater than that.

"Tomatoes are a case in point," says R J Harris. "For tomato plants that are well and truly established and up and running and taking in a great volume of liquid, step up the comfrey-feed ratio to 1:30.

"The result is better plants and a better crop — and grown organically."

10 apply the solution from a watering can equipped with a rose. Do so directly onto the plants' leaves, as a foliage feed, or onto the soil at the base of the plants' stems, as a general moisturiser. Do so in the cool of the evening, to avoid the risk of scorching the watered plants' leaves

11 apply the comfrey stock plus water (1:80) to the plants that benefit by it each time that watering is done. Watering in this way is not moon-oriented

12 when applying comfrey solution as a feed (1:40) and not as a general-purpose moisturiser, do so at **the start of the moon's fourth quarter**

13 awaiting use, the comfrey stock remains in its container. It does not deteriorate when kept thus

---

34

LIKE the Mexican marigold, comfrey stock, derived from the comfrey plant, is one of R J Harris's horticultural tools. Added in homoeopathic quantities to the water that is used for routine watering, it turns watering into the gentlest, most sustained of organic feeding. By means of it, balancing levels of potash, nitrogen and trace elements are supplied to Tresillian's soft-fruit and flower producers throughout the season. The head gardener has found over many years that the treatment is ideal, especially, for geraniums and hanging baskets, and for tomatoes, onions and the bean family.

35

Comfrey emigrated to North America from Britain in the 1600s and quickly populated that continent. Long before that, It was brought to Britain's monastery herb gardens by the Crusaders, who discovered its healing properties, along with many other useful things, in its Middle East homeland. It became known as Saracen's Root; it was valued, medicinally, as a tea to treat colds and bronchitis and as a poultice to aid the mending of broken bones (hence its mediaeval name: 'Knit-bone').

"The Elizabethan herbalists and physicists were never without it," comments R J Harris.

"It was being prescribed right up to Victorian times — and, of course, the Victorian gardeners knew us much as we do, and more, probably, about its horticultural applications."

---

beyond its four weeks' 'brewing' period

14 end the growing season with a fully-charged container of comfrey stock, so that the feed can be applied the moment watering begins in the following Spring. [*Consideration: Spring is*

TIP 52

➔ "Do not grow comfrey in a container," warns R J Harris. "Most containers are too small to accommodate the herb's extensive root system. The result would be a tortured plant. And a container large enough to accommodate the plant's roots adequately would impose well nigh unmeetable manual watering demands."

when the comfrey plants are not sufficiently advanced to be ready for cutting.]

for background information, see
MOON.

COMPOST: *John Innes/1 — types.* There are five types of the John Innes compost, all of them manufactured commercially and available at the horticultural retail outlets, and used by head gardener R J Harris. They are

● the **JI seed compost**
● the **JI No 1 potting compost**
● the **JI No 2 potting compost**
● the **JI No 3 potting compost**.
● the **JI ericaceous compost**

Mr Harris sows almost all of his seeds in the **seed compost**. It provides just enough goodness for germination and for the development of the seedlings' 'baby' leaves.

He uses it, also, for rooting soft cuttings.

It comprises approximately

— 2 parts of loam
— 1 part of sphagnum moss peat,
— 1 part of coarse sand or grit
— fertilisers selected to ensure that the whole equals an authorised nutritional standard.

In general, Mr Harris transplants seedlings and rooted cuttings from the seed compost to the **JI No 1 potting compost,** then to the **JI No 2 potting compost,** and then to the **JI No 3 potting compost**. Some plants find a permanent place, in doors or out of doors, in containers filled with the **JI No 2** or the **JI No 3** potting compost. Others find a permanent home in the garden soil having completed the progression from the **JI No 2** or the **JI No 3** potting compost.

36

For R J Harris, seeds in trays or pots develop most surely into seedlings, seedlings in trays or pots most surely into plantlets, and permanently-potted or containerised plants most surely into life-long healthy beings when they draw their sustenance from the commercially-manufactured medium known as compost — given, that is, the appropriate ambient temperature, amount of sunlight, degree of moisture and location.

The proprietory compost brings, also, an environment that is weed-free (until it is contaminated by exposure to uncontrolled conditions).

The Cornish head gardener's experience leads him to an even more specific conclusion: the most effective of what the uninitiated see as a confusion of branded, garden-centre-available composts are those that bear the name John Innes. These — to pinpoint but one of their many desirable features — are based upon what professionals and packaging refer to as loam and most non-gardeners as soil or earth.

In Mr Harris's view, the specially-treated loam/soil/ earth that is an ingredient of the John Innes composts performs better than the peat that is the principal ingredient of the myriad of non-John Innes composts.

All depends upon the individual plant's appetite, identity and allotted place in the head gardener's overall horticultural plan.

The **JI No 1, JI No 2** and **JI No 3** potting composts consist of approximately

37

'**B**ACK in the 1950s," recalls R J Harris, "when I was an apprentice and every major nursery made its own John Innes composts — and when today's peat-based composts were only just beginning to be heard of — I had to get to work at 5.30 every morning to start up a great big old horizontal boiler to get ready to sterilise the loam that was going to be used in the John Inneses

"First, I had to scrape the clinker out of the fire box, and then I had to light the fire with the kind of steam coal that was used for the railway steam engines of the day.

"It was not until after 8 o'clock that the fire was really going. That was when I took a long-handled, specially-polished shovel I kept for the purpose and put a couple of eggs and rashers of bacon on it and held it over the fire and that was my breakfast.

"The fire box was in two parts, so we could clear out and relight one part while the other was still burning.

"Steam at 180°F or 240 psi was required. Twenty minutes of this saw six level wheel-barrow loads of loam sterilised in a metal container that was attached to the boiler. There were several containers. We emptied one while two or three others were still operating. We kept at it all day."

The loam that the young Harris and his fellow apprentices barrowed and shovelled, paced by the boiler's demands, started out as turfs cut from a selected field of grass and stored in a rick. The rick stood for a year. It was then broken down and forced through a 12cm riddle to remove stones, hard material and surviving roots.

After sterilisation, the loam was combined with peat, sand or grit, lime and fertilisers and passed through a smaller riddle.

"Every single thing we produced each year— thousands of pot plants, tomato plants and cucumber plants, and a million lettuce plants — was grown in one form of John Innes compost or another.

"The sterilisation removed weeds, fungal diseases and soil-borne creatures — all those undesirables that make it impossible to guarantee cost-efficient plant operation and a perfect result in wholesale-trade volumes.

"It goes on today. You will not find anything growing in Nature's untouched soil wherever you go in commercial, greenhouse-based horticulture."

— 7 parts of loam
— 3 parts of sphagnum moss peat
— 2 parts of coarse sand or grit
— fertilisers selected to ensure that the composts equal an authorised nutritional standard.

The presence of loam in all five of the John Innes composts must be emphasised. No other commercially-produced compost is distinguished by this feature.

The head gardener itemises as follows the advantages that spring from the loam's inclusion, and from the general character of the John Innes composts

1 compared to peat (the main constituent of non-loam-based, non-John-Innes composts) loam has the better 'body'. For this reason, it provides a firmer

A 38

Mr J Innes started it all. He lived in the 1800s, an extremely wealthy property and land speculator who, when he died, bequeathed everything he possessed to furthering the improvement of horticulture. An horticultural research institute was the outcome of this generosity, named after him. In the 1930s it started out to rationalise and improve what was then an impossibly numerous and diverse range of manufactured composts — most of them, by today's standards, the product of inadequate horticultural understanding and undesirable manufacturing processes. The John Innes loam-based composts resulted. They gained added significance in connection with food production during the war years of the 1940s. More than half a century later, the Institute, based, as it now is, at Norwich, continues to express its founder patron's belief in research and experimentation.

4 the peat content of the John Innes products combines with the loam and the grit content to give greater water-holding capacity and better drainage. Hence, with John Innes, under- or over-watering is not the calamity that it can be. "To the busy head gardener — who can be as forgetful or as distracted as anyone else — that can be both a reputation saver and a plant saver," comments R J Harris

5 since the loam-based John Innes composts absorb liquids readily, there is either no run-off or hardly any at all when liquid is applied to them slowly and in a controlled manner. Thus, there is almost no loss of applied liquid and no accompanying wetted surface. In this, too, there may be a financial economy: the applied liquid may be an expensive liquid feed

6 the loam-based compost is of help when feeding is delayed. It sustains plant life longer than does the peat-based compost, because the loam contains natural nutrients. It releases these as the plants rooted in the host compost require them

hold when the compost of which it is a part has a cane or a stick thrust into it to support a plant

2 by the same token, loam's 'body' provides a more secure anchorage than does peat for the tall or big-waisted plant that has to spend its life in a container

3 loam takes up water more readily than does peat, and so a container of loam-based compost that has dried out can be re-wetted more quickly and more thoroughly

TIP 53
➔ **The John Innes No 1, No 2 and No 3 potting composts contain lime. Do not use them for lime-hating plants such as heathers, azaleas and rhododendrons. For this kind of plant, buy the compost the plastic-bag container of which bears the words John Innes Ericaceous Compost.**

39

THE association that represents Britain's five John Innes producers issues to garden centres, DIY and hardware stores and other retail outlets the following display and storage instructions:

- *Keep the bags dry and cool*
- *Store them indoors*
- *If stored outside, keep them out of direct sunlight*
- *If stored outside, keep them sheltered from the rain — otherwise, they absorb the rain through their air holes*
- *If stored outside, site them against a north-facing wall*
- *If stored outside, keep them under a canopy or a roof*
- *Cover them with white or light-coloured plastic sheeting to keep them dry — not black sheeting*
- *Stack the bags on pallets or above ground level*
- *Stack them so that air can circulate within and between them*
- *Never stack new deliveries on top of old stock*
- *Rotate the stock*
- *Keep the bags at a distance from heat.*

Behind these strictures is the association's awareness that as manufactured composts age they experience a natural and to-be-expected process of deterioration — all of them, not solely the John Innes composts.

This reality is not to be seen as a product weakness. Given the composition of composts and their purpose, there would be cause for concern if the opposite were the case.

7 the loam that forms the greater part of the John Innes compost is heat-pasteurised. Thus, it is free from weeds, insects and disease

8 the fertilisers with which the John Innes composts are enriched include

- phosphates, for root growth
- nitrogen, for top growth
- potash, for flowering and fruiting
- trace elements, for colour and flavour

9 the John Innes numbers — 1, 2 and 3 — refer to the levels of the nutrients that are present in the composts. The **JI No 1** potting compost has the least amount, whilst the **JI No 3** potting compost has the greatest amount

10 on average, each of the John Innes composts, used correctly, provides sufficient plant food to last for one to two months. After that, usually, a liquid feed is required. The head gardener's preferred feed for this purpose is his own make of comfrey solution, derived from his own make of comfrey stock, which is derived from his own cultivation of the herb comfrey.

If further explanation is required, e-mail R J Harris on *rjh@moongardening.fsnet.co.uk*

40

The sparetime gardener might well wonder: "Why should I use a manufactured compost which costs good money when Nature has provided me with free top soil and a strong, trowel-wielding arm?"

"The answer, in the spirit of true horticulture, lies in the soil," comments R J Harris, "which contains just about every natural thing that sees sown seeds and potted/containerised plants as its rightful prey."

Probably, also, the head gardener points out, Nature's loam does not offer the properties that protect and nourish chosen seeds and plants. That is not the case with the manufactured soil-based composts.

Used correctly, these can do nothing other than encourage germination, support plant development and ensure maximum plant lifespan.

"The money spent on them is recovered in time and seeds saved, in flourishing plants and in protected reputation," says the head gardener.

COMPOST: *John Innes/2 — purchasing.* In the garden centres and the other retail outlets for gardeners, the John Innes composts are available in plastic bags. They range from the easily-carried-in-the-one-hand, 5-litre pack to the largest 25-kilo pack, which is most sensibly moved on a trolley.

All manufactured composts are far from ever-lasting. In addition, they are in risk of being displayed for sale in conditions that do not maintain to the maximum their nutritional and other qualities.

For this reason, the association that represents Britain's John Innes producers, and imposes standards upon them, takes an undisguised interest in the retailers' storage and display conditions. Arising out of this, it recommends for their use a well-publicised code of conduct.

Sell-by dates have not been adopted by the producers of the John Innes composts. It is left to the retail customer to make sure that a purchase is not a carry-over from a previous season's stock.

The association of John Innes compost makers requires that a batch number be shown on each bag of product.

With its help, a particular bag's history can be ascertained should queries arise.

COMPOST: *vegetable waste.* On the Tresillian estate, the voluminous quantities of mixed vegetable waste — including annual weeds that have not gone to seed plus their roots, but excluding perennial weeds and their roots and annual weeds in seed and their roots — is composted in uncontained

---

TIP 54
➔ Whatever the type or grade of manufactured compost that is used, do as R J Harris does and close its plastic bag tightly to keep it moist and to prevent contamination. "Its soil sterilisation must not be lost," Mr Harris warns. "Equally, keep it inside and away from any source of heat, and away from weed killers. Do not keep it from one season to the next. Age is more than likely to disturb the balance of its nutrients. If out-of-season compost is on hand — no matter what its type and make — dispose of it by spreading it as thinly as possible on the garden's beds.

REQUIRED FOR *COMPOST: vegetable waste*

- Two 1m-square (at least) rectangular excavations in, ideally, poor ground, placed side by side and dug down to subsoil level.

- A layer of soft vegetable matter, to line the bottom of one of the two depressions on **the first day of any moon's first quarter**.

- A layer of coarse material, to go on top of it.

- Layers of mixed, soft vegetable matter, added as the year progresses.

- Animal manure in composted or dried form, as an additive as material is added to the heap. Also, but not essentially, wood ash.

heaps activated by the addition of composted animal manure.

To emulate the head gardener's method

1 select a screened or otherwise unobtrusive site (for a compost heap is not a thing of beauty). Locate it, ideally, on ground that is unusable for cultivation purposes or is of poor quality

2 at any convenient time in the month (there is no moon-quarter involvement at this stage), mark out on the chosen site two one-metre squares. Use garden lines. [*Consideration: larger than this is better. The chosen size is determined by the size of the available site and the quantity of available waste*]

3 position the two rectangles side by side and 30cm or so apart

4 ensure that their positions leave sufficient adjacent space for the manoeuvring of a wheelbarrow and the use of a garden fork

5 remove the turf from the two rectangles. Store it elsewhere

6 remove the top soil from the two rectangles. Dig down at least one spade's blade deep, or to sub soil level. Spread the excavated top soil thinly throughout the garden if there is no immediate use for it in connection with other projects

7 on **the first day of any moon's first quarter**, place a layer of soft vegetable material in the bottom of one of the excavated squares. [*Considerations: 1 — this encourages hastened worm activity; 2 —. the first day of the moon's first quarter marks the beginning of the fortnight during which there is the least loss of moisture into the earth from the*

TIP 55

➔ **The vegetable waste that is composted at Tresillian does not include kitchen vegetable waste and egg shells. Mr Harris agrees that this kind of material has a place in urban and suburban compost making, but not where he practices. "It attracts vermin," he says, "and that is a reality at Tresillian. In the town situation, it is less of a problem, perhaps. Even so, one should be wary."**

composting vegetable matter. This is thanks to the upward pressure exerted by the rising water table. Maximum moisture retention within the compost aids the rotting of the vegetable matter]

8 cut coarse vegetable matter into short lengths. Layer it on top of the soft material in the excavation to encourage aeration from the bottom of the heap

9 layer on, next, accumulated vegetable waste in as pre-mixed a condition as can be achieved. If wood ash is available (it is not an essential ingredient), sprinkle it between the layers. Reject the whole of each perennial weed and the top growth of the annual weed that is in seed. Include the annual weeds' roots and the seedless tops of the annual weeds. Maintain the heap's rectangular shape

10 moisten any material that is dry before it is added by first immersing it in water for an hour or two

41

The Tresillian design of compost heap is fully exposed to the air and to the rain. Hence, it is always in the presence of two of the four essential ingredients for successful compost making. The other two — heat and regular turning to achieve air distribution — are achieved by the heap's size and the gardener's fork.

R J Harris agrees that in the average size of suburban garden, the compost bin brings the advantage of neatness and controlled containment.

42

There is no such thing as a standard, universally-utilised John Innes compost recipe. This is despite the fact that the product is the same no matter where it is bought and which of the five officially-recognised manufacturers (see *SUPPLIERS*) produces it. The key to this apparent contradiction lies in the product's loam content. Loam varies in its properties according to where it is found. This makes necessary a balancing variation in the quantities of peat, sand/grit and fertilisers that are mixed with it. In turn, this affects the amount of ground limestone that is added. The limestone counterbalances the acid nature of the peat, thus rendering the compost acceptable to most of plant life.

11 add a thin layer of any kind of composted or uncomposted animal manure from time to time. If this is not available, dust commercial dried manure onto the heap as the vegetable waste is layered on

TIP 56
➔ **When cutting the two depressions into the ground for the heaping of the waste vegetable matter, stack the removed turf neatly grass side to grass side. Leave the stack exposed to the elements for at least one year. Then pass it through a sieve with a 2cm-to-3cm mesh to remove large stones and the surviving weed roots. Spread the resultant good-quality soil thinly throughout the garden.**

12 leave the heap for one year. Throughout the year, continue to layer on material as it becomes available

13 each month of the year — on **the first day of the**

43

On the large, Victorian estates, garden compost was made in considerable volume by rotting waste vegetable matter mixed with hot stable manure — of which there was an over-abundant supply — in metre-deep and at least metre-square pits in the ground.

The technique was modified to meet specific needs. Out-of-season radishes and other salad crops, as example, were produced on the surface of these pits.

"Grape vines in the grape house had their roots trained through gaps in the north wall into a specially-built brick pit," recalls R J Harris.

"Into the pit during the course of the year was tipped all of the waste vegetable matter that could be found together with the animals and birds that died on the estate.

"Their blood content was one of the finest things to feed the grapes.

"You can image what sort of job some unfortunate apprentice had at the end of the year, having to remove most of that because it was spent, and then replacing it with more of the same. Then he had to spread the extracted matter onto the herbaceous borders — minus the bones, of course, which he had to bury.

"That was a very particular kind of compost pit, and not an item of loveliness."

44

The head gardener takes a pragmatic view of weeds in vegetable compost.

"The annual weeds can be added into the heap or the container, roots and all," he comments, "provided that no seeds are involved. Perennial weeds in their entirety are best kept out.

"But you can be sure that weed seeds of every kind will get in, no matter what precautions you take.

"After all, animal manure often comes with a corn or a grass seed content. That is inevitable, given the way that Nature works.

"My philosophy," he says, "is don't worry about it.

"The weeds that do manage to germinate when the compost is applied are all too visible, usually, and pulling them out is the work of a moment.

"In compost, too, their roots have very little 'hold'. So they come out easily and, if they are suitable, can go straight onto the current compost heap."

Mr Harris agrees that, in principle, the gardener's policy should be one of reducing the weed seeds in the composting heap as much as possible.

"'One year's seed is seven years' weed' is an old saying that was drummed into me when I was an apprentice, and it is true."

TIP 57
➔ **"Beware of adding potato peelings to the compost bin or heap,"** says the head gardener. **"Uncomposted, they can result in potato plants in unexpected places in the garden. The bonus of unplanned tubers is not always welcome."**

moon's first quarter, move the heap from one rectangular depression to the other to aerate it. Move the outer material of the original heap to the centre of the new heap as the new heap is formed

14 at year's end, the heap is ready for use. The matter that has not composted fully is placed in the empty excavation, to commence a new heap.

Tresillian's heaps of composting waste vegetation are located outside the kitchen garden in the almost daylong shadow of the north-facing wall. This is where, typically, the offices, workshops and storage rooms are located.

"Within the garden is a place of beauty," comments the head gardener, "where the lady of the house and her guests walk around to smell the sweet peas and all of the other scented blossoms. They are not there to enjoy the aroma of composting vegetable matter."

45

Probably, the rigid, black plastic bin — equipped with a fitted lid — is best for compost making in the small garden. Most local authorities offer it in 100-litre and 120-litre sizes for a subsidised price. For about half the cost, better service can be obtained from an 80-litre black, plastic dustbin which has had its bottom cut off. Turned upside down, it requires a smaller area of ground on which to stand, and is less obtrusive. Unlike the subsidised bin, it can be shaken free from its composting material by one person. This leaves a bin-shaped mini tower of the stuff. The material can then be returned to the bin easily. This is done to achieve the necessary aeration.

Even lower in cost, and as effective, is the 80-litre, plastic, ex-peat or ex-multi-purpose compost sack that has had its bottom sliced open neatly. It is sited as if it were a bin and is supported by two stakes driven into the ground on either side of it. An encirclement or two of garden wire, joining the two stakes, holds it upright. If the sack's interior surface is black in colour, turn it to the outside. It then absorbs heat more effectively. A thin, 80-litre black, refuse sack (or several of them, one encasing the other) slides over the principal sack's top to retain moisture within the composting vegetable matter.

"Just as low-cost," adds Mr Harris, "is the old-fashioned metal dustbin — one that has reached the end of its life and has lost its bottom, or one with the bottom cut out. A black, refuse sack can be slid over it if it has lost its lid."

Whatever the style of the bin that is used, the head gardener advises that its contents be capped with a thick layer of fresh, weed-killer-free lawn mowings. This generates heat, which is passed on to the composting vegetable matter, increasing the bin's internal temperature. The cap also absorbs and retains steam rising from the vegetable matter. Otherwise, the steam condenses on the underside of the plastic lid and drips back into the bin. It cools the bin's contents and, thus, slows or even halts the composting process. Replace the grass cap each time fresh matter is added, or each time the bin's contents are turned to achieve aeration.

> 46
> "I know an old gravedigger," says Mr Harris, "who told me once that he dug an eight-foot-deep grave and found at the bottom of it the growing roots of the weed convolvulus.
>
> "That is a warning to those who put garden compost underground in their flower or vegetable beds.
>
> "If there are living weed seeds in it, do not believe for one moment that they will be killed by depth."

The external, north-facing domain is the least productive of the garden's areas, because the sun reaches it hardly at all. Its lack of warmth makes it ideal for the composting processing, whether applied to vegetable matter or to animal manures, for the coldness reduces the resultant smell and induces the least amount of moisture loss from the composting heaps.

To the head gardener, there is a less demanding, more efficient way to use waste vegetable matter than composting it. Always, somewhere in the walled kitchen garden at Tresillian, there is at least one open, empty, metre-deep trench with a ready-loosened base waiting to be turned into a deep-trench bed *(BED/1)*. Into it goes a fair measure of the redundant vegetable matter, to make the first of the several, varied layers that fill it completely before it is capped with a layer of top soil. The deep-trench bed is R J Harris's king of beds: it produces the superlative crops for which Tresillian is renowned.

For the starting dates of each month's moon quarters see almost any diary — but it is essential to consult *MOON* first of all.

CURRANT: *black, red, white* — bush production, planting and management. Do as described in *FRUIT BUSH/1* to *-/5*. See these sections also for guidance on gooseberry-bush cultivation.

FERTILISER. In Tresillian's Victorian walled kitchen garden and elsewhere in the Tresillian estate in Cornwall, head gardener R J Harris applies in controlled, measured quantities seven organic fertilisers, two animal manures and one vegetable manure. His choice of organic fertilisers is

fish, blood & bone	gypsum
	hoof and horn
bonemeal:	seaweed:
sterilised	calcified
dolomite	seaweed meal
limestone	

The two animal manures are

farmyard manure (a mixture of the product of all of the farm's creatures except horses)	stable manure (solely from horses)

TIP 58

➔ The gardeners of old remembered in general terms which plants to feed with which fertilisers by repeating to themselves the Golden Triangle (so named for reasons that are now lost, even to the Cornish head gardener). The three points of the triangle are
— nitrogen for leaf growth
— phosphate for root growth
— potash for flower and fruit growth.

The one vegetable manure is

mixed vegetable waste from kitchen and garden, rotted — known as garden compost.

In general, these feeds/ conditioners are used at Tresillian as follows

47

The garden bonfire provides potash as long as only wood — anything from bush prunings to tree and hedgerow depletions — is burned on it.
The potash is in the ash that is left over. This must be dry stored the moment it is cold; atmospheric moisture and rain render it almost useless.
A better way is to save the wood for Christmas and enjoy an open fire in the house for a day or two.
The best rates at which to apply wood ash in the garden cannot be suggested: the potash content varies with the type and age of wood burned. A good rule is to apply it liberally, noting that thicknesses of it tend to cake on the soil when applied — especially after rain. Roses love it.
The Tresillian project recently acquired a wood chipper and, for that reason, its timber is no longer burned. Instead, it is shredded and then heaped for about six months. "I like it to break down and neutralise itself by losing its sugar or acid content," says Mr Harris. "Its effect on soil pH is then negligible." After that, it is applied as a moisture-retaining mulch around bushes or as a mulch to subdue weeds, or as path surfacing.

48

'Man-produced and 'man-managed', but not 'man-made', is the rule that head gardener R J Harris observes as far as possible when selecting the fertilisers that he applies in Tresillian's Victorian walled kitchen garden and elsewhere in the Tresillian estate.
"The animal and vegetable manures," he notes, "are much more than solely feeds. They require different thinking and a different approach." They are considered in separate sections in this manual.

FISH, BLOOD AND BONE

Applied it at the rate of 115g to the square metre of bed surface for the hungry ones (eg, the cabbage family). Used for salad crops and generally at the rate of 60g-to-80g to the square metre. Used for potatoes at the rate of 115g to the square metre. Added at the rate of 60g-to-80g to the square metre when earthing up potatoes.
[*Consideration:* *fish-blood-and-bone fertiliser contains fast-acting nitrogen. It also has phosphates. These encourage strong root systems. It is for general-purpose use.*]

TIP 59
➔ In general, the best time to apply feeds of all kinds to the ground is at the start of the moon's fourth quarter. The key to this is the influence of the moon upon Earth's water table. Read *MOON* in conjunction with consulting a current diary to establish moon-phase dates. For propagation instructions, consult the relevant fruit and vegetable sections of this manual.

50

When received at the walled kitchen garden, R J Harris's preferred fertilisers are emptied immediately into individual storage boxes: "made of wood, to keep the material dry," he explains. "Each has a tightly-fitting, shut-down lid and is marked with the fertiliser's name. Left in their plastic bags, the fertilisers deteriorate, either through sweating or through the bags eventually being accidentally punctured and the contents being in risk of contamination." The boxes are stored in the cool of the potting shed. They are replenished the instant they are empty. Thus, no detected deficiency in the soil has to await correction — and the execution of preparatory work does not have to be delayed — as a specific fertiliser's delivery is awaited. R J Harris's fertiliser policy is a pragmatic one: he causes a specific feed to be applied only when there is no doubt that a given lack is to be expected or has been established by a correctly-conducted test, the result of which is beyond question.

BONEMEAL: STERILISED
Used at the rate of 115g-to-145g to the square metre when planting new shrubs and trees.
[*Consideration: sterilised bonemeal slow-releases organic phosphates. It promotes strong root growth during a long period of time.*]

49

The head gardener buys his fertilisers in 25-kilo bags: "the equivalent of the old half-hundredweight bag," he comments.

"Years ago, when I was a young man, we bought them in one-hundredweight bags — 50 kilos.

"That was when there was a fertiliser called guano.

"It was bird droppings from the Seychelle Islands in the Indian Ocean. It was packed in two-hundredweight hessian sacks.

"I can remember carrying many of those in my time as an apprentice."

DOLOMITE LIMESTONE
Used at the rate of 200g-to-250g to the square metre to reduce the soil's acidity, the level of which is first ascertained by means of a soil-acidity testing kit.
[*Consideration: this fertiliser contains calcium and magnesium. Soil acidity-testing kits can be bought at garden centres. They are easy to use when the makers' instructions are followed.*]

GYPSUM
Used to improve the aeration and drainage of heavy clay soils and to make them easier to work. Application: 250g-to-500g to the square metre.

HOOF AND HORN
Applied at the rate of 75g-to-130g to the square metre as a bed dressing for most green vegetables and for the lawns that need to have their colour strengthened.
[*Consideration: it is a slow-acting source of organic nitrogen.*]

51

Where to find the elements

calcium — in dolomite limestone

calcium — in seaweed: calcified

magnesium — in dolomite limestone

magnesium — in seaweed: calcified

nitrogen: *(high release)* — in fish, blood and bone or hoof and horn

phosphates *(quick release)* — in fish, blood and bone

phosphates *(slow release)* — in bonemeal: sterilised

potash *(unreliable source)* — in wood ash

trace elements — in seaweed: calcified

trace elements *(very slow acting)* — in seaweed meal

*This table summarises
FERTILISER.
See specific descriptions in this
section for specific guidance.*

What to give the plants

apples — bonemeal: sterilised

apricots — seaweed: calcified

broad-leafed plants *(quick release)* — fish, blood and bone

cabbage family — fish, blood and bone or seaweed: calcified

courgettes — fish, blood and bone

cucumbers — fish, blood and bone

flower development *(slow)* — fish, blood and bone or bonemeal: sterilised

flowering shrubs — bonemeal: sterilised

fruit development *(slow)* — bonemeal: sterilised

grapes — fish, blood and bone

green vegetables — seaweed: calcified or hoof and horn or fish, blood and bone

lawn — seaweed: calcified or bonemeal: sterilised or fish, blood and bone

lettuces — fish, blood and bone

marrows — fish, blood and bone

nectarines — seaweed: calcified

peaches — seaweed: calcified

pears — bonemeal: sterilised

peas — fish, blood and bone

plums — seaweed: calcified

potatoes — fish, blood and bone

pumpkins — fish, blood and bone

quick-growing plants — fish, blood and bone

root growth: carrots, parsnips, turnips *(slow)* — bonemeal: sterilised

runner beans — fish, blood and bone

salad crops — fish, blood and bone

SEAWEED: CALCIFIED

The head gardener swears by this fertiliser for encouraging stone fruit such as plums. Applied in January at the rate of 115g-to-175g to the square metre, scattered around the affected trees onto the surface of the soil. "The turn-of-the-century way was to grow these fruit trees on builders' rubble for the sake of the lime in the rubble's mortar," explains the head gardener. "Today, cement mortar does not contain the lime that the trees need, so builders' rubble is no longer used." Mr Harris comments: "The increased sweetness imparted to the soil by calcified seaweed creates a better stone. The better the stone, the better the fruit." It is also fed to the cabbages and the others of the brassica family. It is used for this purpose at the rate of 60g-to-80g to the square metre.

[**Consideration:** calcified seaweed contains calcium, magnesium and trace elements. It is a very good soil conditioner.]

SEAWEED MEAL

Used as a lawn food. It gives strong growth and rich colour. It is also excellent as a general feed when applied to the surface of the soil at the rate of 60g-to-120g to the square metre three months before planting and lightly raked in. By planting time, the soil's bacteria have broken it down.

[**Consideration:** seaweed meal is a slow-acting, long-lasting plant food. It is rich in trace elements. It helps to build up the humus of the soil.]

Fruit bush/1 — overview of the production, planting, harvesting and management of the black-currant, the red-currant, white-currant and the gooseberry bush, summarising *FRUIT BUSH/2* to -/5.

Creating a bed for one of these fruit bushes and planting it with a young bush is — in head gardener Harris's practice — a two-year project commencing in October of year one, extending through to October and November of year two and ending in October of year three.

Ensuring, after that, that the mature bush has a fully-productive, problem-free life of at least twenty years' duration entails an annual, three-part maintenance programme.

The total activity falls out as follows

OCTOBER
of year one

Order in fresh stable manure if the proposed soft-fruit bed is to be created in heavy soil. Order in fresh farmyard manure if the bed is to occupy light soil.

Begin to compost the manure.

during
year one

Leave the manure to compost for the whole of the year, for use in October of year two.

OCTOBER
of year two

Insert the fully-composted manure into a double-dug bed designed in principle as described in *BED/3*. Start to create the bed at **the start of the moon's third quarter**. Complete it by **the start of the moon's fourth quarter**.

Order in another batch of fresh manure.

Begin to compost the fresh manure.

52

M R HARRIS urges that his storage regime be applied by the gardener who purchases feeds in small quantities.

"Keep them dry in the tool shed and away from the products — like 'weed-and-feed' and liquid sprays — that might contaminate them.

"And always," he stresses, "be guided absolutely by the maker's instructions printed on the side of the packet or the bottle.

"There is no gain in giving a plant or a crop a bit extra, in the belief that more has got to be better.

"Usually, more is detrimental, both to whatever is being grown in the soil and the soil itself.

"Many of the problems encountered in the garden have their beginnings in years and decades, even, of one well-intentioned gardener after the other adding unnecessary quantities of feed and medication."

NOVEMBER of year two

Take cuttings from a dormant, mature fruit bush at **the end of the moon's fourth quarter**.

Immediately post them in a nursery bed to develop into young bushes. Note that when bush dormancy sets in earlier than November — in October, perhaps — the cuttings may be taken earlier than November and immediately posted in a nursery bed.

during year two

Leave the newly-made bed unused and undisturbed for the whole of the year. Permit it to grow weeds. Uproot the weeds before they set seed.

Do so on a regular basis, thus progressively and largely denuding the bed of its weed content.

Leave the manure to compost for the whole of the year, for use in October of year three.

OCTOBER of year three

Transfer the best of the young bushes from the nursery bed to the double-dug bed. Plant it permanently. Do so at the beginning of **the moon's second quarter**.

Mulch the planted-up bed with the manure that was procured in October of year two, and is now composted.

Order in another batch of fresh manure.

TIP 60

➔ **The head gardener's favourite among the black currants is _Wellington XXX_. "New varieties of currants — as well as of gooseberries — come along all the time," he notes. "What suits one part of the country may not suit another. For the grower who cannot acquire cuttings from a neighbourhood fruit bush, the best guide to what will succeed locally is what is on sale at the local garden centre or nursery."**

53

Prominent among the many kinds of bush fruit produced in the Victorian walled kitchen garden at Tresillian in Cornwall are eight varieties of gooseberry. They are grown in standard as well as bush form.

Three of the varieties are notable for conferring late-June to mid-August cropping. One is *Early Sulphur.* It wins high praise from R J Harris as a "very, very good one for developing into a standard gooseberry."

It is ready in late June or early July: a medium-sized yellow berry with good flavour — "a little over-hairy," the head gardener comments, "but a heavy cropper." It doubles up for use in the kitchen and on the meal table as dessert.

Another is *Careless*: "A mid-July-cropping culinary variety," says Mr Harris, "with a large oval, pale-green, smooth-skinned berry. It has a good flavour, it is a moderately vigorously spreading bush; most garden centres have it."

The third is *Invicta*, another Tresillian gooseberry for the pot: "A very, very late July-August heavy cropper with large, oval, pale-green fruits of a wonderful texture; smooth-skinned, a vigorously-spreading, extremely spiny bush which calls for a steady nerve when you put your hand into it to pluck the fruit."

The *Invicta* gets full marks from R J Harris for its excellent resistance to the gooseberry's *bete noir*, the American mildew.

Begin to compost the manure.

during
year three

Leave the manure to compost for the whole of the year and longer, so that it is available during year four for mulching-layer rehabilitation.

As soon as the young bush becomes fully dormant and enters upon its Winter sleep, spray it with winter tar wash to prevent mildew attack in year three's Spring/early Summer.

In March or April, remove the bed's mulching cover. Weed the bed, water it, feed it with fish, blood and bone fertiliser applied at the rate of 115g to the square metre. Do so at the beginning of **the moon's fourth quarter**.

54

Bush-fruit production in Tresillian's walled kitchen garden fulfils the kind of potential that is not granted to the average urban or suburban garden.

Two conditions bring this benefit: 1) the four, 4m-high walls create in-garden and out-of-garden micro climates. These combine with complementary plant positioning to increase the length of the total harvesting period; 2) the amount of space that is available inside and immediately outside the garden makes possible the development of more plants than most sparetime gardeners see in their gardening lifetime.

These, to enhance production volume and variety even further, comprise a range of types. This confers successive fruiting periods.

Immediately afterwards, rehabilitate the mulch, using the manure put to compost in October of year two.

Remove any berries that form on the young bush. These are the plant's first berries. Make it expend its energies upon below-ground development, not upon first-season fruit.

Spray the young gooseberry bush with Bordeaux mixture on the first signs of an American mildew attack.

OCTOBER of year four

Order in fresh manure.

Begin to compost the manure.

during year four

Leave the manure to compost through the year, so that it is available during year five for mulching-layer rehabilitation.

Wait for the bush to become fully dormant. Spray it with winter tar wash to prevent an American mildew attack.

In January or February, prune the bush. Do so during **the moon's fourth quarter**.

In March or April, remove the bed's mulching cover. Weed the bed, water it, feed it with fish, blood and bone fertiliser applied at the rate of 115g to the square metre. Do so at the beginning of **the moon's fourth quarter**.

Immediately afterwards, rehabilitate the mulch, using the manure put to compost in the October of year three.

Permit the plant to bear a crop of fruit for the first time. Officially, this is its second fruiting season.

Spray the gooseberry bush with Bordeaux mixture on the first signs of an American mildew attack (should that happen).

annually, as from OCTOBER of year five

Order in fresh manure.

Put the manure to compost, for use during the following year to rehabilitate the mulching layer.

Spray with winter tar wash after dormancy to avert mildew attack.

Prune the bush.

Weed the bed, water it, feed it, rehabilitate its manure mulching cover.

Permit the plant to bear a fruit crop.

Spray the gooseberry bush with Bordeaux mixture on the first signs of an American mildew attack.

The entire activity is moon-phase oriented, to ensure that

— the newly-created bed comprehensively absorbs the manure-supplied nutrients

— the young bush's exposure on planting to moisture in the soil is at maximum

— the bush's reaction to pruning is least adverse.

If further explanation is required, e-mail R J Harris on *rjh@moongardening.fsnet.co.uk*

FRUIT BUSH/2 — to prepare to plant a young black-currant, red-currant, white-currant or gooseberry bush. Bed preparation and cuttings production is the initial two-part task in black-currant, red-currant, white-currant or gooseberry bush cultivation as R J Harris proposes it. His method is

1 in a given October, order in a batch of fresh stable manure or fresh farmyard manure.

55

"THE red currant will grow and produce a fine crop completely in the shade and without any sunshine at all," says R J Harris.

"That way its berries are just right for the kitchen.

"Situated in the sun, its fruit's sugar content is higher and so its berries are just right for dessert eating."

Of the many red currant producers that are available today, the head gardener recommends *Red Lake*. "It is a first-class cropper," he says.

"The gooseberry also gives the best of both worlds. Plant it where it gets little sun, and it is perfect for the kitchen. Plant it where there is unstinted light, and it is delicious eaten straight off the bush."

The hidden benefit of this soft-fruit versatility is that shaded and, thus, largely unusable ground can acquire value. At the same time, the cropping season can be lengthened, being given an earlier start by the harvesting of unripe berries.

"The black and the white currants really need all the sunlight they can get," Mr Harris notes.

REQUIRED FOR *FRUIT BUSH/2*

● A fruit-bush site — ideally, but not essentially, with a pH of 6.5 to 7 — to accommodate a double-dug *BED/3*-type soft-fruit-bush bed completed by **the start of an October moon's fourth quarter**.

● Fresh stable or farmyard manure, acquired one year before the soft-fruit-bush bed is created.

● A garden fork, a compost bin or heap, a trench for a deep-trench bed (*BED/1*) or a shallow-trench bed (*BED/2*), if possible.

For the complete instruction, see *FRUIT BUSH/1* to -/5.

[*Consideration: ideally, stable manure is for heavy soil; farmyard manure is for light, sandy soil. If only either one of the two types is available, use it, whatever the type of soil. Its use is better than a lack of the prescribed bed preparation*]

2 set the manure to one side at a suitable spot. Leave it to compost for one year. Earmark it for soft-fruit-bush bed preparation

3 in the following October, choose a site in the garden for a soft-fruit bed

4 ensure that the site

— appears to be well drained

— is at least 2m square if it is to accommodate a single bush

— provides sufficient space if it is to accommodate two or more bushes stationed at least 1.5m from each other in rows 1.5m apart with a general surround which is about 1m in width

— is not embraced by the current crop-rotation system

5 note the site's character and be aware of the category of berries that it will produce. [*Considerations: 1 — if the site is fully exposed to the sunlight, it produces fully-ripened berries, which are fit to eat raw, straight from the bush. Equally, the same berries are ideal for cooked dishes when picked in a less-than-ripened state. Plucking the less-than-ripened berries for the kitchen can be seen as fruit thinning in aid of achieving, later, perfect and the largest-possible, fully-ripened berries; 2 — if the site is constantly in the shade and, as a result, is also a cold site, it produces, at best, less-than-ripened berries fit only for the kitchen; 3 — if the site is partially shaded, partially sunlit, it produces like the fully-sunlit site at a later time in the garden's production timetable; 4 — this awareness offers planned flexibility in harvesting. It also enables the otherwise ignored shaded, cold areas to be productive to a degree instead of being omitted from the overall garden plan*]

6 check that the site's top soil has a pH reading of between 6.5 and 7

7 create a bed at the chosen site as described in *BED/3*. Use the one-year-old, composted manure that was acquired as fresh manure one year ago. Vary *BED/3*'s method in the following ways

— make each trench as deep as twice the length of a spade's blade

— plan, in advance, what to do with the sub-soil, hard material and rubbish that is excavated as the double-depth trenches are dug

— loosen the bottom of each double-depth trench especially thoroughly with a garden fork. [*Consideration: good drainage is a 'must' so far as the roots of the soft-fruit bush are concerned. This is the only opportunity that the gardener has throughout the plant's very long life to create this essential condition*]

— dispose of the surplus top soil, if there is any, by spreading it as thinly as

TIP 61
➔ **Reduce preparation time from two years to one by purchasing composted manure. It is available by the sack from the garden centre. A bonus is a very useful stock of re-usable plastic sacks and a material that is much easier to store and to handle than is the raw version. The disadvantage is the cost that is involved. Comparatively, this can be very high.**

possible on all of the available garden beds. [*Consideration: the completed bed does not have a raised surface, unlike the single-dug bed*]

8 ensure that the fruit-bush bed is embarked upon at **the start of the October moon's third quarter.** Ensure that it is completed by **the start of the October moon's fourth quarter**. [*Consideration: this is the time in the month of the maximum reception by the soil of added nutrients such as those delivered by buried, composted manure. The process is repeated monthly*

56

'Buy a pH-testing kit from the garden centre and use it according to its maker's instructions," the head gardener advises.

"If a properly carried out test reveals that pH6.5-to-pH7 or a reading very close to that is not available, search elsewhere for a bush-fruit bed site that does have it.

"This is much easier — and certainly cheaper, more reliable and, for the gardener, much less demanding physically — than trying to wreak a permanent change in an unsuitable pH.

"If the ideal pH is not to be found, get as close to it as you can.

"If nothing at all like it is available, give up all idea of bush-fruit production and concentrate upon the possible, whatever that is — or take what your soil has to offer and be ready for less-than-top-quality results and a bit of a battle to achieve them."

57

Of all British bush fruits, the gooseberry has the strangest of places in Britain's social history. For the pot, it is best unripened. The affluent Victorians grew it, therefore, adjacent to the north-facing and, hence, almost sunless wall of the kitchen garden along with the cherries and the red currants that were destined for kitchen use. Thus was increased the productivity of an unavoidably inhospitable growing area. The dessert gooseberries, to be taken from the bush or the standard to be eaten raw, were grown to full ripeness elsewhere, in total sunlight.

Unripened and, hence, green, bullet-hard gooseberries travelled well and withstood rough handling. Piled high on the greengrocer's shelves and available during a long period, they created in the Victorian city-dwelling poor a misunderstanding which endures among non-gardeners to the present day. Not knowing of the existence of fully ripened gooseberries — which were, and still are, unfit for retail selling — the majority of the populace never questioned but that the fruit in its natural state was unfit for consumption until softened by sustained boiling and sweetened by the addition of considerable amounts of sugar.

until the bed is planted-up one year later, thanks to the moon's cycle and the water table's reactions to that cycle. This ensures that comprehensively-nourished and moistened soil receives the young soft-fruit plantlet when it is installed permanently in the bed]

58

"OF COURSE," concedes the head gardener, "I do understand that so far as Mr and Mrs Gardener are concerned, the age of double digging has gone.

"Insist on that, and most people will say that it is easier to go to the supermarket for their soft fruit."

Mr Harris does not disagree that, in all probability, 'Mr and Mrs Gardener' will find that the pH of their garden — should they take the trouble to investigate it — is sufficient for the development of one or two unremarkable bushes.

"It is a fact," notes the head gardener, "that simply digging a hole at a convenient spot and earthing in a purchased bush's roots and then relying on an occasional feed of something or other from the garden centre will produce a colander or two of acceptable berries for a few seasons."

Pruning, he agrees, could be forgotten, as could be the other forms of correct bush and bed maintenance.

"Nothing comes for nothing, however," the Cornish head gardener comments, "so you can be sure that there is a battle each year with the weeds and, after a time, that becomes a losing battle,

"Also, when there is a rain shortage, there is an endless to-ing and fro-ing with watering cans. Or this proves to be too much of a burden, and reduced crops of moisture-starved, shrunken berries are accepted as Mother Nature's norm.

"Even so, for all that," notes R J Harris, "there *are* more important things in life than striving for perfection in soft fruit.

"The bushes that disappoint after a time can always be replaced by bought-in new ones, which can be treated in the same way.

"They provide acceptable crops for a few years, start to fail and then are replaced once again — often without thought being given to the need to change the planting site.

"That is not horticulture as I was taught it, and as I still practise it."

9   ensure that the surface of the completed bed is in the coarsely broken, ploughed-field-like state that is specified in *BED/3*.
[*Consideration: this inaugurates the process of fertility enhancement which the head gardener seeks continually as a background to everything that he does in the garden*]

10   coinciding with the completion of the soft-fruit bed, order in another batch of the fresh manure. Store it where the initial batch was stored. Leave it to compost for one year. Earmark it for the mulching of the surface of the new bed in one year's time

11   leave the new bed unused for one year. Throughout the year, methodically, permit its surface to grow weeds until they are just short of setting seeds. Remove them at this stage or slightly earlier.
[*Consideration: by this environment- and garden-friendly and very low-cost means, reduce considerably the bed's future weed population. Do so before the*

59

M R HARRIS acknowledges that the making of his style of soft-fruit bed creates a great amount of hard work for the sparetime gardener. He agrees that his advocacy of double digging is likely to meet with a less than rapturous reception from the 'no-dig' school of gardening.

"A black- or a red-currant bed," he insists, "is set up to do its job for twenty-plus years, so thoroughness has got to be the watchword of the day.

"You have but the one opportunity to deal with the weeds, which is essential if the developing, and then mature plants, are not to have to compete constantly with the enemy for moisture and nutrients. That opportunity is offered only before permanent planting takes place.

"You have but the one opportunity to get that layer of nutritious, moisture-trapping, moisture-retaining, fully-composted manure at the right depth beneath the young plants — which get the best possible start with its help as they struggle to achieve maturity.

"Again, once planting has taken place, that opportunity has gone.

"Show me," says Mr Harris, "an easier way to achieve all of that, and I shall adopt it gladly."

bed's surface becomes difficult to reach into because of the presence of one or more soft-fruit bushes.]

12 use a garden fork when de-weeding. In the process, tread on the bed's surface as little as possible. Reinstate trodden-on areas as soon as they are created, to remove harmfully rain-trapping and air-excluding depressions. Maintain as far as possible the bed's original rough, broken surface

13 compost the annual weeds that have not set seed, together with their roots. Or place them in the trench that awaits development into a deep-trench bed (*BED/1*) or shallow-trench bed (*BED/2*), if there is one in the garden

14 off site, destroy or dispose of the annual weeds that have managed to set seed,

together with their roots. Do the same with the perennial weeds and their roots, and the grass growth and its roots

15 in the November following the October creation of the double-dug bed, one month later, commence fruit-bush cuttings' production and development as described in *FRUIT BUSH/3*. Do so at **the end of the November moon's fourth quarter**. [*Consideration: November is specified because the bush from which the cuttings are taken must be fully dormant*

TIP 62
➔ **The mature soft-fruit bush has a twenty-year-plus, fruit-bearing life span: "So when deciding where to locate its bed, keep in mind that it will be there for all of that length of time," the head gardener advises.**

before the secateurs are applied as described in FRUIT BUSH/3. If dormancy arrives earlier than November, the cuttings may be taken correspondingly earlier.]

for background information, see *MANURE, MOON, pH, SOIL.*

F**RUIT BUSH/3 — to produce a young soft-fruit bush.** Using a nursery bed, head gardener R J Harris converts a fruit-bush cutting into a young fruit-bush which is ready for posting permanently in the bed that is described in *FRUIT BUSH/2.*

The Cornishman's programme is

1 in November — when **the moon is at the end of its fourth quarter** — look for new growth on an established soft-fruit bush. The bush has fully shed its leaves, is dormant, and has gone into its Winter sleep. [***Consideration:*** *if dormancy arrives before November, cuttings may be taken correspondingly earlier*]

2 the new growth is growth which has developed in the season now over. It grows out of the end of an existing branch. Existing branches are of firm and well-ripened wood. The new growth is obvious by virtue of its freshness and newness, its pale-green colour, its comparative slenderness and its fragility

3 ignore any new growth that springs from the bush's main stem or stems

4 the chosen existing-branch-plus-new-growth is as straight as possible

REQUIRED FOR *FRUIT BUSH/3*

● An established, dormant soft-fruit bush, secateurs, a nursery bed, a garden line, coarse sand, a watering can, water, 1:40 comfrey solution, a garden spade.

For the complete instruction, see *FRUIT BUSH/1 to -/5.*

5 the new growth has at least five buds or bumps on it. These are just above where the new growth emerges from the existing branch. They are noticeable eruptions at which leaves grew

6 focus on the point where the new growth emerges from the existing branch. Count four or five leaf buds or bumps back along the existing branch towards the centre of the bush. Cut with secateurs just beyond the fourth or fifth leaf bud or bump. Apply a 45° cut

TIP 63
➔ **If preferred, insert fruit-bush cuttings into John Innes No 2 potting compost in 15cm pots instead of into a nursery bed. Do so, one cutting per pot. House in an open cold frame or at a protected spot in the garden for the duration of the year-long development from cutting to very young bush. Close the frame when frost strikes or when there is prolonged, heavy rain. Increase the protection against these conditions when the pot is in the open. Otherwise, manage in all ways as described in *FRUIT BUSH/3.***

7 remove the new-growth end of the cut-off, old-plus-new-branch. Do so just above the fifth leaf bud on the new growth. Apply a 45° cut with secateurs.
[**Consideration:** *this produces a cutting which is about 30cm in length and consists of old-plus-new growth*]

8 repeat the operation until ten or a dozen fully-prepared cuttings have been created

9 take the cuttings to a nursery bed. This is an unused, narrow strip of one end of a *BED/3*-type bed which is in the first, second or third year of its four-year life span

10 select the nursery bed's site so that its presence for one year does not impede the continuation of the current crop-rotation system.
[**Consideration:** *the fourth-year bed is not used for this purpose. The area in which the fourth-year beds are located is subject, as from October and November, to the upheaval caused by the installation of the crop-rotation beds required to begin a fresh, four-year crop-rotation programme. The upheaval would affect adversely newly-installed cuttings*]

11 level the nursery bed's surface. Use a garden fork. Follow by using a rake. Move the surface of the ground backwards and forwards with the rake's tines. Criss-cross it in the process. Use the full length of the rake's handle. Aim for a rake-tine depth of very

coarse earth crumbs, evenly laid out

12 de-earth the rake frequently, to keep its tines unblocked

13 remove the stones that are trapped by the rake's unblocked tines. Store these for use in connection with other projects in the garden.
[**Considerations: 1** — *cost-conscious gardening aims always to conserve useful resources that may be difficult to obtain at some point in the future. Sometimes, stones are an irreplaceable ingredient in garden projects, and merit the small amount of storage space that they occupy when conserved;* **2** — *the stones that slip through the rake's unblocked tines are of the size that is required by the soil. They are an aid to drainage. They act as a moisture-retaining mulch. At all times, but especially in Summer, they release during the night the heat that they absorb during the day, relatively warming the section and its contents;* **3** — *the stones that are gathered*

TIP 64
➔ **Be sure to wait for total leaf drop before removing cuttings from a soft-fruit bush. Pruning — of which removing a cutting is an expression — is done only when the branches of such a bush are bare and apparently lifeless. Better, it is done at the end of the moon's fourth quarter during the bush's dormancy. This is when the water table exerts the least upward pressure, causing the least bleeding of sap when the secateurs are applied.**

by the rake's regularly de-earthed tines are likely to be too large to be wanted in the soil; 4 — generally, if no stone removal is desired, use a hoe when a bed's surface is being turned. The hoe's shape prevents it from gathering stones of any size]

14 for a better, more easily achieved breaking down of the particles of the bed's surface, use R J Harris's preferred four-tined cultivator. Do so as if it were a rake. Reduce the coarse crumbs of the soil to crumbs which are as fine as the four-tined cultivator is capable of producing. Whether a rake or a cultivator is applied, penetrate the surface with it as deeply as its tines permit. [**Consideration:** *of the many manually-operated cultivators that are available for this purpose, the head gardener uses the long-handled tool that has three, four or five long, curved tines. In the hands of a practised operator, the three-tined cultivator provides a coarse tilth, the four-tined a less coarse tilth, and the five-tined a fine tilth. Also, being much less prone to clogging and having far fewer and more widely-spaced tines than the rake, all three cultivators ignore the essential small stones that the initial raking leaves in situ]*

15 open a slit in the nursery bed's surface. Use a sharpened garden spade. To do this

— position a 2m-long garden line on the nursery bed

— do so centrally, so that subsequent hoeing, for weed suppression/moisture raising, may be done easily and without harm to the bed's contents

— position the cutting edge of a sharpened spade at the beginning of the line as if about to commence digging. Hold the spade upright

— drive the blade of the spade vertically into the earth to a depth of about 20cm

— withdraw the spade gently. At the same time, rock it backwards and forwards once or twice, gently, so that the slit opens at the top to a width of about 8cm

— extend the opened slit, in the same way, until it is some 150cm long

16 drop a 2cm-to-3cm thickness of coarse sand into the bottom of the slit, to act as a drainage point

17 place the prepared cuttings into the slit at 15cm intervals. Their old-wood sections go in first. The ends of these dip into the coarse sand at the bottom of the slit. The new-growth sections stand vertically proud of the surrounding bed's surface. Each shows three or four leaf buds or bumps above the surface

18 close up the slit around the cuttings. Firm the earth, so that the cuttings have adequate support. Create a depression at the base of the cuttings by this means. The depression directs rain water down towards what will be the cuttings' developing root systems

19 water the cuttings well. Use a watering can fitted with a medium rose. Use water containing comfrey stock in the ratio 1:40

20 leave the cuttings in the nursery bed, undisturbed, for one year until the following October. Hoe the bed regularly during the year, to keep the bed free from weeds

21 water the nursery bed, from time to time, with water containing comfrey stock in the ratio 1:40. As the weeks pass, most (at best) of the ends protruding from the ground, or a few of them (at worst), show signs of life. By Summer, the successful cuttings develop into very young fruit bushes. By October, a year after their insertion into the nursery bed, they are ready to be transplanted to the waiting soft-fruit-bush bed. Like the cuttings, this is one year old.

for background information, see *COMFREY/1 to -/3, MOON, ROTATION.*

FRUIT BUSH/4 — to plant a young soft-fruit bush. The head gardener's method is

1 a day or two before **the start of the October moon's second quarter**, examine the one-year-old fruit-bush plantlets in their nursery bed

REQUIRED FOR *FRUIT BUSH/4*

● A nursery bed in which grow one-year-old soft-fruit plantlets.

● A permanent bed for one or more one-year-old soft-fruit plantlets.

● A watering can with a medium rose, water, a garden fork, a garden spade, a wheelbarrow, a garden bucket, a flexible tape measure, sterilised bonemeal, composted manure, soft string, garden canes, 1:40 comfrey solution garden gloves.

For the complete instruction, see *FRUIT BUSH/1 to -/5.*

2 check that they are bare of leaves and, hence, dormant and into their Winter sleep

3 if this is not the case, wait one month until a day or two before **the start of the November moon's second quarter**

TIP 65
➔ **If possible, when planting two or three fruit bushes in the one bed, station them the recommended 150cm or more apart in a north-to-south single line. This ensures that the ripening fruits receive maximum sunlight; one bush does not throw its shadow upon its fellow as the sun moves across the sky. If a greater number of bushes is in parallel rows in a north-to-south orientation, the plants are best staggered in relation to one another, so that, largely, shadows fall upon empty ground. Space the rows 150cm apart.**

60

Red gooseberries feature in Tresillian's kitchen garden's fruit-bush area under R J Harris's supervision. The variety that the head gardener singles out for praise because of its flavour is *Whinham's Industry*: "It is a very late July-to-mid-August fruit for eating cooked or uncooked. It is beautiful off the bush on a hot, sunny afternoon; it is a medium-to-large oval, dark red berry, and only slightly hairy."

Mr Harris notes with regret that it is susceptible to American mildew.

4 at this time, leaf drop is assured. Check, then, that the young bushes are

— in an unfrozen state

— standing in nursery-bed soil that is neither frozen nor waterlogged

5 if the young plants are frozen and/or waterlogged, postpone their removal to their new home until the New Year. Seize the earliest month in which the required three conditions are met. Then, proceed as follows

6 subject the soil in the nursery bed around the stems of the young fruit bushes to the most thorough of soakings. Use a watering can filled with water from a mains tap or a rainwater butt. Do not use comfrey solution

7 apply water repeatedly until the roots could not possibly be in the presence of a greater amount of moisture.

[*Consideration:* this is not to suggest that conditions of flooding are the aim. The considerable quantity of water that is applied is present as absorbed water, not standing water]

8 water at the end of the day, so that the plants' roots are not subjected to the cold dousing — and, as a result, traumatised — during the comparatively higher daytime temperature

9 suspend operations for the following 48 hours. (*Consideration:* this ensures that by the time any one bush is lifted out of the nursery bed, its roots are fully moisture-charged]

10 use the 48-hour pause to plan the planting out. At the bed designated to receive a young fruit bush, place a cane upright in the ground where it is proposed to position the young plant. Use a cane of sufficient length to show at least 150cm above the ground's surface

11 stand well back and, from a number of observation

TIP 66
➜ **Blackbirds love a mulching layer. They rummage in it for the worms that it draws to the surface, tossing it to all points of the compass. Reduce their mayhem by pinning down a width of fine-mesh chicken wire around the perimeter of the mulch. What the birds do within the chicken-wire edging does not matter; their scatterings remain on the bed or fall on the wire netting.**

points, examine the cane's position

12 if necessary, adjust the position until it can be seen that the proposed position of planting is the best from every point of view

13 after the 48-hour pause — by which time **the moon has just begun its second quarter** (creating ideally moist conditions within the waiting permanent bed) — tie a length of string around the base of the stem of the best of the bushes. Do so at nursery-bed surface level. Leave a generous end of string on each side of the knot.

14 lift the young plant from the nursery bed. Use a garden fork. Ensure that its roots are not damaged. Leave the rejected bushes in the bed to be dealt with later

15 gently remove the earth from the young bush's root system. Do so on the nursery bed, so that the removed soil falls back upon the bed's surface. Do so, also, by hand, and with very great care. Ensure, thus, that no young weeds are attached to the roots and are conveyed to the bush's permanent home

16 take the selected bush (or more than one, if several are

61

The head gardener rejects the suggestion that the newly-planted-up, soft-fruit-bush bed must have a considerable volume of water added to it before it is covered with its first or rehabilitating mulching layer.

Lack of this step being taken, it is sometimes held, results in dry earth beneath a blanket that retains rain and does not release it to the ground beneath.

"With the correct bed preparation, and with the planting-out taking place in October or November, there is sufficient moisture in the soil," he says.

"A whole year's rains plus the Autumn rains that have just arrived will have done — and will do — an adequate job of wetting.

"Moreover, the gravitational pull of the new moon's early days raises the water table during the new plants' early days, increasing the moisture content of the bed's manure 'sponge'.

"No more water need be added. Not unless," he qualifies, "for some unknown reason, there is a very, very, very dry spell.

"I must say that in all my time I have yet to experience that."

---

to be planted) to its new habitat. Place it flat on the ground, with care

17 with care, so that no damage is done, measure with a flexible tape measure the length of the young plant's longest root

---

TIP 67
➔ **If buying a containerised young soft-fruit bush from a garden centre, select the one that provides the longest available length of leg between soil and first branch. This is the one that, with correct pruning, will provide the least troublesome bed management.**

62

AS he waits for 48 hours for the soft-fruit plantlets in the nursery bed to become fully moisture-charged prior to being moved to their permanent home, the head gardener decides whether to transplant them during or at the end of the chosen day.

"My mind is made up for me by the state of the weather," he says.

"The aim, whatever else happens, is activity as early as possible in the moon's second quarter — be that in October or in November.

"You never know what to expect during either of these months until the given day arrives and declares itself.

"If the day is at all a warmish one — and October can bring such days — I work at the end of it. Then," he explains, "the day's warmth has cooled down and evaporation in the garden has reduced to its lowest point.

"The young plants in their new home lose less moisture than if transplanted earlier on. Also, they have the cool of the night in front of them, not the remainder of a warm day. The reduction in evaporation continues. As a consequence, they are under minimum stress during their initial hours of recovering from transplantation. This increases their chances of survival and of fulfilling their potential.

"Moisture, after all," Mr Harris notes, "is the plants' life blood. Reduce it, and they are that much closer to death.

"On the other hand, if the chosen day brings seasonably cool or cold conditions, I do my planting out at any time, for the difference between the daytime's and the evening's moisture loss is hardly anything to speak of."

18 remove the stand-in cane from the bed and dig with a garden spade a hole where the cane was inserted. The hole measures in diameter twice the length of the bush's longest root. It is a spade blade in depth

19 place the excavated soil in a wheelbarrow. Position the wheelbarrow within easy reach

20 ensure that as the hole attains its final depth, the underground manure layer is not disturbed and scattered

21 when the hole is complete, add to the excavated soil in the wheelbarrow 50g of sterilised bonemeal. Mix the two together thoroughly

22 fill a garden bucket with soil plus sterilised bonemeal

63

THERE are at least forty varieties of gooseberry. Some fruit earlier than others. "This provides scope for planting for successive crops," suggests R J Harris. "With planning, it is possible to have bushes and/or standards that come to peak condition between late June and early August. They offer fruit for the kitchen, fruit for eating raw when fully ripe, and fruit that serves both purposes." Most of the forty are available from the specialist nurseries, the catalogues of many of which give detailed planting and cropping guidance.

taken from the wheelbarrow and position the bucket conveniently close to the planting hole

23 thoroughly loosen the soil at the bottom of the hole with a garden fork.
[**Consideration:** *this ensures that there is no hard pan upon which water can collect after planting has been completed, and be detrimental to the bush's root system*]

24 add 50g of sterilised bonemeal to the loosened earth at the bottom of the hole. Mix the two together thoroughly

25 place the centre of the stand-in cane on the string that is tied around the plantlet's stem. This is the point at which the plantlet emerged from the surface of the nursery bed

26 position the cane at right angles to the stem, thus forming a cross

27 tie the cane to the stem with a temporary knot

28 hold the young bush upright and place its roots in the prepared hole

29 rest the ends of the cane on the bed's surface on the two sides of the hole. Ensure,

---

64

'Leaf mould is a good substitute for manure as a mulch on the new fruit-bush bed," says the head gardener. "So is spent mushroom compost. You might even get a crop of mushrooms. One always looks for the benefits in everything.
"But," the head gardener warns, "avoid wood chips. "You never know which trees the chips have come from, so you never know what they may or may not do to the pH of the bed.
"By that means, uncertainty about growing conditions is introduced.

"Uncertainty has no place in good horticulture. "Failing all else," he suggests, "an application of chemical-free straw bought from a reliable source is better than nothing. "Never," he points out, "use hay. Hay is dried grass and in it are all the seed heads of the dried grass.
"That is the last thing you want on a bed that has had every last weed stripped out of it at the cost of a considerable amount of physical effort." If no other material is available for mulch

purposes, apply a thickness of weed-killer-free lawn mowings rather than leave the bed surface bare. If these can be composted mowings, so much the better.
R J Harris admits to having heard of a thickness of newspapers being used as a mulch, weighed down with stones against the wind and renewed as it perishes.
"It is all right," he concedes, "provided that the unsightliness of it as it decomposes can be accepted, as well as the extra workload of renewing it."

65

The head gardener notes that the rooted fruit-bush cutting that is containerised (whether bought-in or home-raised) can be permanently planted out in any month of the year (provided, of course, that it is done at the start of the moon's second quarter). The young plant's roots remain in the compost in which they have developed and, consequently, suffer no disturbance and very little trauma when being installed in their new home.

There is, however, need for full watering of the rooted cutting prior to transplantation. Two hours after the watering, or longer, the plantlet and its compost root ball slide smoothly from their container into the waiting, correctly-prepared bed — into a place formed with the aid of an empty pot that is a twin of the one containing the young plant.

The result is a perfect transplantation, in which a young bush's stem rises from a rain-gathering depression and the bush has very little idea that it is in an unfamiliar place.

66

'The disadvantage of the containerised fruit bush plantlet," observes Mr Harris, "is that its convenience can lead to the temptation to skip bed preparation.

"A water-treated, de-containered young bush can be popped in anywhere with so much ease that the matter of its future development can be overlooked.

"At first the young plant seems to thrive, of course.

"Not until a few seasons have come and gone does the absence of preparation become apparent in a less-than-healthy adult, poor yields and, perhaps, pest and disease problems.

"Motto," says Mr Harris.

"'Preparation is an investment.'

"Support it with correct maintenance and it will bring dividends for the life-span of the mature plant."

thus, that the bush is planted at its original depth

30 support the young plant in that position with one hand

31 with the other hand, take the soil-plus-bonemeal from the bucket and return it to the hole, spreading the bush's roots to their fullest extent at the same time

32 gently raise and lower the bush as the earth is returned to the hole. Ensure by this means that the soil falls neatly in and around the crevasses of the root system. Ensure, also, that no air pockets are created within the root system and the returned earth

33 once the plant is sufficiently supported by its root system and the cane, use both

TIP 68
➜ **Always wear garden gloves when handling bone meal and mixing it into soil, to avoid the risk of skin irritation.**

67

The mulching layer's main purpose when placed on the fruit bushes' new bed immediately after planting is not that of adding nutrients to the soil. It does that, of course, the head gardener points out, but the role is a subsidiary one.

For maximum return, the fruit bush must have its feet constantly in a thoroughly moistened bed — a bed which is never permitted to dry out.

The mulch helps considerably to ensure that, imposing, as it does, a moisture-retaining layer upon the bed's surface. This reduces evaporation.

The manure layer placed underground at the double-dug stage of bed preparation completes the process.

"If moisture is not kept where it can help to convey nourishment to the roots, the plant will be less than healthy and, hence, vulnerable to all the evils that Nature is capable of throwing at it," says Mr Harris.

"Even more disappointing, its berry crop is reduced in quantity and quality."

---

hands to firm in the returned earth until the young bush is as when it grew in the soil of its nursery bed — and, ideally, within a shallow, rain-collecting depression

34 remove the stand-in cane from the stem. Remove the string from the stem

35 when all transplanting has taken place, give the ground immediately around the newly-planted bush a thorough watering. Use the watering can with a medium rose. First add comfrey stock to the water in the ratio of 1:40

36 spread a thickness of at least 8cm of composted manure over the whole of the surface of the fruit-bush bed. Stop it just short of touching the plant's stem, to prevent above-surface root formation.
(**Consideration:** *the manure used is the fresh manure put to compost a year ago*]

37 remove the rejected bushes from the nursery bed. Pass on the usable ones to neighbours and relatives, or dispose of them off site

38 coinciding with the insertion into the permanent bed of the soft-fruit plantlet/s, order in another batch of the

---

68

GARDEN compost receives only grudging acceptance from the head gardener as a possible mulch material for the newly-planted-up soft-fruit-bush bed.

"It can be very, very sticky, unsightly stuff," he comments.

"Unless it is well decayed it can be a bit of a nuisance when you go in among the plants to work around them."

The mulch's other important task is to repel weeds.

"Garden-made waste-vegetable compost can be riddled with weed seeds," Mr Harris comments.

fresh manure. Park it conveniently. Leave it to compost for one year. Earmark it for mulching-layer rehabilitation in one year's time.

for background information, see *COMFREY/1 to -/3, FERTILISER, MANURE, MOON.*

F RUIT BUSH/5 — **to develop a young fruit bush into a mature fruit bush, to maintain a mature fruit bush.** The head gardener's method is as follows

1 remove the very few berries that may appear on the new bush during the first year of its life in its permanent bed. By this means, make it concentrate its energies on below- and above-ground development

2 at the end of the new bush's first year in its new home, on **the final day of the November moon's fourth quarter** (at best) or on any of the approximately eight days of **the November moon's fourth quarter** (at worst), look for new branches on the fruit bush. [*Consideration: these are the branches that have developed in the season just ended. They appear, in the main, at the end of existing branches. Recognise each one by its obvious freshness, newness, pale-green colour and comparative slenderness and fragility*]

3 leave these new branches alone if they do not extend beyond the parent plant's allotted growth space. They bear, unseen, next year's fruit

REQUIRED FOR *FRUIT BUSH/5*

- One-year-old composted manure for mulching layer rehabilitation at **the start of the March or April moon's fourth quarter.**

- 115g to the square metre of fish-blood-and-bone fertiliser, applied to the soft-fruit bed at **the start of the March or April moon's fourth quarter.**

- A garden hoe, a hand fork, a de-weeding tool, a watering can, a wheelbarrow, 1:40 comfrey solution, a garden rake, secateurs.

For the complete instruction, see *FRUIT BUSH/1 to -/5.*

4 shorten each new branch — at any point in its length and by as little as possible — only if it extends outside the plant's allotted growth space. Use secateurs

TIP 69
➔ **Bush fruit must be picked the moment it is ripe. There is, Mr Harris points out, an even better time to harvest it. That is when full ripeness coincides with the afternoon of a warm, sunny day and the end of the moon's second quarter. Then, the fruit carries maximum juice and, hence, maximum flavour. It is at its worst, by the same token, when picked fully ripened on a rainy, dull day during the moon's fourth quarter. Unripened berries, for the pot, may be picked at any time: "although, even with these," he adds, "catching a sunny afternoon and the end of the moon's second quarter brings an improvement."**

70

IN

R J Harris's horticultural practice, the freshly-planted soft-fruit bush is brought to maturity and kept in peak condition and at peak fruiting by four annual treatments

— pruning
— feeding
— re-mulching
— spraying to prevent mildew.

A possible fifth treatment is curative spraying, to combat a mildew attack that proves too strong for the preventive spraying to avert.

The result of the annual prune is a bush which is supported upon a single, branch-free stem about 15cm in height. The bush is goblet-shaped, with an empty centre. It possesses no branches which will not bear fruit next season. It fits snugly within its designated growth area. It offers effortless management beneath its lowest branches. In the case of the gooseberry, it offers pain-free berry harvesting.

Supremely, the annual pruning leaves the plant with the desire to produce new growth. This ensures an annually rejuvenated plant. Potentially, such a plant has a very long life ahead of it.

The pruning also places the plant's life under threat. It reacts to this by seeking to ensure its future. This it does by increasing its seed production. A by-product of this process is an increased number of berries for the gardener's consumption.

69

Prune in November, December,

January or February. Choose the first of these that provides the three essential conditions

— when the bush is bare of leaves, indicating that it has entered upon its Winter sleep

— when the weather is not freezing

— when the bush's branches are not in a frozen state.

Note that the November prune and the February prune are possible only when the bush is dormant and leafless.

the plant, or the one that is of malformed shape]

7 prune off most of it. Leave a short length of it attached to its parent branch. This short length bears three or four

5 look for the branch that crosses another branch

6 of the two crossing branches, select the one that is clearly of least service to the plant.
[*Consideration: this is the shorter of the two, or the weaker of the two, or the one that grows into the centre of*

TIP 70
➜ **Bush fruit can be bottled, and very successfully. See Panel 116 for a general-purpose instruction, which calls for no special bottling equipment and utilises every-day, domestic cooking utensils.**

71

"AT PRUNING TIME, the condition of the weather is of paramount importance," stresses R J Harris. "Rain does not matter. Wind does not matter. But only the most foolhardy of gardeners cuts into a plant that is frozen or when the weather is freezing."

In Cornwall, the head gardener's home county, January and February are guaranteed to be suitable for work with the secateurs. "But no later," he comments, "because by the middle or the end of February the plants show signs of life."

For those in Yorkshire or Shropshire, or Lancashire or Kent, his advice is "prune in November immediately after leaf drop if weather conditions permit. If they do not, prune during the following February or March before the new leaves begin to show.

"Good general counsel in horticulture is always work with the elements, not against them," the head gardener says.

bumps from which, clearly, leaves or berries grew

8   look for branches that show signs of decay

9   prune off the whole length of the decay-bearing branch, even if it appears to have non-decayed parts

10   look for any branch that keeps the light and air from the heart of the bush

11   prune off most of it — but leave a short length of it attached to its parent branch. This short length

bears three or four bumps from which, clearly, leaves or berries grew

12   look for branches appearing on the stem of the bush, below the upper branches. Remove them, restoring the stem's 15cm-plus-long, branchless state

13   look at where the plant's main stem emerges from the ground

14   look for new branches growing from the ground close to the base of the stem

15   remove the soil from around the stem. Do not damage the stem or the plant's roots

16   look for the points where the new branches grow from the main stem

17   cut at these points, removing the whole of each new branch

TIP 71

➔   **The soft-fruit-bush areas of the Victorian walled kitchen garden at Tresillian in Cornwall are not protected against the birds. It does not matter if they augment their diet with snatched berries, so voluminous is the fruit-bush crop. For the garden with no more than one or two bushes, however, any bird attack, no matter how slight, is significant. Low-cost, heavy-gauge, light-weight, black plastic net of close mesh suffices to keep them away. Simply throw it fully over the individual bush and pin down or weight its edges to prevent the marauding birds from trapping themselves within its folds.**

72

The mulching layer traps moisture within the fruit-bush bed, so that the bed is never dry — or is as close to that perfect state as it is possible for it to be. "The rule of thumb for all top fruit is that the biggest percentage of its content is water," points out Mr Harris. "The more moisture that can be retained within the bed and around the root systems the juicier and tastier is the fruit and the more prolifically does the plant bear."

18 replace the soil. Leave the base of the plant as it was originally.
[**Consideration:** *this base-of-stem stage of the pruning maintains the single, branch-free stem that distinguishes the ideal bush*]

19 dispose securely off site of all removed branches or parts of branches.
[**Consideration:** *totentially, this material is a disease/pest carrier*]

20 in March or April of the young plant's first year, in the driest weather that is available — and at **the start of the moon's fourth quarter**, — move out of the way what is left of the bed's mulching layer. Use a rake. Expose the bed's surface completely. Take care not to damage the young bush's stem

21 remove all weeds from the bed. On a small bed use a hand fork or a preferred specialist de-weeding tool. On a large bed use a hoe.

Do not damage the plant's stem or roots. Tread on the bed as little as possible. Immediately reinstate any trodden-on areas, using a hoe or a rake

22 saturate the bed with comfrey solution which is in the ratio of one part of comfrey stock to forty parts of mains water or water taken a water butt. Use a frequently replenished watering can. Subject the bed to the most thorough of soakings.
[**Consideration:** *the aim is to saturate the plant's roots. This is to ensure the effectiveness of the next stage: feeding. The controlling factor at this point is the gardener's patience and stamina. It is not possible to over-water the bed and the young bush (or bushes, if more than one has been permanently planted)*]

23 immediately — so that there is no loss of moisture due to

TIP 72
→ The 'sponge' that is so important a part of each of R J Harris's three types of bed acts as a food store for no more than three seasons once a plant has sunk its roots into it. Hence, after season three, the annual mulching layer of manure and dressing of fertiliser assume two additional roles: the former takes over from the 'sponge' the task of retaining moisture and making it available to the plant's roots; the two combine to leach rain-driven nutrients into the top soil around the affected plant to boost the steadily diminishing underground larder.

73

AMERICAN MILDEW is the principal curse of the
gooseberry bush. Says R J Harris: "The disease appears on the leaves in the form of white spores. These then extend to the forming, young berries. It is carried on the wind. It follows very, very hot days and cold nights, and especially when there is thundery weather and much humidity.

"It is yet another demonstration that town-area gardens suffer from problems of this kind because of their close proximity to each other — and suffer from them very rapidly, indeed.

"A disease or a pest thriving at one end of the road — which is much more likely to be there, in any event, because of the intensive gardening of varying qualities that has gone on for decades and generations — expands to the other end before you know where you are.

"At Tresillian, where the estate's gardens are isolated, the opposite is the case, and we suffer much, much less."

Gooseberries are not spoiled by American mildew. When the spores have been removed by thorough washing, the berries are fit to be consumed: "although," says Mr Harris, "if nothing is done to prevent the attacks — and if they are accepted, year after year, as an unavoidable feature of soft-fruit production — the affected leaves can be detrimental to the well-being of the plant and that, in turn, can affect the quality of the fruit. And repeated uncorrected attacks can result in a permanently sickly plant bearing berries of increasingly inferior quality."

A visit by American mildew is accounted for, usually, by an ineptly-executed or insufficient or omitted winter tar wash treatment.

"The instant the first dusting of spores is detected, Bordeaux mixture must be sprayed on according to its maker's instructions," says R J Harris. "Several sprayings may be necessary to eradicate the disease."

evaporation — spread evenly onto the saturated bed surface 115g of fish-blood-and-bone fertiliser to the square metre. Work it in well with the hand fork, the rake or the hoe. Avoid the plant's roots

24 immediately, bring back onto the bed the remains of the initial mulch

25 add to it fresh mulch — if possible, but not essentially, of the same kind. Achieve a 7cm-to-8cm thickness on

the whole of the bed's area. Stop the mulching layer just short of the bush's main stem.

TIP 73
➜ "Wear protective gloves when pruning gooseberry bushes," advises R J Harris. "The work goes forward so much more quickly. Even those branches that have grown during the season just closed, and are very, very young and tender, carry thought-provoking spines."

[**Considerations: 1** — *if the mulching layer touches the main stem, it provokes the growth of above-ground roots. The plant then becomes weakened;* **2** *— the added mulch material is drawn, ideally, from the batch of manure ordered in a year ago, which has been composting for the past year*]

26 spray immediately after the feeding and re-mulching stages — and whilst the bush is fully dormant and is minus its leaves. Use a winter tar wash, according to its maker's instructions. Deliver it, preferably, via a pressure sprayer.
[**Consideration:** *in the case of gooseberry bushes, this preventive treatment makes an American-mildew attack unlikely*]

27 coinciding with the pruning, feeding and mulching-layer rehabilitation of the soft-fruit bed, order in another batch of fresh manure. Store it and leave it to compost for one year. Earmark it for the re-mulching of the surface of the bed in one year's time

28 repeat the total pruning, feeding and mulching-layer rehabilitation and manure-procurement programme annually for the life of the bush or bushes

29 permit the young bush to fruit for the first time during its second year in its permanent home. Permit it to fruit annually thereafter

30 as the seasons pass, look for very dark-brown, gnarled branches at the annual pruning stage. Expect to see them only in the bush that is several years old

31 prune them off. Cut where each begins, no matter where in the total plant that is.
[**Consideration:** *do not worry if these old branches have young-looking branches attached to them. All must go. Only by this means can the bush be rejuvenated and protected from the encroachment of unproductive old age.*]

for background information, see
COMFREY/1 to -/3, FERTILISER, MANURE, MOON.

GOOSEBERRY — bush production, planting and management. Do as described in *FRUIT BUSH/1 to -/5*. See these sections also for guidance on black-currant, red-currant and white-currant bush cultivation.

LETTUCE/1 — as a catch crop, grown in the space between developing rows of pea and dwarf-french-bean plants. Adopting head gardener R J Harris's policy and approach, proceed as follows

1 at the earliest moment in the season, procure the preferred variety/ies of lettuce seed

2 in early February (there is no moon-quarter involvement at this stage), and working under cover

— loosely fill a small seed tray with John Innes seed compost

- Empty ground between developing rows of principal crops such as peas and dwarf french beans.

- Chosen lettuce seed, for development into seedlings in a tray.

- 60g to the square metre of fish-blood-and-bone fertiliser applied each month at **the start of the moon's fourth quarter** prior to planting out lettuce plantlets at **the start of the next moon's second quarter**.

- John Innes seed compost. John Innes No 2 potting compost.

- Seed trays, water, a watering can with a fine rose, a folded newspaper, a seed dispenser, a 6-mm garden sieve, labels, a cold frame, cold greenhouse or conservatory, sacks, redundant blankets or fleece, thick, bared copper wire or short lengths of copper tubing, a hoe, a redundant biro for use as a small dibber, a redundant table fork for use as a transplanting 'tool'.

For the complete instruction, see *LETTUCE/1* and -/2.

— lightly brush the hand across the top of the tray to level off the compost

— tap the base of the tray, gently yet firmly, two or three times upon the workbench top. By this means, settle the surface of the compost until it is level with the base of the rim that is moulded into the top of the tray

— add more compost, if necessary, to compensate for under-filling

— gently add water to the compost's surface until the whole of the compost is thoroughly moistened. Use a can fitted with a fine rose. Do not disturb the surface of the compost as the water is added

3 cover the tray with a folded newspaper. Place it in a protected place. Place a packet of the chosen lettuce seeds alongside it. Leave both undisturbed for twenty-four hours.
[**Considerations:** **1** — *this enables the compost to become comprehensively moistened;* **2** — *the newspaper reduces evaporation. It is folded to increase its rigidity and to reduce its area to one that is slightly larger than the top of the tray. Newspaper is*

TIP 74
→ The 'sponge' that is so important a part of each of R J Harris's three types of bed acts as a food store for no more than three seasons once a plant has sunk its roots into it. Hence, after season three, the annual mulching layer of manure and dressing of fertiliser assume two additional roles: the former takes over from the 'sponge' the task of retaining moisture and making it available to the plant's roots; the two combine to leach rain-driven nutrients into the top soil around the affected plant to boost the steadily diminishing underground larder of plant goodness.

74

There is general agreement that mystery surrounds the origins of the lettuce. The ancient Greeks knew, ate and wrote about it. So did the Romans. Doubtless they included its seeds in their food parcels to Britain. Certainly, it was being mentioned by the English of mediaeval times.

Equally unrecorded is the period during which today's forms evolved. Of these, the cos type hearts up, is tall, is less demanding of space and, arguably, offers the finest of lettuce flavours. It happens also to be the most troublesome to grow. The cabbage type also hearts up, but hugs the ground and, spreading, is more demanding of space.

cheaper, safer and more convenient than a sheet of glass. Unlike condensation-dripping glass, it does not encourage any kind of undesirable condition of the compost's surface; **3** *— the process also enables compost and seeds to arrive at a common ambient temperature. Overall, seed germination is encouraged by this means*]

4 after the twenty-four-hour pause, remove the newspaper

5 open the packet of chosen lettuce seeds over the uncovered tray.
[***Consideration:*** *this ensures that accidentally-spilled seeds drop onto the compost and, hence, are not wasted*]

6 transfer some of the lettuce seeds to a seed dispenser of the kind that enables controlled sowing. It is obtainable from any garden centre. Fill the dispenser without touching the seeds with the fingers.
[***Consideration:*** *the seeds are not crushed by pressure applied by the finger tips. This helps to achieve the highest possible amount of germination*]

7 distribute onto the surface of the moistened compost a number of seeds according to how many lettuces you expect to consume by one means or another during one month?

8 space the seeds as widely as possible

9 pass some of the John Innes seed compost through a 6-mm garden sieve to produce powdered compost. Return the residue of the compost to the compost bag

10 dribble the powdered compost onto the scattered seeds. Do so through the finger tips. Do so as thinly as possible.
[***Consideration:*** *by this means, achieve a covering the depth of which is no more than twice the thickness of the individual seed. This is standard practice when*

TIP 75
➔ **Remove the roots as well as the body of the lettuce plant when harvesting. Remove any bolting lettuce in its entirety before it can set seed. The cos lettuce does not object to having its outer leaves removed before, in due course, it is fully uprooted.**

75

The lettuce, the spring onion and the radish are head gardener R J Harris's preferred plants for filling ground left empty by the deployment or removal of principal crops.

At a pinch, all three cope with any soil conditions and the smallest area of available soil. Hence, in Mr Harris's planning, they fall outside the crop rotation programme and are introduced at any time within the growing season into any empty places in any of the beds that he creates for specific crop developments.

He opts for catch crops from seeds sown in pots or trays and developed to plantlet stage, instead of from seeds sown in the ground. This is because usable results are achieved more quickly. This is not simply an obviously good idea. It is a requirement. Ground that becomes available for a catch crop sometimes is not available long enough for development from seed to mature plant.

At Tresillian, the walled kitchen garden is constantly equipped with pots or trays of catch-crop plantlets awaiting a permanent home.

sowing seeds, whether into compost or garden soil]

11 return the surplus powdered compost to the compost bag

12 label the tray, so that, later, there is no doubt about what is growing in it and when it was sown

---

If further explanation is required, e-mail R J Harris on
rjh@moongardening.fsnet.co.uk

13 re-cover the tray with the folded newspaper

14 place the sown, covered tray in a protected, darkened place. Ensure that in this place the temperature level cannot rise higher than 12°C to 15°C (55°F to 60°F).
[*Consideration: when sown lettuce seeds' ambient temperature exceeds this level, germination is reduced. Also, the seeds that manage to germinate develop into plants of reduced quality*]

15 ensure that, from that moment, the compost remains evenly moist and never dries out. Apply water with a can fitted with a fine rose. Until mature seedlings have been developed, use water that is kept always beside the tray. Beyond the mature-seedling stage, mains water or water from a butt is suitable.
[*Consideration: by this means, the water is at the same ambient temperature as the compost during the crucial stages of germination*

TIP 76
➔ **The earliest of the planted-out young lettuce may be at risk from the frost. Be ready to cover them by night with fleece (the easiest and also feather-light, so weigh it down against the wind), cloches (the most expensive) or plastic sheeting arranged over improvised wire hoops and then tucked into the soil to resist the force of the wind (the cheapest and most troublesome). Remove the protective covering the moment it is judged to be unnecessary.**

76

Lettuce can be cooked, a fact which is often overlooked, so entrenched in users' minds is the imagine of the plant as solely a salad base or as a decorative adornment of prepared dishes.

Steaming is simplest. In a basket set over a little boiling water in a saucepan, it softens in about ten minutes and can be served as if it were any other steamed, green vegetable. Lettuce soup — especially the delicious chilled variety —takes a little longer, but recipes for it are common. Peas served with lettuce are different: the total mix is chopped spring onions, lettuce, peas, chopped mint and a little sugar, the whole stir-fried in butter and seasoning.

It all helps to answer the question What can we do with the weary, end-of-season lettuce, including that which has gone to seed? — other, that is, than committing it to the compost bin or the trench for the next deep-trench or shallow-trench bed.

and early growth. Thus, germination and seedling development are not inhibited by sudden, traumatic temperature changes]

16 remove the newspaper and examine the tray daily

17 look for the first hint of green growth showing through the dark brown of the moist compost. Replace the newspaper each time no development is discerned

18 when growth is detected, remove the newspaper

permanently and place the tray in full light in a protected place

19 daily, watch for the appearance of two baby leaves on each of the developing seedlings

20 when this happens, fill another tray with John Innes No 2 potting compost. Use the same method as before. Do so where the tray of seedlings is located, so that the two share a common ambient temperature

21 water the tray's compost content as before. Do so where the seedlings are located

22 cover the new tray with a folded newspaper. Leave it for twenty-four hours, so that its compost becomes comprehensively moistened

23 make very shallow holes in the new tray's compost with the smallest of dibbers. Space the holes 5cm apart

TIP 77
➔ **If possible, insert lettuce plantlets into the ground during the evening of the correct moon day, not during the day itself. This is a plant that loves to be cool when young. It also loves its full measure of moisture. Both conditions are at their most available after the comparatively warm day has dwindled into the comparatively cold evening, and evaporation has reduced. Overall, the result is better lettuce.**

in rows 5cm apart.
[**Consideration:** *a redundant biro makes a suitable dibber for this purpose*]

24 transfer the lettuce seedlings to the John Innes No 2 potting compost in the new tray. Do so as follows in respect of a single seedling

— hold one of the seedling's two leaves between forefinger and thumb

— do so as gently as possible. Do not touch the seedling's stem

— tease the seedling out of its compost bed. Do so with utmost gentleness. Use a redundant table fork (the head gardener's preferred 'tool' for this purpose) to separate the compost at the seedling stem's base and to detach the seedling's single, hairlike root. Sacrifice adjacent seedlings in the process, if that is unavoidable

— lower the seedling's root into a waiting dibbered hole in the other tray's potting compost

— leave as much of the seedling's stem proud of the compost's surface as when it grew in the seed compost

25 gather the potting compost around the root, still using the redundant table fork. Bed the seedling in — again, as gently as possible

26 fill the tray in this fashion. Station it where the seedlings have always been stationed, in full light

27 when the seedlings' two leaves have increased to a minimum of four and the seedlings have become plantlets, place them in their tray in a cold frame, cold greenhouse or conservatory to harden off

28 adjust the protective enclosure's ventilation so that, regularly, there is a change of air

29 during the early weeks of this February/March season, shut the protective enclosure by night to protect against the frost. In the case of the cold frame and the very small greenhouse, be ready with coverings such as sacks or fleece or redundant blankets to increase the night-time — and, if necessary, the day-time — protection. Weigh them down against the force of the wind

30 when hardening off the plantlets on a conservatory window sill, be ready for them to lean towards, and stretch up to, the window panes. Compensate for this by turning the tray through 180^{0} each time leaning becomes apparent

31 the plantlets are suitable for planting out after several days of hardening off

32 repeat the seed-to-plantlet programme each month throughout the growing season until June or July. Commence at the beginning of each month. There is still no moon-quarter

77

Transplanting lettuce plantlets from tray to garden soil

— In the late afternoon or early evening, thoroughly water the place in the bed to which the young lettuce is to be transferred. Use a watering can fitted with a medium rose.

— At the same time, gently lower the tray containing the plantlets into a depth of water. Do so until the top of its growing medium is just below the water's surface.

— Hold the tray there until air bubbles stop rising from the medium's surface. (*This signals that complete water penetration has taken place.*)

— Remove the tray to a shaded patch of soil — not a hard surface. There, permit the surplus water to drain away. (*This avoids creating the conditions that the garden's 'undesirables' may convert into a temporary residence or, at worst, a breeding place.*)

— Wait for at least two hours. (*This ensures that comprehensive moistening takes place and that, as a result, root systems and targeted bed area soak up as much water as they are capable of absorbing and retaining.*)

— Form in the soil at the designated spot the space required to accommodate a plantlet-bearing square of the growing medium in the tray.

— Make the space slightly wider, broader and deeper than is required.

— Hold a plantlet in the tray very gently by one of its leaves. Do not hold it by its stem. (*No matter how gently pressure is exerted when the stem is held, it is crushed. This causes the death of the young lettuce.*)

— Cut with a narrow-bladed, sharp knife a square of the growing medium that is at the base of the plantlet's stem.

— Carefully extract the square of medium. Use the knife as a lifting tool. Place the square of medium, plus its resident plantlet, into the waiting hole in the garden soil.

— Gently firm the soil around the square without disturbing it, and without leaving space beneath it or alongside it.

— Ideally, ensure that when the square of medium is settled in, its surface is slightly below that of the surrounding soil.

— Gently and thoroughly apply water at the base of the newly-established plantlet. Use a small watering can fitted with a fine rose. (*At this stage, watering fuses the soil to the medium in which the plantlet has developed, enabling its roots to begin drawing in moisture and nutrients at the earliest moment. Also, the watering causes the plantlet to be securely embedded in the soil and, thus, anchored firmly to it.*)

involvement.

[*Consideration: the monthly production of lettuce plantlets may entail 'over-production'. It is more important, however, to have usable plantlets always to hand on a monthly basis for transplanting at* **the start of the second quarter of the moon** *when suitable ground area becomes unemployed. In any event, in the presence of a compost bin (and, possibly, of non-vegetable-growing neighbours), no surplus vegetable matter need be viewed as 'waste'*]

33 when the weather conditions improve, lodge the plantlets' tray in a protected, well-lit place in the garden

34 guard against slug/snail attack by encircling the base of the plantlets' tray with thick, bared copper wire. Alternatively, post short lengths of copper tubing around the tray's base. Or improvise, with the result that there is a water barrier between the pests and the tray and the young lettuce plants developing in it

35 be alert for planting-out opportunities as from the first moment that the peas and the dwarf french beans are sown/planted out into their prepared sections of a first-year, single-dug bed (BED/3)

36 transplant the lettuce plantlets from their tray to between-rows ground on the day that the first dwarf french beans and peas are sown/planted out — ie, at **the start of the moon's second quarter** in the

month of sowing/planting out. See panel for an effective method of planting out the young lettuce plants

37 when planting out, favour the youngest lettuce.

[*Consideration: the young ones adjust themselves to a change of environment more readily than do the older ones. Also, when settled in, they develop into better lettuce*]

38 space the lettuce 22cm apart. Plant in single rows where the available space is 60cm wide. Plant in double rows where the available space is more than that. Space double (or multiple) rows 20cm apart. Stagger the planting positions.

[*Consideration: planting in rows runs counter to the vogue for planting out haphazardly. The regimented approach aids general management. In particular, it simplifies hoeing*]

39 after making the first insertions of lettuce plantlets, repeat the operation each month for as long as between-rows

TIP 78

→ **The more speedily lettuce is grown, the better is its flavour. That is why the head gardener gives this lowly plant the very best of growing conditions, never failing to begin with fish-blood-and-bone fertiliser. It is also why he favours beginning with young plants in the garden, not seed sown into the ground. He also never fails to observe the correct moon phases when feeding and planting out.**

ground is available and for as long as weather/soil conditions and the progress of the season make it possible

40 insert the plantlets, each month, at **the start of the moon's second quarter**. [*Consideration:* it is likely that the second and third lettuce insertions coincide with the second and third sowings of the pea and dwarf-french-bean seeds]

41 before the second and before each subsequent planting out, dress the surface of the targeted ground with fish-blood-and-bone fertiliser at the rate of 60g to the square metre. Do so at **the start of the fourth quarter of the moon** that precedes the second-moon-quarter planting out

42 turn in the fertiliser lightly. Use a hoe. [*Consideration:* 60g is specified — not the more usually applied heavier first feed — in the knowledge that the targeted ground was fully fed in support of the first sowing of the principal crop's seeds. This full feed supported, also, the first lettuce plantlets to be inserted. The reduced applications in support of the second and later insertions express R J Harris's determination to avoid the common mistake of over-feeding the soil]

43 harvest the lettuce when it is mature, not before. [*Consideration:* unlike most vegetable plants, lettuce has its best flavour when fully-grown. This is when its heart

is at maximum size and density. The stage immediately beyond that is seed-head development, when the plant begins to become bitter and unpalatable]

44 throughout, hoe regularly to prevent weed-seed germination and to raise moisture to the surface of the ground around the inserted lettuce plants' roots (as well as those of the principal plants)

45 sacrifice the lettuce additions when the pea and/or dwarf-french-bean section providing them with a home is cleared of its principal plants. [*Consideration:* when the legumes come to an end, their bed is emptied in readiness for the rotation-oriented Autumn dig. Any 'lodgers' permitted to overstay their welcome and linger on, such as spinach and lettuce and other salad crops, make digging impossible and, thus, disrupt the crop-rotation system.]

for background information, see
BEAN: dwarf french/1 to -/3,
FERTILISER, MOON,
PEA/1 to -/3, ROTATION.

LETTUCE/2 — as a top-quality crop from seedlings, produced within the crop-rotation system and using the most ground-demanding method.
Proceed as follows

1 at **the end of the September moon's third quarter**, create the bed that is described in BED/3. [*Consideration:* three

REQUIRED FOR *LETTUCE/2*

- A section of a first-year *BED/3* for use as a lettuce producer.

- 115g to the square metre of fish-blood-and-bone fertiliser, applied to the lettuce section at **the start of the March or April moon's fourth quarter**.

- Lettuce plantlets pots, for planting out monthly 22cm apart in rows also spaced 22cm apart, commencing at **the start of the following April or May moon's second quarter**.

- A garden fork, a rake, a four-tined cultivator (if possible), fleece, cloches or an improvised tunnel made of wire hoops covered by plastic sheeting, a compost bin or heap, a trench awaiting development into a deep-trench bed (see *BED/1*) or a shallow-trench bed (see *BED/2*), a garden spade, a hoe.

For the complete instruction, see *LETTUCE/1* and -/2.

conditions help considerably to as good as guarantee success in lettuce production. They are well-worked top soil, a manure 'sponge' beneath it, and plenty of moisture. BED/3 provides all of these]

Visit *R J Harris's Moon Gardening*'s companion web site **www.moongardening.fsnet.co.uk** to keep in touch with the results of the head gardener's latest experimental archaeological projects and developmental work in the walled kitchen garden at Tresillian in Cornwall.

2 commencing on the first day of the following February (there is no moon-quarter involvement at this stage), produce at the start of each month — and have constantly available — the lettuce plantlets the production of which is described in *LETTUCE/1*. Do so until June or July

3 at **the start of the March or April moon's fourth quarter**, earmark a section of *BED/3* for use as a lettuce section. [**Consideration:** *if March's soil is unworkable, wait for April's. If this is not improved, wait for May's. Begin the seedlings-tray production in February, and continue it, despite this*]

4 ensure that the section

— is no more than large enough to accommodate the required number of lettuce plantlets. [**Consideration:** *these deliver a harvest that extends through Summer into Autumn, thanks to successive, monthly insertion of plantlets posted 22cm apart in rows also 22cm apart*]

TIP 79

➔ **Seize every opportunity to grow lettuce as a catch crop from plantlets, in preference to starting from seed and giving it its own bed. Inserting waiting young plants into soil prepared for other cultivation is more quickly done, and with much less effort, than starting with no bed and an unopened packet of seeds. Also, space is saved.**

78

At Tresillian, in the walled kitchen garden, an often-used combination of lettuce is *All The Year Round, Webb's Wonderful* and *Oak Leaf* sown in regimented rows in areas separated by temporary paths on the bed's surface to facilitate hoeing. The combination and the lettuce types are typically Victorian; they help to achieve the return to those times that R J Harris works for constantly.

Equally often, planted nearby are spinach, kohlrabi and maincrop potatoes with a scattering of Mexican marigolds and pot marigolds to perplex the pests as well as to add colour.

— provides access to each of its four sides for management and harvesting.
[**Consideration:** *the access acknowledges that adjacent sections within BED/3 are, or are to be, earmarked for other crop production*]

5 clear the section of weeds. Use a garden fork

6 compost the annual weeds that have not set seeds, together with their roots. Or place them in the trench that awaits development into a deep-trench bed (*BED/1*) or shallow-trench bed (*BED/2*), if there is one in the garden

7 off site, destroy or dispose of the annual weeds that have set seeds, together with their roots, the perennial weeds and their roots, and the grass growth and its roots

8 at the same time as de-weeding the lettuce section-to-be, use the garden fork to level its surface. Break up the large clods formed by the use of a garden spade when *BED/3* was created, and that have thwarted Winter's attempts to reduce them in size

9 follow by using a rake. Move the surface of the ground backwards and forwards with the rake's tines. Criss-cross it in the process. Use the full length of the rake's handle. Aim for a rake-tine depth of very coarse earth crumbs, evenly laid out

10 de-earth the rake frequently, to keep its tines unblocked

11 remove the stones that are trapped by the rake's unblocked tines. Store these for use in connection with other projects in the garden.

TIP 80
➔ **Lettuce plantlets left over at the end of the season have three uses: their leaves — although small — are suitable for salads, plucked from the container as required; the young leaves can be used as recipe ingredients; the young plants in their entirety can go into the compost bin or heap and/or the trench that awaits development into an over-wintering deep- or shallow-trench bed. The redundant John Innes No 2 potting compost is spread thinly on the garden's beds (which is how all redundant composts may be turned to good account). The empty containers are washed clean with Jeyes fluid and returned to store.**

79

Lettuce wins high praise from R J Harris for its gardener-friendly qualities

"Wherever there is unemployed ground not affected by the rotation system, make it earn its keep by giving you lettuce with next to no trouble right through the season," he says.

"Fork it over well to loosen the surface, de-weed it at the same time, feed it 115 g of fish-blood-and-bone to the square metre and then get a fine tilth and sow seeds into 12mm deep drills when the moon is in its second quarter. Repeat the sowing each month.

"Thin the seedlings and then the plantlets until there is a 22mm spacing between the maturing plants.

"After that, keep harvesting."

The head gardener lists points to note:

1) lettuce seeds germinate best when not over hot. "So use slightly shaded areas, if possible, when seed sowing."

2) the appropriate moon quarters must be observed when first feeding the soil and then when sowing the seeds

3) guard against the slugs and snails by positioning bare copper wire or copper tubing close to the developing plants.

[*Considerations:* **1** — cost-conscious gardening aims always to conserve useful resources that may be difficult to obtain at some point in the future.
Sometimes, stones are an irreplaceable ingredient in garden projects, and merit the small amount of storage space that they occupy when conserved; **2** — the stones that slip through the rake's unblocked tines are of the size that is required by the soil. They are an aid to drainage. They act as a moisture-retaining mulch. At all times, but especially in Summer, they release during the night the heat that they absorb during the day, relatively warming the section and its contents; **3** — the stones that are gathered by the rake's regularly de-earthed tines are likely to be too large to be wanted in the soil; **4** — generally, if no stone removal is desired, use a hoe when a bed's surface is being turned. The hoe's shape prevents it from gathering stones of any size]

12 dress the raked-level surface of the lettuce section with 115g to the square metre of fish-blood-and-bone fertiliser. Work it in lightly. Use the rake. Restore the level surface

13 achieve a less coarse tilth on the lettuce section's surface. Do so by re-applying the rake if no other tool is

TIP 81

➜ **The cold frame can produce lettuce for Winter- and Spring-time consumption. Sow the seeds sparsely into its floor at the start of the September moon's second quarter. Do so into drills 12mm deep and 22cm apart. Ventilate by day, shut up by night and add protection if frost is about. Thin after four-leafed development. Harvest as often as the produce is ready, taking when the plants are still young. Spring onions can be grown in the cold frame, sown at the same time.**

available. Move its head in all directions methodically. Seek a greater breaking down of the coarse particles of surface earth

14 for a better, more easily achieved breaking down of the surface particles, use R J Harris's preferred four-tined cultivator. Do so as if it were a rake. Reduce the coarse crumbs of the soil to crumbs which are as fine as the four-tined cultivator is capable of producing. Whether a rake or a cultivator is applied, penetrate the surface with it as deeply as its tines permit.
[*Consideration: of the many manually-operated cultivators that are available for this purpose, the head gardener uses the long-handled tool that has three, four or five long, curved tines. In the hands of a practised operator, the three-tined cultivator provides a coarse tilth, the four-tined a less coarse tilth, and the five-tined a fine tilth. Also, being much less prone to clogging and having far fewer and more widely-spaced tines than the rake, all three cultivators ignore the essential small stones that the initial raking leaves in situ*]

15 at **the start of the April or May moon's second quarter**, make the first

---

80

Lettuce has joined the long, long queue of the plants that have suffered the F1-hybridisation fate.

As a result of the F1 treatment, affected plants are mirror images of one another. They are the products not of seeds but of bits of themselves. That is why the gardener cannot expect to repeat them by collecting seeds from them in the time-honoured way. Their seeds do not reproduce true to F1 type. Only a further purchase of seeds wins a repeat of the original plant.

This makes sense on commercial levels. Seed sales are increased. The fruit and veg retailer benefits, as well, by receiving vegetables in uniform sizes all harvested at the one grower-dictated time. The same applies to hard fruit, which comes uniformly armour-plated against damage and calculatedly unripened to give long shelf life.

Be it said, hybridisation helps to guarantee food for the masses. Notably, it has given to the world wheat, barley and oats the yields of which have been increased ten-fold or more.

Nothing, however, in the head gardener's opinion, equals home-garden produce for flavour and nutritional value. That is so in the case of the common-or-garden, un-F1-manipulated lettuce.

---

transplantation of plantlets to the lettuce section of first-year the *BED/3*. Be guided by the weather/soil conditions when deciding in which month to do this. See the panel in *LETTUCE/1* for an effective method of planting out lettuce plantlets

16 favour the youngest plantlets.
[*Consideration: the youngest plantlets adjust themselves to a change of*

environment more readily than do the older ones. Also, when settled in, they develop into better lettuce]

17 space the plantlets 22cm apart in rows also spaced 22cm apart. Stagger the planting positions in relation to one another. Plant in regimented rows in order to simplify hoeing and general management. Do so speedily, yet gently.
[***Consideration:*** *when removed from their host compost, the roots of the young lettuce dry quickly, especially in windy conditions. Hence, they must be exposed to the elements for the shortest possible time]*

18 protect this first planting out if frost threatens. Use fleece, cloches or an improvised tunnel made of wire hoops covered by plastic sheeting the two long edges of which are tucked into the ground to resist wind pull. Remove the protective coverings the moment the weather conditions indicate that they are no longer necessary

19 repeat the initial planting out on a monthly basis. Do so each time **at the start of the moon's second quarter**. Progressively fill the section. Occupy the whole of the growing season in this way

20 progressively harvest the lettuce when it is mature, not before.
[***Consideration:*** *unlike many vegetables — which are better for the table when picked young — lettuce has its best flavour when fully-grown. This is when its heart is at maximum size and density. The stage immediately beyond this is seed-head development, when the plant begins to become bitter and becomes increasingly unpalatable]*

21 throughout, hoe regularly to prevent weed-seed germination and to raise moisture to the surface of the ground around the inserted lettuce seedlings' roots

22 when over-production occurs, harvest for the non-vegetable-growing neighbours, the compost bin, the trench awaiting development into a deep-trench bed (*BED/1*) or a shallow-trench bed (*BED/2*), or cooked dishes

23 empty the lettuce section by the **start of the September or October moon's third quarter**

24 with a garden spade, methodically dig over the empty surface to the depth of the spade's blade. Achieve an appearance that is as close as possible to that of the surface of a ploughed field. Make this a part of the Autumn dig of the total *BED/3* area. Ideally, complete the total dig by **the start of the moon's fourth quarter**. Do not feed the section. It bears no more crops until the new season. Then, together with the remainder of dug-over *BED/3*, it embarks upon its second year in the R J Harris crop-rotation system.

for background information about
***LETTUCE/2*, see**
FERTILISER, MOON, ROTATION.

MANURE/1: how mixed farmyard manure and stable manure work.

The more fertile top soil is, the better it enables plants to grow and to flourish. Manure — usually, fully-composted manure — increases top soil's fertility in the following ways

1 it opens and keeps open the top soil's structure. It does this by

— being bulky, especially when it is mixed with straw

— feeding. and hence increasing, the top soil's worm and insect population

2 worms and insects create an aerating structure within the top soil by tunnelling and forming passageways. The more of them there are, the more of their tunnels and passageways there are

---

82

Sub soil is an inferior growing medium principally (but not solely) because its dead vegetable- and animal-matter content does not decay.

This is due to the absence of bacteria, the soil-borne agent that causes decay.

Bacteria are not present because sub soil — due to its position deep beneath the top soil — is unable to receive air and warmth and — sometimes — moisture. These are the ingredients without which bacteria cannot exist.

"This is why the under layers of woodland soil form such an unsatisfactory growing medium," says Mr Harris. "They are rich in thicknesses of leaves — but they lack air, due to leaf compaction, and that lack of air results in a lack of warmth.

"Not until the gardener goes to work with spade and fork does air get in and, with it, warmth and moisture. These enable the bacteria to feed on the leaves, causing them to decay and, thus, create a medium for successful plant growth."

81

"Most gardeners know instinctively that animal manure is good for the soil," says Mr Harris. "The trouble is, some of them apply the 'more has got to be better' rule, and use far too much of the stuff.

"I have known cases where, ground area for ground area, up to five times as much has been applied as a farmer puts on his fields.

"This is a waste of effort as well as a waste of money and feed. And it does the soil no good at all."

---

3 the tunnels and passageways and the openness created by manure's bulk admit air

4 the more of this infrastructure there is, the more air is present in the top soil

5 air draws in warmth

6 air draws in moisture (which is retained for longer by the top soil because of manure's natural moisture retentiveness)

83

THE garden spade and the garden fork offer the best form of manure, says R J Harris.

"Understandably, very few sparetime gardeners know this. Professional horticulturists have known it for centuries.

"The word 'manuring' comes from the word 'manoeuvring'," the head gardener explains, "and 'manoeuvring' was once a regularly-employed technique. Spade or fork dug into the soil, lifted it, turned it and replaced it in a broken form.

"The word 'manoeuvring' came from the ancient French 'maynoverer', which came from the Latin 'manu operari' or 'work by hand'.

'It just goes to show that turning the soil by hand — like so much in horticulture — goes right back to ancient times and has come to us an unchanged technique.

"Deep digging — or manoeuvring — or bastard trenching, as it was also once known — is by far the best way to enable essential air and, hence, warmth and moisture to get into the soil to encourage the bacteria that break down the dead animal and vegetable materials.

"This applies throughout the moon month. But it applies especially during the moon's third and fourth quarters. This is when the sinking water table makes the top soil more ready to draw in whatever is applied to it, including air, warmth and moisture.

"The marvel of it is that manoeuvring increases soil fertility without the addition of any kind of plant food," says the head gardener. "That must make it the lowest-cost treatment, financially speaking."

7 air, warmth and moisture make it possible for bacteria to be in, and to thrive in, top soil

8 bacteria decompose the vegetable and animal matter that is present in top soil

9 decomposed vegetable and animal matter plus air, warmth, moisture and the nutrients added to the top soil by the manure create the environment that plants must have if they are to succeed

10 supporting this process are the nutrients produced by the worms and the insects as they consume, digest, ingest and excrete their fellow creatures.

The best time to insert manure and any other feed into top soil is when the moon's third quarter begins.

This is when the moon's gravitational pull begins to weaken. As a result, it permits the level of the water table to fall.

Nature notoriously abhorring vacuums, a drawing-in effect results. This encourages additives to be more deeply, more compre-

TIP 82
➔ **Compost stable manure by stacking it on the ground for a few weeks (no container is necessary, unless one happens to be available) and leaving it uncovered and undisturbed. It need not be turned. Ideally, make the stack on the first day of the moon's first quarter.**

hensively absorbed into the top soil's structure.

The process gathers pace until the next new moon, a fortnight or so later. Then, the satellite planet's pull upon Earth begins to strengthen, raising the water table's level and, by its upward pressure, decreasing the top soil's receptivity.

Complementing this natural process is the practical reality that the best time to apply feed is when the top soil is most charged with moisture.

This, again, is when the moon's third quarter begins.

Then, the previous fortnight's increasing gravitational pull has raised the water table's level and increased the top soil's moisture content.

MANURE/2 — **managing the material.** The head gardener recommends the following way to make fresh farmyard manure (not stable manure) suitable for use in the garden and to minimise its smell

1 receive the manure from farmyard or other supplier in plastic sacks.
[**Consideration:** *by this means avoid the wheelbarrowing of delivered loose material from where it is tipped to where it is to be stored. Avoid, also, by this means, close proximity to a malodorous substance*]

2 wheelbarrow the plastic sacks to a timber bin of the kind that was once advocated as the best type for composting waste vegetable matter

3 make the bin a generous cubic metre in size. Give it the construction form of a Canadian log cabin. Design

84

' IT'S a fantastic job, of a cold, frosty morning, to get stuck in with a good fork and transfer the composting manure from one point to another to aerate it and thus increase its bacteria and insect population," says R J Harris.

"When I was an apprentice in the 50s, it was standard practice for the young boys to go out every month at the start of the day and turn a big heap of the stuff.

"We used to layer it with leaves and other vegetable matter."

Rain makes no difference to this ancient process. The farmers, indeed, tip cartloads of unprotected material into the corner of a field in the Spring and Summer and leave it there for twelve months before spreading it.

"Years ago," recalls Mr Harris, "when it was all horse-and-cart work, they used to dot cartloads all over the field in small heaps and leave them to compost. Then, later, the men would come in with forks and spread it to where it was needed."

it so that the slotted-together timbers do not introduce gaps into its sides.
[**Consideration:** *this reduces the loss of moisture from the composting manure and serves to retain heat*]

4 alternatively, use a black plastic vegetable-waste composter of the kind that is available from most local authorities, at a subsidised price, or from the garden centres.
[**Consideration:** *this has the advantage of maximum*

85

"**K**NOW what you are buying when you buy in manure," cautions the head gardener.

"Stable manure — the product of the horse —must not have wood shavings in it. It *must* be straw based.The shavings are detrimental when dug into the garden soil.

"Refuse pig manure if it is offered all by itself. It almost certainly contains toxic substances, which got into it from the feed that the pigs were given by the farmer. These substances are not wanted where food is grown."

Mr Harris suggests that some gardeners may prefer to buy commercially-produced, bagged manure.

"This is not the popular dried manure, which is poultry-based, usually, and seen as a feed, not a conditioner," he comments.

"It is composted horse manure or composted farmyard manure. It is ready for use, it measures up to stated standards, and it is in a very convenient form for handling and storage.

"Its only disadvantage is that it is not cheap.

much waste vegetable matter as is available. If none is available, have a bale of straw to hand, acquired in advance. Add it in loosened form, until a strawy mix is arrived at. [*Consideration: the first day of the moon's first quarter begins the fortnight during which the least loss of moisture into the earth from the stored manure can be expected. This is due to the rising water table, which exerts upward, repelling pressure. Maximum moisture is a requirement in composting manure. It provides the all-important bacteria and insect life with one of the four elements it needs if it is to live and to convert its habitat into a fertility-enhancing medium. The other three are air, warmth and vegetable matter*]

7 prevent the escape of odours from the filled timber bin by covering the surface of the manure with a 8cm-to-10cm thickness of leaf mould, top soil, peat, upside-down turfs, lawn mowings (non-weed-killer-treated),

moisture retention. It also possesses maximum heat attraction and retention, due to its colour]

5 park the sacks at the bin or container until **the first day of the moon's first quarter**, or as close to that day as can be managed

6 on that day, empty the plastic sacks into the bin or container. As this is done, mix in with the manure as

TIP 83
➔ **The head gardener acknowledges: "Certainly, soil is bound to be fed and thus improved when stable or farmyard manure in its original, bulky state is applied to it in an unthinking manner. And results can be expected, of course. But, for truly splendid returns, and for truly improved top soil, it pays to compost correctly and to apply the correct amounts at the correct moon times."**

weighted-down straw or gravel.

[**Consideration:** *the plastic composter has a lid, which serves this purpose. Place a weight on the lid, so that Winter's winds cannot remove it*]

8   leave the binned/ containered material to age for one year or, better, two years.

[**Consideration:** *this lengthy period gives the bacteria within it full opportunity to feed upon the vegetable matter that is present. This induces the process of decay that renders the manure beneficial when it is added to the garden's top soil*]

9   once per month during the year of composting — as **the moon begins its first quarter** — remove the capping or lid from the manure and transfer it to a similar container placed immediately alongside.

[**Consideration:** *by this means add air and, thus, warmth to the material. This lends support to, and causes an increase in, the transforming activity of the bacteria.*]

After the first transference, expect the well-known odours of manure to have reduced almost to nothing

10   alternatively, after removing the surface capping, de-assemble the timber bin from around the manure stack (this facility is the advantage of the Canadian-log-cabin style of design)

If further explanation is required, e-mail R J Harris on
rjh@moongardening.fsnet.co.uk

and re-assemble it immediately alongside. Transfer the composting manure as the timbers of the bin are re-assembled

11   in either case, replace the protective capping

12   alternatively, employ two plastic composters — the one always filled and the other always empty as it awaits the next manure transference.

MARIGOLD: *Mexican/1* — **from seeds to half-hardy plantlets in a heated greenhouse; hardening off in a cold frame.** Using the head gardener's preferred method, proceed as follows

1   on any day in early February, adjust the greenhouse's heating system's temperature level to 18°C-20°C (65°F-68°F)

2   at the same time, assemble in the greenhouse, on a workbench top

- a packet of Mexican marigold seeds
- two seed trays
- John Innes seed compost
- John Innes No 1 potting compost
- a container to hold sieved compost
- a 6mm garden sieve
- a room thermometer, which remains on the workbench top, where the work is done
- a piece of absorbent material

3   also in the greenhouse, have a water container that is

REQUIRED FOR *MARIGOLD: Mexican/1*

• A heated greenhouse, Mexican marigold seeds, seed trays, John Innes seed compost, John Innes No 1 potting compost, a container to hold sieved compost, a 6mm garden sieve, a room thermometer, a water container, water, a piece of absorbent material, a newspaper, a seed dispenser, garden labels, a dibber, a small, sharp knife, a cold frame, sacking or fleece or redundant blankets.

For the complete instruction, see *MARIGOLD: Mexican/1 to -/3.*

— large enough in area at the top to permit the lowering into it of a compost-filled seed tray

— filled to the top with water

4 wait for 24 hours, to ensure that the assembled aids share the greenhouse's temperature

5 fill the one seed tray with the John Innes seed compost to within 10mm-to-12mm of its top. Level the compost's surface

6 consolidate the compost by tapping the base of the tray gently once or twice on the workbench top

7 if necessary, add material to raise the level of the compost to within 10mm-to-12mm of the tray's top

8 lower the base of the filled tray into the container of water until the tray's top is just above water level. [***Consideration:*** *moisture enters the tray through the drainage holes in its base. This effects a moistening without the disturbance to the compost's surface that would be caused by the use of a watering can — no matter how fine the can's rose*]

9 wait for a count of ten. Lift the tray out. Do this several times. Pause between each dipping to allow the surplus water to drain back into the water container

---

86

When making holes in the potting compost to receive the transplanted seedlings, Mr Harris uses one of his kit of several home-made, ash-wood dibbers. "The gardener can get a professional's dibber at a very low price at any garden centre," he observes. "It is made of plastic, usually. It has a wide base at one end for large seedlings and a narrow base at the other for small seedlings.

"It is a neat little job and well worth buying if DIY wooden dibbers are not possible."

---

10 note that, in stages, the colour of the compost's surface changes from an even light brown to an even dark brown. When this colour is arrived at, the compost is correctly moistened

11 place the tray on a piece of absorbent material on the

workbench top.
[*Consideration: the
absorbent material soaks up
the final drainings*]

12 cover the tray with a folded
newspaper. Leave it on the
workbench top, undisturbed,
for 24 hours.
[*Considerations:* **1** — *this
enables the compost to
become comprehensively
moistened. It also arrives at
the greenhouse's temperature
of* 18°C-20°C *(65°F-68°F);* **2**
— *the newspaper reduces
evaporation. It is folded to
increase its rigidity and to
reduce its area to one that is
slightly larger than the top of
the tray. Newspaper is
cheaper, safer and more
convenient than a sheet of
glass. Unlike condensation-
dripping glass, it does not
encourage any kind of
undesirable condition of the
compost's surface;* **3** — *the
24-hour pause also enables
compost and seeds to arrive
at a common ambient
temperature. Overall, seed
germination is encouraged*]

13 whilst waiting, pass some of
the seed compost through
the 6mm garden sieve to
remove lumps and hard
material from it. Place the
sieved, powdered compost in
a container situated
conveniently on the
workbench top

14 after the 24-hour pause,
remove the newspaper
covering from the compost-
filled tray. Open the packet
of Mexican marigold seeds
over the tray.
[*Consideration: this ensures
that accidentally-spilled
seeds drop onto the compost
and, hence, are not wasted*]

87

'To me," says head gardener
R J Harris, "the Mexican
marigold's unique qualities make
it an indispensable tool for
gardening as well as an unusual
plant for propagation."

The special value of the plant
lies in its roots. They have the
ability to deter eelworm (a
potential curse of the potato
crop), mice and moles, couch
grass, bind weed and ground
elder.

In doing so, the roots of the
individual plant are effective for
roughly 2m in all directions. This
overall advantage, the Cornish
head gardener believes, is better
achieved by this environment-
protective, almost cost-free,
fauna-friendly and non-invasive
means than by what can be
bought — and expensively — at
the garden centre and sprayed
on.

---

15 still working over the tray,
transfer some of the seeds to
a seed dispenser of the kind
that enables controlled
sowing without contact
between seeds and fingers.
Fill the dispenser without
touching the seeds with the
fingers. [*Considerations:* **1**
— *the seeds are not crushed
by pressure applied by the
finger tips. This helps to
ensure germination, since
crushed seeds do not
germinate;* **2** — *a seed
dispenser is obtainable from
any garden centre*]

16 post the seeds onto the
surface of the moistened
seed compost. Do so
sparsely, so that, after
germination, the resultant
seedlings are markedly

widely separated from each other

17 dribble the powdered compost onto the seeds through the finger tips. Do so as thinly as possible. [**Consideration:** *by this means, achieve a covering the depth of which is no more than twice the thickness of the individual seed. This is usual practice when sowing seeds — whether into compost or garden soil*]

88

Head gardener R J Harris raises his Mexican marigold plantlets in the heated greenhouse that is against the south-facing wall of Tresillian's kitchen garden. "It is a half-hardy South American plant," he says, "and must have an early, protected start if it is to have a long growing season in the garden keeping all manner of undesirables at bay."

His seed supplier, Suffolk Herbs (see *SUPPLIERS*) reports that South American Indians rely on the Mexican marigold for mosquito control as well as for protecting their potato crops from eelworm. They also dry its leaves and flavour soups and meat dishes with them.

18 return the surplus powdered compost to the compost bag

19 label the tray, so that, later, there is no doubt about what is growing in it and when it was sown

20 re-cover the tray with the folded newspaper. Leave the covered tray on the workbench top

21 ensure that, from that moment, the compost in the tray remains moist. Use the dipping method of watering that was used at the outset

22 examine the tray at least twice daily

23 the moment that there is a hint of green growth showing through the dark brown of the moist seed compost, remove the newspaper covering. Leave the uncovered tray

permanently in full light on the workbench top. Ensure that the greenhouse continues to be heated at 18°C-20°C (65°F-68°F)

24 watch for the appearance of two 'baby' leaves on each seedling

25 when either one of the two 'baby' leaves is large enough to be gripped — with utmost gentleness — between forefinger and thumb, fill and moisten the other seed tray with John Innes No 1 potting compost. Do so as when preparing the first tray

26 cover the newly-filled tray with a folded newspaper, as before

27 at the same time, water the seedlings in their tray. Use the dipping method to do so

28 leave dipped seedlings and newspaper-covered tray on the workbench top in the heated greenhouse for at least 24 hours, so that their

For the starting dates of each month's moon quarters see almost any diary — but it is essential to consult *MOON* first of all.

compost can become moistened evenly throughout and can arrive at the greenhouse's temperature of 18°C-20°C (65°F-68°F)

29 after the 24-hour wait, remove the folded newspaper from its tray

30 make 24 holes in four rows of six in the fully-moistened potting compost. Use a suitably-sized dibber. Shape each hole to take a square of compost

31 ease one seedling at a time — rooted in a square 'nest' of its moist seed compost — out of the seedling tray. Hold it by nothing other than one of its 'baby' leaves. If necessary, sacrifice one or two adjacent neighbours in the process. Use a small, sharp knife to cut out — and to help to lift out — the square of host compost

32 do not touch the seedling's stem.
[*Consideration: a stem that is held is certain to be a crushed. That kills the young plant. A plant is able to grow a new leaf to replace a damaged or removed leaf. It cannot grow a new stem*]

33 transfer the square of compost and its contained seedling to one of the prepared holes in the potting-compost-filled tray

34 gently firm in the square of compost and its seedling. Use the knife as a firming-in tool

35 continue to transplant in this way until all of the

waiting holes in the potting compost are filled

36 label the planted-up tray, indicating what has been transplanted and when.
[*Considerations: 1 — the fully-grown Mexican marigold plant protects against pest and weed over a radius from its stem of about 2m; 2 — whether or not the plantlet tray's 24 plantlets are sufficient to meet the garden's needs only the responsible gardener can decide; 3 — it is recommended that no less than a full, single tray is developed. The surplus of plantlets, if there is one, may be offered to neighbours. added to the compost bin, or placed in the trench that waits development into a deep-trench bed (BED/1) or a shallow-trench bed (BED/2). Their roots, too, may be composted*]

37 remove the now-unemployed seedling tray from the greenhouse. Spread its compost contents thinly over a garden bed. Wash and dry it and return it to store. Remove the other aids and materials for proper cleaning and storage

38 leave the tray of young plants in full light on the workbench top to grow on in the heated greenhouse. Maintain the temperature at the 18°C-20°C (65°F-68°F) level. Do so until each plantlet bears at least four leaves

39 with the weather by this time improved, move the plantlets in their tray to a cold frame.

[*Consideration: if the weather is not improved, wait until it is — which could well be no earlier than mid-April. The plantlets come to no harm in the heated greenhouse as they wait for improved weather conditions*]

40 open the cold frame's top fully during the day

41 close it fully at about 1600 hours and cover it with several layers of sacking or fleece or redundant blankets to shut out the night-time cold

42 on a daily basis, monitor the tray's compost for moisture. Water whenever necessary. Use the dipping method. [*Consideration: mains water may be used, first placed in a container having a suitably-sized top. More conveniently, water in a fully-filled, external water butt may be used. In this case, the tray is lowered into the water via the butt's open top. Water temperature level is not of significance at this relatively advanced stage of plant development*]

43 leave the plantlets in the cold frame for about one month, so that they become almost fully hardened off

44 remove them from the cold frame. Expose them day and night to the elements in a sheltered spot in the garden for two or three days. They become fully hardened off and ready to be posted out in the garden according to the pest/weed/vermin-deterrent needs of the plants to be protected.

for background information, see COMPOST: *John Innes/1* and *-/2*, SUPPLIERS.

MARIGOLD: **Mexican/2 — from seeds to half-hardy plantlets and hardening off without the aid of a heated greenhouse and cold frame.** Do as the head gardener would do were not Tresillian's walled kitchen garden equipped with a heated greenhouse and cold frames, and proceed as follows

1 on any day in late February, and noting that there is no moon-quarter involvement at this stage, take over a room in the house, or a garden room, which will not be

— required for any other purpose for the following month, at least

— entered or used during that period by any person other than the responsible gardener

2 note that a room that possesses

— a west-facing window is ideal

— a south-facing or a south-west-facing window is acceptable, provided that the window has a light curtain drawn over it permanently

3 note that the room not to be used is the one with a window facing directly east or directly north

4 note that in the usable room, single-, double- or triple-glazing makes no difference to its effectiveness

REQUIRED FOR *MARIGOLD: Mexican/2*

● A heated room with a west-, south- or south-west-facing window, Mexican marigold seeds, two seed trays, John Innes seed compost, John Innes No 1 potting compost, a container to hold sieved compost, a 6mm garden sieve, a room thermometer, a water container, water, a piece of absorbent material, a newspaper, a 6mm garden sieve, a seed dispenser, garden labels, a dibber, a small, sharp knife.

For the complete instruction, see *MARIGOLD: Mexican/1* to *-/3*.

5   close the window fully and keep it closed during all of the propagation period, to obviate draughts

6   turn on the room's central-heating radiator/s or bring in portable heating equipment

7   raise the room's temperature to 18°C-20°C (65°F-68°F) by night and by day and keep it at that level for all of the time that seedlings and plantlets are propagated

8   ensure that on the work surface at one and the same time — so that when used they are all at the room's temperature level — there are

- a packet of Mexican marigold seeds
- two seed trays
- John Innes seed compost
- John Innes No 1 potting compost
- a container to hold sieved compost
- a 6mm garden sieve
- a room thermometer, which remains on the work surface top, where the work is done
- a piece of absorbent material

9   also have in the room a water container that is

— large enough in area at the top to permit the lowering into it of compost-filled seed tray

— filled to the top with water

10   wait for 24 hours, to ensure that the assembled aids share the room's temperature

11   working in the room, with its door fully closed, fill one seed tray with the John Innes seed compost to within 10mm-to-12mm of its top. Level the compost's surface

12   consolidate the compost by tapping the base of the filled seedling tray gently once or twice on the work surface top

13   if necessary, add material to raise the level of the compost to within 10mm-to-12mm of the tray's top

14   lower the base of the filled tray into the container of water until the tray's top is just above water level. [***Consideration:*** *moisture enters the tray through the drainage holes in its base. This effects a moistening without the disturbance to*

the compost's surface that would be caused by the use of a watering can — no matter how fine the can's rose]

15 wait for a count of ten. Lift the tray out. Do this several times. Pause between each dipping, to allow the surplus water to drain back into the water container

16 note that, in stages, the colour of the compost's surface changes from an even light brown to an even dark brown. When this colour is arrived at, the compost is correctly moistened

17 place the tray on a piece of absorbent material on the workbench top. [*Consideration: the absorbent material soaks up the final drainings*]

18 cover the tray with a folded newspaper. Leave it, undisturbed, on the work surface for 24 hours. [*Considerations: 1 — this enables the compost to become comprehensively moistened, and to arrive at the room's temperature of 18°C-20°C (65°F-68°F); 2 — the newspaper reduces evaporation. It is folded to increase its rigidity and to reduce its area to one that is slightly larger than the top of the tray. Newspaper is cheaper, safer and more convenient than a sheet of glass. Unlike condensation-dripping glass, it does not encourage any kind of undesirable condition of the compost's surface; 3 — the 24-hour pause also enables compost and seeds to arrive*

at a common ambient temperature. Overall, seed germination is encouraged]

19 whilst waiting, pass some of the seed compost through the 6mm garden sieve to remove lumps and hard material from it. Place the sieved, powdered compost in a container situated conveniently on the work surface

20 after the 24-hour pause, remove the newspaper from the compost-filled tray. Open the packet of Mexican marigold seeds over the tray. [*Consideration: this ensures that accidentally-spilled seeds drop onto the compost and, hence, are not wasted*]

21 still working over the tray, transfer some of the seeds to a seed dispenser of the kind that enables controlled sowing without contact between seeds and fingers. Fill the dispenser without touching the seeds with the fingers. [*Considerations: 1 — the seeds are not crushed*

TIP 84
➔ **Some gardeners are more confident transferring potted plantlets than they are transferring trayed plantlets to permanent positions in the garden. If this is preferred, transplant the seedlings not to plantlet trays but to 70mm-to-80mm pots — one per pot — filled with 24-hour-moistened John Innes No 2 potting compost. Manage the pots in all respects as if they were trays. This applies whether the propagation takes place in a heated greenhouse or heated spare room**

by pressure applied by the finger tips. This helps to ensure germination, since crushed seeds do not germinate; 2 — a seed dispenser is obtainable from any garden centre]

22 post the seeds onto the surface of the moistened seed compost. Do so sparsely, so that, after germination, the resultant seedlings are markedly widely separated from each other

23 dribble the powdered compost onto the seeds through the finger tips. Do so as thinly as possible. [***Consideration:*** *by this means, achieve a covering the depth of which is no more than twice the thickness of the individual seed. This is usual practice when sowing seeds — whether into compost or garden soil]*

24 return the surplus powdered compost to the compost bag

25 label the tray, so that, later, there is no doubt about what is growing in it and when it was sown

26 re-cover the tray with the folded newspaper. Leave the covered tray on the work surface

27 ensure that, from that moment, the compost in the trays remains moist. Use the dipping method of watering that was used at the outset

28 position the newspaper-covered, sown tray as far as possible from the window, so that the sunlight cannot reach it

29 examine the tray daily

30 the moment that there is a hint of green growth showing through the dark brown of the moist seed compost, remove the newspaper covering. Ensure that the room remains at 18°C-20°C (65°F-68°F)

31 throughout the day, keep the uncovered seed tray on the window-sill

32 turn the tray at regular intervals to compensate for the developing seedlings' desire to stretch towards the light and, thus, become distorted and 'leggy'

33 at night, return the uncovered seed tray to where it was originally, away from the window-sill

34 keep the compost in the seed tray moist at all times

35 watch for the appearance of two 'baby' leaves on each seedling

36 when either of the two 'baby' leaves is large enough to be gripped gently between forefinger and thumb, fill and moisten the other seed tray with John Innes No 1 potting compost. Do so as when preparing the first tray

---

Visit *R H Harris's Moon Gardening's* companion web site
www.moongardening.fsnet.co.uk
to keep in touch with the results of the head gardener's latest experimental archaeological projects and developmental work in the walled kitchen garden at Tresillian in Cornwall.

37 cover the newly-filled tray with a folded newspaper, as before. Locate the covered tray well away from the window-sill

38 at the same time, water the seedlings in their tray. Use the dipping method to do so

39 leave the dipped seedlings and the newspaper-covered tray for at least 24 hours, so that the latter's compost becomes moistened evenly throughout and arrives at the room's temperature of 18°C-20°C (65°F-68°F)

40 after the 24-hour wait, remove the folded newspaper from its tray

41 make 24 holes in four rows of six in the fully-moistened potting compost. Use a suitably-sized dibber. Shape each hole to take a square of compost

42 ease one seedling at a time — rooted in a square 'nest' of its moist seed compost — out of the seedling tray. Hold it by nothing other than one of its 'baby' leaves. If necessary, sacrifice adjacent neighbours in the process. Use a small, sharp knife to cut out — and to help to lift out — the square of host compost

43 do not touch the seedling's stem.
[***Consideration***: *a stem that is held is certain to be a crushed. That kills the young plant. A plant is able to grow a new leaf to replace a*

For the starting dates of each month's moon quarters see almost any diary — but it is essential to consult *MOON* first of all.

damaged or removed leaf. It cannot grow a new stem]

44 transfer the square of compost and its contained seedling to one of the prepared holes in the potting compost-filled tray

45 gently firm in the square of compost and its seedling. Use the knife as a firming-in tool

46 continue to transplant in this way until all of the waiting holes in the potting compost are filled

47 label the planted-up tray, indicating what has been transplanted and when
[***Considerations***: **1** — *the fully-grown Mexican marigold plant protects against pest and weed over a radius from its stem of about 2m;* **2** — *whether or not the plantlet tray's 24 plantlets are sufficient to meet the garden's needs only the responsible gardener can decide;* **3** — *it is recommended that no less than a full, single tray is developed. The surplus of plantlets, if there is one, may be offered to neighbours. added to the compost bin, or placed in the trench that waits development into a deep-trench bed (BED/1) or a shallow-trench bed (BED/2). Their roots, too, may be composted*]

48 remove the now-unemployed seedling tray from the room. Spread its compost contents thinly over a garden bed. Wash and dry it and return it to store. Remove the other aids and materials for proper cleaning and storage

49 throughout the day, keep the uncovered tray of seedlings on the window-sill

50 at night, return it to where it was originally — away from the window-sill

51 turn the tray when it is located on the window-sill at regular intervals to reduce stem 'legginess' and distortion

52 maintain the room's temperature at the 18°C-20°C (65°F-68°F) level at all times.

53 continue until each plantlet bears at least four leaves

54 turn off the heating permanently and permit the room to cool

55 with the weather by this time improved, during the day move the plantlets in their tray to a protected, sunny location in the garden. At the night, return them to the unheated room and position them away from the window-sill. [*Consideration: if the weather is not improved, wait until it is — which could well be no earlier than mid-April. The plantlets come to no harm in the unheated room as they await improved weather conditions. During this period of waiting, locate the plantlets on the window-sill by day and away from it by night. Maintain the anti-'legginess' regime*]

56 maintain this garden-by-day/room-by-night procedure for several days and nights

57 during this hardening-off period, ensure that the tray's compost is never permitted to dry out. Moisten by means of the dipping method

58 when required, the plantlets are stationed permanently in the garden according to the pest/weed/ vermin-deterrent needs of the plants to be protected.

for background information, see *COMPOST: John Innes/1* and *-/2,* *SUPPLIERS.*

MARIGOLD: *Mexican/3* — **applying the hardened-off plantlet in the garden, to repel pest and disease.** Using the head gardener's method, proceed as follows

1 in April, May or June, at **the start of the moon's second quarter**, thoroughly water the compost in the tray containing Mexican marigold plantlets. Use the dipping method and mains or butt water.

89

'O f course," Mr Harris reminds, "the moment hardening off is considered for the Mexican marigold, allowance must be made for weather conditions.

"The half-hardy — which this plant is — is a tender creature, designed by Nature for climates other than ours.

"If the British weather is throwing its worst at the garden, the hardening-off stage must be delayed until conditions improve.

"It does not matter if the plantlets grow on a little in their tray or trays as a result of this."

90

RJ HARRIS, speaking in the walled kitchen garden at Tresillian one late November: "Here we are, nearly December, and our Mexican marigolds are still trying to flower. They now exceed 4m in height, and with the night-time frost that we have just had I came out this morning expecting to see them black and shrivelled.

"Not a bit of it. Here they were, standing proud in the Winter sunshine and looking lovely.

"A couple of people came round the garden with me yesterday and they said 'Well, what is that?' and I told them and they said they had never seen or heard of anything like it."

[*Consideration:* warm enough weather/soil conditions is the aim, bearing in mind that the Mexican marigold is a South American, half-hardy plant, which does not have sufficient time in which to mature if planted after July]

2 ideally, water the plantlets' compost in the mid-to-late afternoon.
[*Consideration:* this makes it likely that the planting out of the Mexican marigold takes place in the relative coolness of the very late afternoon or early evening. Thus, it enters its new environment when there is least evaporation of moisture and, hence, the garden soil is at its most moist. This is when, also, the plant begins its new life with the immediate advantage of the coming night-time hours of maximum moisture and lack of moisture-evaporating, day-time warmth]

3 put the watered tray of plantlets to one side in the garden in the open air where it drips onto soil, not onto a hard surface.
[*Consideration:* by this means avoid creating standing water and, hence, habitat for disease and pest]

4 at the same time, thoroughly water the targeted planting-out sites.
[*Consideration:* the locations of these are decided by the developments to be protected. In the case of the potato — the plant with which the Mexican marigold is most often associated — the ideal site for a single marigold is found in the 60cm gaps that lie between the potato trenches. It is inserted into the soil at least 3.5m from the next marigold]

5 wait for at least two hours for tray and planting-out sites to become comprehensively moistened

6 transfer plantlets from tray to permanent positions as

TIP 85
➔ **"You transplant only when the host medium and the targeted medium are fully moist — never, never when one is or both are dry," advises the Cornish head gardener. "Try that, and you can count on it that your young plants will either never recover from the operation and fade away, or suffer a check that takes them a long time to get over."**

'The seed that is germinated and developed in a greenhouse or a conservatory or a spare bedroom in trays, pots or containers — i e, not in open ground, upon which Nature exerts control —does not benefit by being sown or taken care of according to any phase of the moon," says R J Harris.

"As a developing plantlet in the ground, it does benefit from moon-influenced management at planting-out time and soil-feeding time.

This applies as much to the Mexican marigold as to any other plant."

91

---

when promoting seedlings to plantlets in heated greenhouse, spare room or garden room

7 do so without prior soil preparation where

— couch grass, bind weed and ground elder are to be deterred

— eelworm is to be deterred

— mice and moles are to be deterred

noting that the roots of the mature Mexican marigold deter for approximately 2m from the plant's stem in all directions

8 through the Summer months, permit the plant to develop to its maximum height of at least 2m. Staking is not required

9 cut the plants at ground level after frost has destroyed them

10 remove their roots from the ground. Cut the roots into small pieces and use them, together with the plants' stems and heads, as compostable vegetable matter.

[*Considerations:* **1** *— do this even when the heads contain seeds. Being of a half-hardy plant, the seeds will not germinate if they survive the composting process and find their way into the garden soil;* **2** *— left in the ground to rot, the roots of the Mexican marigold — which are very large — are likely to impede the fertilising, pre-Winter dig of the affected bed.*]

for background information, see
MARIGOLD: mexican/1 and *-/2,*
MOON, PLANTS: compatible,
SUPPLIERS.

MOON. The moon month (or moonth) is made up of four quarters. These are referred to in this manual as the first, second, third and fourth quarter. In diaries — unhelpfully, so far as gardeners are concerned — they are referred to as 'new moon', 'first quarter', 'full moon' and 'last quarter'.

On the first day of the first quarter (new moon), the strength of the moon's gravitational pull upon

---

SIMPLIFYING THE CONFUSION

as seen in most diaries	as seen in this manual
New Moon	**First Quarter**
First Quarter	**Second Quarter**
Full Moon	**Third Quarter**
Last Quarter	**Fourth Quarter**

Earth is at its weakest. The pull increases from that lowest point as the first quarter develops into and becomes the second quarter. At the end of the second quarter (full moon) and the start of the third, the gravitational pull is at its strongest.

When the third quarter begins, the strength of the pull starts to reduce. It goes on reducing through the third quarter and then through the fourth quarter. At the end of the fourth quarter, the gravitational pull is

---

93

One of the wonders of the Internet is www.googol.com/moon/. This beautifully illustrated web site offers more facts about the satellite planet than most people could ever need — which, be it said, is a criticism of it. The weight and size of the facts that can be extracted from it constitute a barrier.

However, all is pardoned by the site's home page. This presents in the simplest way the state of the moon on each day until the end of 2015. It is a 'must' for the moon gardener who takes annual planning seriously.

---

once again at its weakest.

This is when the moon is once again new and at the start of another first quarter.

The Earth's water table responds to this phenomenon. It rises as the strength of the m o o n ' s gravitational pull increases. It falls back as that s t r e n g t h decreases.

As the water table rises, it exerts an upward pressure. This causes the moisture beneath the garden soil to rise. This, in turn, results in an increased moisture content at the level where gardeners do their gardening.

As the water table falls back, the pressure decreases and the top soil's moisture content reduces.

This unfailing act of Nature — which is of greatest significance during Summer's diminished rainfall and increased activity in the garden — can be of help to the aware gardener in the following ways.

Preparation

Begin the soil manoeuvring that is the essence of the fertilising Autumn dig at the start of the moon's fourth quarter. The fallen and still falling water table releases pressure upon the dug soil and causes it to be at its most receptive to air and air-borne higher temperatures. This combination encourages increased vegetable-processing activity by the creatures of the soil and, thus, enhances the process that results in increased fertility.

92

'During the whole of my time with the walled kitchen garden and the estate at Tresillian — now almost twenty years — I have never had cause to instruct that water be applied to soil or plant for the purpose of irrigation," says head gardener R J Harris, speaking in 2002. "This has been during some of the driest spells that the British Isles has experienced.

"Water has been used only as an aid to feeding."

The statement expresses the reality that correctly-practised moon-oriented management removes or considerably reduces what can be one of gardening's most wearisome and/or expensive chores. This is true no matter what the gardener's methods (or lack of them).

94

A bonus of moon gardening is that fertiliser applied at the correct moon time — at the start of and during the fourth quarter — can be reduced by as much as 50% of the manufacturer's recommended volume or weight.

The moon's final phase is when its 'pull' on Earth diminishes to its weakest strength. In conse- quence, the water table beneath Earth's surface is permitted to slip back to its lowest level.

As the water table recedes, it draws to a deeper depth the fertiliser that is applied at the time. There is improved dispersal and, hence, there can be a reduction in the quantity used.

A consequently additional bonus is a reduction in the chemicals' build up that causes the now acknowledged problems to both wild life and mankind. For, every drop of run off created by fertiliser application (and *over* application, of which many gardeners are guilty) adds to that build up.

In farming, this reality can be of significance — financially as well as environmentally.

with the thoroughly absorbed feeds (applied at the start of the previous fourth quarter) to encourage the germination of these slow developers and, subsequently, enhance their ability to survive.

Sowing the seeds of above-ground developers such as cabbages

Sow at the start of the moon's second quarter. The following week or so of by now well- moistened growing medium combines with the thoroughly absorbed feeds (applied at the start of the previous fourth quarter) to create the conditions that encourage the rapid germination that these comparatively fast developers require. It also, subsequently, enhances their ability to survive.

Pruning

Perform surgical operations upon plants when there is the least resultant loss of sap. This is when the moon is in its fourth quarter. Then, the water table has almost completely fallen. It exerts the least upward pressure. This, in turn, causes the least discharge of sap from the secateured plant.

Feeding

Add manure and fertilisers to the soil at the start of the moon's fourth quarter — on the first day, ideally, or as close as possible to that time. The falling water table releases pressure upon the dug soil and encourages the more thorough and deeper absorption of additives.

Sowing the seeds of below-ground developers such as carrots

Sow at the start of the moon's first quarter. The following fortnight or so of gradually increasing moisture combines

TIP 86

➜ **Diaries indicate each month's new moon with a black disc. They indicate its full moon with an open circle. Their 'first quarter' — shown after the new moon —and their 'last quarter' — shown after the full moon — are presented graphically as slim crescents. Gardeners are advised to base their planning for gardening activity not upon this confusing presentation form but, simply, upon the first, second, third and fourth quarters of the moon.**

95

The head gardener's belief in the efficacy of his design of underground 'sponge' (referred to throughout this manual whenever his way with preparation is under discussion) increases the significance of the moon's influence upon Earth's water table.

The 'sponge' is positioned beneath the inserted plant at an appropriate depth. It collects and conserves downward descending rain water. It acts as a reservoir from which the plant's roots draw moisture even during the driest of dry spells.

Importantly, it also collects and retains moisture that results from the rising water table — moisture that falls back and out of reach of plants' roots when there is no 'sponge'. Hence, the 'sponge' has a dual purpose and so is doubly valuable to the gardener who makes it a feature of soil preparation.

Harvesting the above-ground developers such as cabbages

Take leaves, or remove the whole plant from the soil, when one or the other is at its most juicy and, consequently, most flavoursome. This occurs at the end of the moon's second quarter. At this time, the water table is at its highest level. Its increased pressure induces the greatest moisture content in the top soil and in everything that is in it.

Harvesting the below-ground developers, such as carrots, that are to be stored

Remove these roots or tubers from the soil when the moon begins its fourth quarter. Then, the water table has almost completely fallen. It exerts the

96

Some moon gardeners harvest their crops in the hours of darkness.
"I know of a farmer in Somerset who swears by harvesting his potatoes and root vegetables by the tractor's headlights," comments Mr Harris. "He argues that the moon's gravitational pull is stronger by night than by day, and so puts more moisture into the crops. More moisture means more flavour, so he reckons he has an improved product that warrants a better price.

"Of course, he does this at full moon, which is the time of the highest level of the water table and the greatest amount of moisture in the top soil. And night time is the coolest time, so everything — including his crops — retains more moisture than during the day."

The head gardener views the practice with uncertainty.

"There is a cost to be paid," he notes. "Night-time harvesting is harvesting by artificial light, and that is both anti-social and tricky. Also, how do you persuade staff to work that kind of overtime? — not to mention overtime rates of pay.

"Above all, is the slight improvement in flavour won by night-time harvesting — and it is only slight — worth all of that? This is considering that the way of gardening I advocate brings so many improvements anyway, among them flavour improvement.

"I have decided not to go down that road on a regular basis."

97

One of R J Harris's rules is that feeds be added to the soil ten days or so before the sowing of seeds or the insertion of plants. The result is that the new arrivals are received by a beneficial distribution of the supplements throughout the soil.

Carried out in accordance with the rules of moon gardening, the adding of feeds is done at the start of the moon's fourth quarter. This is when the soil is at its most receptive to additives.

The moon's fourth quarter commences roughly ten days before the beginning of the ideal moon period during which to sow or to plant — the moon's first and second quarters.

This particular symmetry gives an indication of the overall symmetry and helpful discipline that is brought to gardening's ways and means by a practical observance of the moon's phases.

Arising out of this, a moon-oriented calendar drawn up by the gardener to cater for his or her horticultural needs and aspirations is extremely helpful.

least upward pressure. This, in turn, results in the least moisture content in the top soil and in the targeted plants growing in it. The plants are at their driest — the condition that enables the longest possible storage period. The drier the stored root or tuber, the more is rot held at bay. An improvement upon this result is won when two further steps are taken: 1) harvesting is done at the very end of the day; 2) the lifted roots or tubers are transferred immediately into store. By this means, the produce is not exposed the sun, and when stored is as firm as when removed from the soil.

Harvesting the below-ground developers, such as carrots, that are to be consumed immediately

Harvest these roots or tubers when the moon is at the end of its second quarter or the commencement of its third. At this time the water table is at its highest level. Its pressure increases the top soil's moisture content to the maximum, inducing the maximum amount of sap — and, hence, flavour — within the individual units of the gathered crop. An improvement upon this is harvesting at this moon time in the cool of the end of the day or of the night. Then, there is a general reduction of evaporation. The harvested crops retain even more sap and, in consequence, even more flavour.

Harvesting fruit

Allowing for the reality that all fruit is best picked the moment it is ripe, harvest soft and hard fruits when the moon is at the end of its second quarter or the commencement of its third. At this time the water table is at its highest level. It exerts the most pressure upon the plant's roots, inducing the maximum flow of sap within the plant and its fruit and, hence, the greatest amount of fruit flavour. An improvement upon this is harvesting in the cool of the end of the day. Then, there is reduced evaporation — from harvested crops as well as from soil.

Planting out

Insert plantlets, young bushes and young trees into the soil at the start of the moon's second quarter. The existing heightened moisture content — thanks to the rising water table — plus the following week or so of further moisture increase, encourages enhanced plant development. Improve upon this by planting in the cool of the end of the day. Then, there is reduced evaporation and, hence, greater retention by the soil of moisture. Added to this is the increased pressure upon the inserted plant's roots, exerted by the rising water table. It induces increased sap flow and, hence, more rapid, more thorough take-up and ingestion of nutrients. Overall, this combines with the increased moisture in the soil to maximise the benefits experienced by the plant during the traumatising days of its introduction to its new habitat. Overall, the rising water table encourages growth because its upward pressure enhances the rising of the sap within the affected plant. Hence, it can be accepted that plants (and all living things) are at their strongest and most desirous of survival when the moon is at the end of its second quarter and the start of its third quarter — when, in short, it is full.

O NION/1 — producing onion plantlets; locating and preparing the onion-producing bed. Mr Harris produces award-winning onions in two stages: as August-sown seeds developing over-Winter into plantlets in a sheltered nursery bed which is not embraced by the walled kitchen garden's crop-rotation system; as Spring plantlets developed into mature onions in a section of the head gardener's single-dug bed (BED/3) in the first year of the bed's four-year life span. This is when the nutrients and the moisture of its 30cm-or-so thickness of fully-composted animal manure, placed a spade's depth beneath its surface, are untapped.

REQUIRED FOR *ONION/1*

- A section of a first-year *BED/3* for use as an onion producer.

- A small nursery bed — outside the crop-rotation system and unfed for at least one season — for onion-plantlet production.

- Onion seeds, sown sparsely in drills spaced 30cm apart in the nursery bed at **the start of the August moon's first quarter**.

- 60g to the square metre of calcified seaweed or wood ash, applied to the onion section at **the start of the September moon's fourth quarter**.

- A hoe, a rake, a compost bin or heap, a five-tined cultivator (if possible), a garden line, a seed dispenser, garden labels, a trench for a deep-trench bed or shallow-trench bed (if possible), a garden spade, a garden fork, 30cm-long, end-of-row marker sticks.

For the complete instruction, see *ONION/1* and -/2.

Accompanying the onion in the first-year *BED/3* are broccoli, the cabbage family, cauliflower, kale, kohlrabi, leek, savoy, spinach, swede and turnip as well as this manual's highlighted dwarf french bean and pea and — for a part of the tenure of these two — the broad bean sown in the previous Autumn. Each is in its own, adjacent section of first-year *BED/3*.

Proceed as follows to produce onion plantlets

1 in late July, decide where to locate a small nursery bed for the production of onion plantlets. Its site

— provides soil which has been unfed for at least the previous season (and for longer, if possible). Hence, the nursery bed is located outside the total area affected by the crop-rotation programme. [**Consideration:** *fertiliser is applied to all of the beds in the crop-rotation area at least once per season as a part of the crop-rotation regime. This disqualifies them from use as an onion nursery bed*]

— in size and in proportions is large enough only a seed drill of, at most, 2m in length. [**Consideration:** *more than this length of sowing is likely to result in far too many mature onions for most households*]

— is as sheltered as possible, so that Winter's and early Spring's harsh conditions have as little impact as possible upon the onion seedlings and the onion plantlets that develop from the seedlings

— provides access for convenient management and plantlet harvesting

2 at **the start of the August moon's first quarter**, clear the nursery-bed site of its weed growth. Use a garden fork

3 compost the annual weeds that have not set seeds, together with their roots. Or place them in the trench that awaits development into a deep-trench bed (*BED/1*) or shallow-trench bed

(*BED/2*), if there is one in the garden

4 off site, destroy or dispose of the annual weeds that have set seeds and their roots, the perennial weeds and their roots, and the grass growth and its roots

5 at the same time as de-weeding the site of the onion nursery-bed-to-be, use the garden fork to level its surface

6 follow by using a rake. Move the surface of the ground backwards and forwards with the rake's tines. Criss-cross it in the process. Use the full length of the rake's handle. Aim for a rake-tine depth of very coarse earth crumbs, evenly laid out

7 de-earth the rake frequently, to keep its tines unblocked

8 remove the stones that are trapped by the rake's unblocked tines. Store these for use in connection with other projects in the garden. [**Considerations: 1** — *cost-conscious gardening aims always to conserve useful*

TIP 87
➔ **From the moment the onion seed is sown in the ground to the moment the fully-matured bulb is lifted for storage, no water is applied to either section or plant at Tresillian. The nursery bed is sufficiently moist, thanks to the current season's rains. The principal planting-out area has inserted beneath it a thick moisture-trapping and moisture-retaining 'sponge' of fully composted manure.**

resources that may be difficult to obtain at some point in the future. Sometimes, stones are an irreplaceable ingredient in garden projects, and merit the small amount of storage space that they occupy when conserved; **2** — the stones that slip through the rake's unblocked tines are of the size that is required by the soil. They are an aid to drainage. They act as a moisture-retaining mulch. At all times, but especially in Summer, they release during the night the heat that they absorb during the day, relatively warming the section and its contents; **3** — the stones that are gathered by the rake's regularly de-earthed tines are likely to be too large to be wanted in the soil; **4** — generally, if no stone removal is desired, use a hoe when a bed's surface is being turned. The hoe's shape prevents it from gathering stones of any size]

9 achieve a less coarse tilth on the nursery bed's surface. Do so by re-applying the rake if no other tool is available. Move its head in all directions methodically. Seek a greater breaking down of the coarse particles of surface earth

10 for a better, more easily achieved breaking down of the surface particles, use R J Harris's preferred five-tined cultivator. Do so as if

it were a rake. Reduce the coarse crumbs of the soil to crumbs which are as fine as the five-tined cultivator is able to produce. Whether a rake or a cultivator is applied, penetrate the surface with it as deeply as its tines permit.

98

The *Bedforshire Champion, the Ailsa Craig* and the *Oakley*, the latter dating from 1800, are the head gardener's favourite onion types. He finds that they grow and store well, and have mild flavours.

The first is his award winner. He has shown it innumerable times at Cornwall's major shows, and with it has taken more prizes than he can remember.

He established a record when one of his exhibits displayed twenty-four *Bedfordshire Champions* each weighing about 2k.

"In the kitchen," he points out, "they are equally good.

"Their size in no way diminishes their flavour and — I am quite sure — their nutritional value."

[**Consideration:** of the many manually-operated cultivators that are available for this purpose, the head gardener uses the long-handled tool that has three, four or five long, curved tines. In the hands of a practised operator, the three-tined cultivator provides a coarse tilth, the four-tined a less coarse tilth, and the five-tined a fine tilth. Also, being much less prone to clogging and having far fewer and more widely-spaced tines than the rake, all three cultivators ignore the essential small stones that *the initial raking leaves in situ*]

11 do not feed the nursery bed. Do not water it. Do not incorporate garden compost into its surface.
[**Consideration:** *the seed needs the minimum of nutritional value and moisture in order to be able to germinate. Hence, an over-supply of both of these can inhibit its ability to spring*

99

The onion ranks amongst the oldest and most valued of vegetables. It is supposed to have been widely distributed in pre-historic times in Western Asia. It has been so long in cultivation that its native country is unknown. What is certain is that the ancient Greeks, the Romans (who took it to Britain, it is thought) and the Egyptians grew it extensively.

It was grown in Britain at the time of the early herbalists, who knew it as a herb and valued it for its medicinal qualities. The sailors of bygone days, who had yet to discover lemons and limes, prized it as a scurvy deterrent. For centuries, ordinary men and women looked to it to help them to ameliorate the awfulness of their daily meals.

If more of it were eaten today, believe many nutritionists, today's potassium lack in the human diet would not be as prevalent and as potentially damaging as it is.

---

into life. It is as a seedling or as a plantlet striving for maturity that it requires to be nourished]

12 still at **the start of the August moon's first**

quarter, position a garden line in the nursery bed. Make it as long as the seed drill is required to be — no more than 2m. Trace the drill along the line. Make it a generous centimetre deep. Use the edge of a hoe or a suitable stick.
[**Consideration:** *the head gardener finds that the end of his five-tined cultivator's handle is ideal for this task*]

13 sow the chosen onion seeds into the drill. Do so as sparsely as possible. Use a seed dispenser obtained from a garden centre. Fill it from the seed packet without touching the seeds.
[**Consideration:** *fine seed sown by hand is in risk of being crushed by the fingers. Crushed seed is unlikely to germinate*]

14 cover the sown seeds by carefully reinstating the soil and gently firming the drill with the back of a rake.
[**Consideration:** *leave a space of 30cm between drills if more than one drill is sown*]

15 place a durable, marked label at one end of the drill, declaring what is sown in it and when

16 insert a 30cm marker stick half way into the ground at each end of the drill. Before applying any tool to the nursery bed, link the sticks with a line and, thus, know where the onion-seed drill has been positioned

17 leave the sown onion seeds to develop through Winter into seedlings and then into plantlets. Maintain a strictly

100

In the days of Queen Victoria, when the walled kitchen garden at Tresillian was at its production height, the onion was grown from seed. Today's onion set was unknown.

Head gardener R J Harris's aim is to return the kitchen garden to its former times and practices, which is why his starting point is the seed and the kind of onion bed that was used in the mid 1800s: a single-dug expanse of raised top soil based upon a layer of fully-composted farmyard manure.

Mr Harris acknowledges that the onion set considerably eases the burden upon today's sparetime gardener, and provides a guarantee of passable results.

"In no way, though, can its results match the bulb that is once again the Tresillian speciality," he claims, "neither for size and weight, nor for flavour."

weed-free nursery bed by hoeing at frequent intervals. [*Consideration: in a bed as small as is the nursery bed, only a small number of maturing weeds is sufficient to rob seriously the onion seedlings of moisture and nutrients. Unchecked, the weeds diminish the seedlings' ability to achieve their potential, with a consequent deleterious effect upon the quality of the harvested onion*]

18 by **the end of the September moon's third quarter**, establish a single-dug bed according to *BED/3*

19 earmark a section of this *BED/3* for use as a principal

onion developer. This *BED/3* section

— is in an open, sunny situation. [*Consideration: the onion is sun-hungry. Given insufficient sun, it lacks size when fully-grown and stores poorly*]

— is not low-lying and, thus, not liable to become water-logged in very rainy conditions

— offers a medium, well-drained soil

— is not close to, or overhung by, trees or bushes

20 decide on the onion section's size by noting that

— onion plantlets are posted 15cm apart in rows which are 30cm apart

— four parallel rows of plantlets, and no more, are established to form a block of planting. Increased planting is achieved by lengthening the rows, not by adding extra rows. [*Consideration: this makes it easy for the rows to be reached into for management and harvesting purposes. Thus, walking on the onion section during the growing season is avoided*]

— ideally, the rows are oriented north to south. [*Consideration: aligned thus, no one onion top casts a shadow upon its neighbour's bulb*]

21 the moment that the new BED/3 is complete, dress the surface of the section that is to be used as an onion section with 60g per square metre of calcified seaweed or wood ash. Turn it into the surface. Use a spade to do so, not a fork. Thus, maintain the very rough, ploughed-field-like surface that was formed when BED/3 was created. Leave BED/3, including the onion section-to-be, for the birds to feed on and to Winter's rigours.

for background information, see BED/1 to -/3, COMPOST: vegetable waste, FERTILISER, ROTATION.

O NION/2 — **planting out onion plantlets; maintaining, harvesting, storing mature onions.** Equipped with a burgeoning onion nursery bed and a bed prepared for the development of mature onions (see ONION/1), the head gardener grows prize-winning onions according to the following method

1 at **the beginning of the February moon's fourth quarter**, clear the weeds from the earmarked section of the first-year BED/3 that is for onion production

2 this onion section-to-be almost certainly bears few Winter-grown weeds. Remove these and dispose of all of them off site. [*Consideration: these weeds are too few in number to merit the time that has to be given to separation into matter for composting and matter for destruction. However, if every available*

scrap of vegetable matter is prized for composting or other re-use, the time is found to separate the weeds and to apply them appropriately. See later for the correct approach to the carrying out of this chore]

REQUIRED FOR *ONION/2*

- The section of the first-year *BED/3* that is for use as an onion producer.

- Onion plantlets in a nursery bed, which are moved from it at **the start of the March or April moon's first quarter** and posted in the prepared onion section 15cm apart in no more than four rows spaced 30cm apart.

- 115g to the square metre of fish-blood-and-bone fertiliser, applied to the onion section at **the start of the moon's fourth quarter** prior to the planting out of the onion plantlets.

- 60g to the square metre of fish-blood-and-bone fertiliser, applied to the onion section as a boosting feed at **the start of the fourth moon quarter before 21 June**.

- A garden fork, a compost bin or heap, a trench for a deep-trench bed or shallow-trench bed (if possible), a rake, a hoe, a four-tined cultivator (if possible), a garden line, a dibber for planting out plantlets, a small trowel, shallow trays for onion storage (ideally, but not essentially, with wire-netting bottoms), a dry, airy, well-lit place to store onions in trays.

For the complete instruction, see *ONION/1* and -/2.

3 if February's weather/soil conditions place the garden out of bounds, postpone commencing onion-section preparation until **the start of the March moon's fourth quarter**

4 in this case, the onion section-to-be almost certainly bears weeds which have potential as vegetation for re-use or destruction. If so, remove them from the section's surface. Use a garden fork to do so

5 compost the annual weeds that have not set seeds, together with their roots. Or place them in the trench that awaits development into a deep-trench bed (*BED/1*) or shallow-trench bed (*BED/2*), if there is one in the garden

6 off site, destroy or dispose of the annual weeds that have set seeds and their roots, the perennial weeds and their roots, and the grass growth and its roots

7 at the same time as de-weeding the site of the onion section-to-be, use the garden fork to level its surface

8 follow by using a rake. Move the surface of the ground backwards and forwards with the rake's tines. Criss-cross it in the process. Use the full length of the rake's handle. Aim for a rake-tine

depth of very coarse earth crumbs, evenly laid out

9 de-earth the rake frequently, to keep its tines unblocked

10 remove the stones that are trapped by the rake's unblocked tines. Store these for use in connection with

---

101

'There is nothing wrong with regimenting the planting of vegetables," argues R J Harris. "It simplifies management and reduces physical workload.

"What is wrong is leaving the drawn up ranks without defences."

In the walled kitchen garden at Tresillian the 'defences' take the form of 'walls' of adjacent plantings which are well disposed to each other and are rotated together or close to each other for that reason.

Thus, in the first-year *BED/3*, the onion crop, planted out in serried ranks, affords protection to the nearby carrot and parsnip crops — each of these in its own section of a third-year *BED/3*. Surrounding the whole is a single-line perimeter of pot marigolds.

"The combination bewilders the carrot fly and the onion fly and helps to keep the parsnip maggot at bay," explains Mr Harris. "It also matches perfectly my rotation system, and looks very pretty, indeed."

---

other projects in the garden. [*Considerations: 1 — cost-conscious gardening aims always to conserve useful resources that may be difficult to obtain at some point in the future. Sometimes, stones are an irreplaceable ingredient in garden projects, and merit the small amount of storage space that they occupy when* conserved; **2** — *the stones that slip through the rake's unblocked tines are of the size that is required by the soil. They are an aid to drainage. They act as a moisture-retaining mulch. At all times, but especially in Summer, they release during the night the heat that they absorb during the day, relatively warming the section and its contents;* **3** — *the stones that are gathered by the rake's regularly de-earthed tines are likely to be too large to be wanted in the soil;* **4** — *generally, if no stone removal is desired, use a hoe when a bed's surface is being turned. The hoe's shape prevents it from gathering stones of any size*]

11 still at **the start of the February or March moon's**

fourth quarter (depending upon the prevailing weather/soil conditions), dress the surface of the onion section-to-be with 115g to the square metre of fish-blood-and-bone fertiliser. Work it in lightly. Use a rake

12 achieve a less coarse tilth on the onion section's surface. Do so by re-applying the rake if no other tool is available. Move its head in all directions methodically. Seek a greater breaking down of the coarse particles of surface earth

13 for a better, more easily achieved breaking down of the surface particles, use R J Harris's preferred four-tined cultivator. Do so as if it were a rake. Reduce the

102

Once upon a time, R J Harris recalls ("long, long before my time"), the head gardeners in the private estates grew their onions in the same bed year in, year out.

"So much so," says Mr Harris, "that if you walked into one of those walled gardens of old, you could tell at a glance where the onions were produced. You looked for the surface area that was considerably higher than the rest of the garden, and that would be it.

"Endless seasons of single-'spit' trenching and then stuffing with manure followed by a reinstatement of the top soil created a permanently and increasingly raised bed."

This was despite those gardeners of old knowing, in most cases, about the need to rotate crops as a way of countering pest, disease and nutritional deficiencies.

"It all came to a sudden halt when a new disease called white rot infested not only onions but onion beds as well," says Mr Harris. "In fact, once in the bed, it stayed there, waiting for the next planting out.

"That was when onion rotation was adopted as a general practice."

Tresillian's head gardener believes that, unknown to yesterday's seed producers and their customers, the old onion varieties were resistant to the disease.

"Increasingly," he explains, "the old timers were abandoned in favour of new types — which did not have that resistance, perhaps — and so, over time and through ignorance, the resistance was lost and the disease received encouragement."

coarse crumbs of the soil to crumbs which are as fine as the four-tined cultivator is capable of producing. Whether a rake or a cultivator is applied, penetrate the surface with it as deeply as its tines permit. [*Consideration: of the many manually-operated cultivators that are available for this purpose, the head gardener uses the long-handled tool that has three, four or five long, curved tines. In the hands of a practised operator, the three-tined cultivator provides a coarse tilth, the four-tined a less coarse tilth, and the five-tined a fine tilth. Also, being much less prone to clogging and having far fewer and more widely-spaced tines than the rake, all three cultivators ignore the essential small stones that the initial raking leaves in situ*]

14 at **the start of the March moon's first quarter** (or April's, if weather/soil conditions necessitate this), adjust no more than four garden lines on the onion section. They are 30cm apart. With them, form a planting-out block which can be reached into easily for management from each of its four sides

15 use a dibber or a small trowel to make planting-out holes 15cm apart along each of the four lines. Stagger the planting-out positions

16 ensure that the individual planting hole is able to accommodate the individual plantlet's roots without cramping or distortion

17 carefully ease a few onion plantlets at a time out of the nursery bed. Use a garden fork to do so, with great care

18 separate the removed, few plantlets by gently teasing apart their intermingled root systems. Take care not to damage the root systems. Also, do not damage the plantlets' green top growth. This is 15cm-to-18cm in height

19 immediately, insert the plantlets into the onion section. Ensure that each, once gently yet firmly settled into the soil, is at its original planting level. [*Consideration: it is important that the plantlets' roots are not exposed to the drying wind or to the sunshine for a second longer than can be helped*]

20 from within ten days or a fortnight of planting up the onion section, hoe its surface thoroughly at least once per week — whether or not it is inhabited by young weeds. [*Consideration: this prevents weed germination and, in consequence, weed infestation. It also, importantly, raises moisture*

TIP 88
➜ **The earlier the onion plantlets can be inserted into the ground, the more rings they are likely to form before the year's longest day arrives and they cease ring development. Hence, early-planted onion plantlets tend to grow into bigger onions — given correct pre-planting preparation and management.**

to the surface. There, with weed removal, there is no competition for the moisture. This helps the onions to swell and, thus, increase in size]

21 hoe in the late afternoon or early evening, if possible, when conditions are cooler. [**Consideration:** *this is when there is the least moisture evaporation. As a result, there is increased return in moisture recovery for a given amount of effort]*

22 at **the start of the fourth moon quarter that occurs immediately prior to 21 June**, dress the surface of the onion section with 60g to the square metre of fish-blood-and-bone fertiliser. Work it in lightly with a hoe. [**Consideration:** *21 June is the year's longest day. On or about this day, the maturing onion stops forming its rings and embarks upon thickening them. The extra feed of fertiliser applied at this time provides additional nutrients just when they are needed]*

23 as from August, watch for the onions' tops to lie flat on the ground. When this happens, turn them, so that, on the ground, they point to the north. [**Consideration:** *this increases the bulbs' exposure to the sun, thus hastening their ripening]*

24 in September, at **the end of the moon's second quarter** carefully insert a fork beneath each onion and lever it up, slowly, until its roots are detached from the soil. Do not disturb it further. Leave it in situ in its raised position for the following two or three days. [**Consideration:** *at this time of the moon's cycle, the water table is at its highest level and, consequently, the moisture content of the top soil is at its greatest. This, in turn, makes the onions at their juiciest and, hence, their most flavoursome. Thus, they are at their best for harvesting]*

25 lift each onion away from the soil completely and place it on its side

26 every other day afterwards, turn it from one side to the other to expose different sections of it to the atmosphere and, thus, encourage its bulb to dry

27 when the onion's top growth has withered completely, remove the onion from the ground and, by hand, clean off the dried earth and redundant foliage

28 remove the redundant foliage from site and destroy it

29 immediately place the harvested onions in shallow trays (ideally, but not essentially, with wire-netting bottoms). Locate the trays in a dry, airy, well-lit storage place

30 inspect the stored onions regularly throughout Winter. Remove for immediate use or disposal any that show signs of deterioration

31 empty the onion section of the first-year *BED/3* by the **start of the October moon's third quarter**

32 with a garden spade, methodically dig over the section's empty surface to the depth of the spade's blade. Achieve an appearance that is as close as possible to that of the surface of a ploughed field. Make this a part of the Autumn dig of the total BED/3 area. Ideally, complete the total dig by **the start of the October moon's fourth quarter**. Do not feed the section. It bears no more crops until the new season. Then, together with the remainder of dug-over BED/3, it embarks upon its second year in the R J Harris crop-rotation system.

for background information see COMPOST: *vegetable waste, FERTILISER, ROTATION.*

PARSNIP — **preparation, sowing, management, harvesting, storage.** Head gardener R J Harris devotes the whole of the growing season — March/April to August/September — to producing the parsnip in its own section of his single-dug bed (BED/3), his deep-trench bed (BED/1) or his shallow-trench bed (BED/2) during the fourth and final year of these three bed's four-year life span of employment according to his crop-rotation programme.

The beds have borne crops during each of the previous three years. Their top soil has received major loosenings and, hence, fertility-enhancing aerations at least three times with spade and fork. Their manure content is more than three years old and, hence, almost fully dissipated.

The well-worked top soil and the dissipated manure render the year-four BED/1, BED/2 and BED/3 ideal

REQUIRED FOR *PARSNIP*

- A section of a year-four *BED/1, BED/2* or *BED/3* for use as a parsnip producer.

- 115g to the square metre of fish-blood-and-bone fertiliser, applied to the parsnip section at **the start of the moon's fourth quarter** in the month preceding the month of the first parsnip-seed sowing.

- Parsnip seed, sown in the parsnip section at **the start of the moon's first quarter in March, April, May, June and July**.

- *Orange King* or *Scotch Prize Calendula* pot marigold seed and spring onion seed sown at **the start of the moon's second quarter** in the month of the parsnip-seed sowing.

- A hoe, leaf mould (if possible), a garden fork, a rake, garden lines, mint or thyme (if possible), a pressure spray, a filter, a 6mm garden sieve, wood ash (if possible), garden labels, small bushy twigs (if possible), a compost bin or heap, boxes for root storage, dry sand or dry peat, a place to house boxes containing stored roots, a trench for a deep-or shallow-trench bed (if possible).

for the growing of root crops. Accompanying the parsnip in the year-four BED/1, BED/2 and BED/3 are this manual's highlighted beetroot and carrot, each in its own section.

For splendour, R J Harris's parsnips almost equal the onions (see ONION/1 and -/2) with which he wins awards year after year.

To achieve his parsnip results, do as follows

1 at the earliest moment in the season, acquire the seeds of the selected variety of parsnip, and of spring onions and the pot marigold the packet of which is marked, usually, *Calendula*.
[**Consideration:** *look for R J Harris's* recommended *Orange King or* Scotch Prize. *If these are not available, procure any old-fashioned pot marigold*]

2 at **the start of the February moon's fourth quarter**, earmark for parsnip development a section of one of the three year-four beds

3 make the earmarked section large enough, and appropriately positioned

— to house the required number of parsnip rows spaced 30cm from each other.
[**Consideration:** *in ideal weather/soil conditions, five monthly parsnip-seed sowings in the one season are expected. Hence, the single monthly sowing is not excessive. Probably, a drill per month which is two metres in length provides a large enough total crop— or pro rata if the growing season starts late due to adverse weather/soil conditions*]

— to accept a four-sided, right-angled border of a single line of pot marigold flowers around each

---

103

The parsnip — one of the most accommodating and patient of crops — is that rare vegetable, a native of the British Isles, which did not attain its present form until the gardeners of the Middle Ages took it in hand.

The results can be seen at their most impressive on the display benches of today's horticultural shows up and down the country. There, groups of three or four matched 120cm-long-plus specimens retaining full flavour are not unusual. They are grown by enthusiasts, most of whom are prepared to undertake the preparation of the necessary deep parsnip bed at least two years before showing. These are growers many of whom contrive special growth conditions and techniques involving lengths of drainage pipe, special composts and endless tender, loving care.

---

month's sowing of one or more rows of parsnip seeds. Each side of the border keeps a 50cm distance from the nearest row of parsnips or nearest parsnip-row end

— to ensure that the section provides access to each of its four sides for management and harvesting. The access acknowledges that adjacent sections for other crop production exist, or are to exist, within *BED/1*, *BED/2* or *BED/3*

4 the February-initiated parsnip-section-to-be almost certainly bears only very few Winter-grown weeds. Remove these with a fork. Dispose of all of them off site.

104

The carrot fly and the parsnip fly are foes to be taken seriously. In the face of successful onslaughts of the grubs of these pests, many a gardener has given up trying to produce these two root crops.

The key to confusing and thus deterring the questing egg layers is the sending of as many unhelpful and contrasted signals as possible at the one time.

In addition to acting upon this section's suggestions, alternate carrot and parsnip rows in the one bed. Their soil/nutritional/management needs are almost identical. See *CARROT*.

[*Consideration: these weeds are too few in number to merit the time that it takes to separate them into matter for composting and matter for destruction. However, if every available scrap of vegetable matter is prized for composting or other re-use, the time is found to separate them and account for them appropriately*]

5 a March- or April-initiated parsnip-section-to-be (unfriendly weather/soil conditions having enforced a postponement of gardening) almost certainly bears weeds which have potential as vegetation for re-use or destruction. If so, remove the weeds. Use a garden fork

6 compost the annual weeds that have not set seeds, together with their roots. Or

place them in the trench that awaits development into a deep-trench bed (*BED/1*) or shallow-trench bed (*BED/2*), if there is one in the garden

7 off site, destroy or dispose of the annual weeds that have set seeds and their roots, the perennial weeds and their roots, and the grass growth and its roots

8 at the same time as de-weeding the parsnip section-to-be, use the garden fork to level its surface. Break up the large clods formed by the use of a garden spade when the bed was Autumn-dug, and that have thwarted Winter's attempts to reduce them in size

9 ideally, dress the surface of the parsnip-section-to-be with a thickness of fully-composted leaf mould. Turn it in to the depth of a garden fork.
[*Consideration: omit this if leaf mould is not available. With leaf mould, the resultant crop is a superior one*]

10 follow by using a rake. Move the surface of the ground backwards and forwards with the rake's tines. Criss-cross it in the process. Use the full length of the rake's

TIP 89
➜ **The parsnip hates heavy, wet, clayey, cold soil and poor drainage — although it does its best in even these inhospitable conditions. Lighten such soil by first of all digging in finely-sifted coal ash or peat or fully-composted leaf mould.**

handle. Aim for a rake-tine depth of very coarse earth crumbs, evenly laid out

11 de-earth the rake frequently, to keep its tines unblocked

12 remove the stones that are trapped by the rake's unblocked tines. Store these for use in connection with other projects in the garden. [*Considerations:* **1** — *cost-conscious gardening aims always to conserve useful resources that may be difficult to obtain at some point in the future. Sometimes, stones are an irreplaceable ingredient in garden projects, and merit the small amount of storage space that they occupy when conserved;* **2** — *the stones that slip through the rake's unblocked tines are of the size that is required by the soil. They are an aid to drainage. They act as a moisture-retaining mulch. At all times, but especially in Summer, they release during the night the heat that they absorb during the day, relatively warming the section and its contents;* **3** — *the stones that are gathered by the rake's regularly de-earthed tines are likely to be too large to be wanted in the soil;* **4** — *generally, if no stone removal is desired, use a hoe when a bed's surface is being turned. The hoe's shape prevents it from gathering stones of any size*]

13 still at **the start of the February moon's fourth quarter**, dress the surface of the rake-levelled parsnip-section-to-be with 115g to the square metre of fish-blood-and-bone fertiliser. Lightly rake it into the surface. Restore the level surface

14 achieve a less coarse tilth on the section's surface. Do so by re-applying the rake if no other tool is available. Move its head in all directions methodically. Seek a greater breaking down of the coarse particles of surface earth

15 for a better, more easily achieved breaking down of the surface particles, use R J Harris's preferred five-tined cultivator. Do so as if it were a rake. Reduce the coarse crumbs of the soil to crumbs which are as fine as the five-tined cultivator is able to produce. Whether a rake or a cultivator is applied, penetrate the surface with it as deeply as its tines permit. [*Consideration:* of the many manually-operated cultivators that are available for this purpose, the head gardener uses the long-handled tool that has three, four or five long, curved tines.]

TIP 90
➔ "Buy the *Guernsey Half Stump* if you can find it when shopping for parsnip seed," advises R J Harris. "It is one of the old-fashioned ones. It grows to about 30cm long, and has a fantastic sweet flavour." Other varieties to win the head gardener's recommendation are *The Student*, *Hollow Crown* and — his favourite for show purposes — *Tender & True*. "Expect lengths of between 45cm and 60cm with this one," he says.

In the hands of a practised operator, the three-tined cultivator provides a coarse tilth, the four-tined a less coarse tilth, and the five-tined a fine tilth. Also, being much less prone to clogging and having far fewer and more widely-spaced tines than the rake, all three cultivators ignore the essential small stones that the initial raking leaves in situ]

16 at **the start of the March moon's first quarter**, at a spot which is 50cm away from — and parallel to — one edge of the parsnip-section-to-be, position a garden line. It is as long as the intended first parsnip row is long

17 do this, ideally, on the morning of what promises to be a fine, dry day

18 excavate a 12mm-deep drill, following the garden line. Do so with the edge of a hoe or with a suitable stick. *[**Consideration:** achieving a drill that is 12mm (half an imperial inch) deep is not easy. The aim, for maximum seed germination, is too shallow a drill rather than too deep a drill]*

19 leave the drill open and unsown from morning until late afternoon. *[**Consideration:** the parsnip seed gets its best start in comparatively warm soil. The exposure of the open drill to the sun and the air throughout the day helps to achieve this]*

20 ideally, just before sowing, spray the drill with a mint or thyme solution to help to deter the parsnip fly. Make the solution by boiling a handful of chopped mint or thyme in a litre of water. Filter the resultant liquid when it is cold, to remove the herb particles. Spray as a fine mist with a pressure spray. *[**Considerations: 1** — omit this stage if neither herb is available; **2** — do not filter the solution, if time presses. Fill a cup with it and gently discharge it along the length of the drill. Keep back as much as possible of the herb particles. The few of these that escape into the drill do no harm]*

21 sow the parsnip seeds into the drill in the late afternoon of the chosen day. Do so in sets of three. Station the sets of three 15cm apart. Position these very large seeds with the tips of the fingers. Touch them as little as possible, to reduce the risk of inflicting damage and, thus, diminishing their ability to germinate

22 fill in the drill by hand with finely sieved earth. Ideally,

---

TIP 91
➔ **When a seed drill has been opened in readiness for sowing: 1) insert a 30cm-long stick into the ground at each end of the open drill; 2) leave half of the stick showing above the surface; 3) sow the drill, 4) reinstate the drill. Later, place lines between the sticks over the invisible, sown seeds so as to know where not to ply the hoe. Use the same technique when sowing seeds into dibbered holes.**

do so with sieved earth in which one part of wood ash has been added to four parts of earth. Use a 6mm garden sieve.
[*Considerations:* 1 — *omit the wood ash if it is not available. With wood ash, the resultant crop is a superior one;* 2 — *omit the sieved earth, if time presses. Instead, move the in-situ soil back into the seed drill. Use a rake, with care*]

23 if more than one row of parsnip seeds are sown, position the rows so that they are parallel to each other. Space them 30cm apart

24 mark one end of each row with a durable label. Note on it what has been sown and when

25 cover the row with a carefully-placed, loose layer of small, bushy twigs.
[*Consideration:* the top growth of this early sowing is vulnerable to the early season's uncertain weather conditions. The twigs provide protection]

26 at **the start of the March moon's second quarter**, position four garden lines around the March sowing. The lines form a right-angled box. The box's four sides are 50cm away from the nearest parsnip row or parsnip-row end. Site one of the two long sides of the box at the edge of the parsnip section. Thus, position it 50cm away from the first parsnip-seed row

27 excavate a 12mm-deep drill, following the four garden lines. Do so with the edge of a hoe or with a suitable stick

28 sow the drill with pot marigold seeds. Station sets of two seeds 15cm apart. Use the finger tips to do so. Touch these very large seeds as little as possible in order not to risk inhibiting germination. Do not thin when germination is achieved. Permit both seeds to reach maturity .
[*Consideration:* 1 — *these marigolds are very vigorous in germination and in growth. For this reason, the thinnest of sowings is required;* 2 — *the aroma of these flowers helps to confuse and, thus, deter the parsnip fly as it quests for egg-laying territory;* 3 — *ensure that the 50cm spacing from the nearest parsnips is observed. This makes it unlikely that the fully-grown pot marigolds deprive the parsnips of sunlight. Also, flopping pot marigolds do not damage the parsnips' tops*]

TIP 92
➔   **If a February initiation of parsnip development is not possible because of adverse weather/soil conditions, postpone activity until March or April. Nothing is lost. Be sure to observe in the month of commencement the start of the fourth moon quarter for the preliminary feeding, and — in the following month — the start of the first moon quarter for sowing the parsnips. Follow this, at the start of the second moon quarter, with the sowing of the protective marigolds and spring onions.**

105

The head gardener counsels: "In the colder parts of the country, it pays to warm the area where the parsnip seeds are to be sown. Do this as from the end of February."

Cloches can be used. Line them up over where the drills are to be made. Leave them in situ until the start of the March moon's first quarter. Then form the drills and sow.

"This is if soil and weather conditions permit," comments R J Harris.

Bad conditions may enforce a wait until March/April: "or even April/May.

"If a March sowing is achieved, leave the cloches on as the young plants grow. In this case, protective twigs over the drill are not necessary.

"Remove the cloches the moment warmer conditions arrive."

Cheaper and simpler than cloches is heavy-gauge, clear, plastic sheet. Place a strip of this over each drill site, instructs the head gardener. Use improvised, hooped wire supports to keep it from touching the earth's surface. This obviates condensation and, consequently, undesirable humidity.

Tuck the edges of the plastic strip into the soil to prevent wind lift. Keep it in place over the sown drill and then the first growth until the season warms up.

29 repeat the parsnip sowing in its entirety at **the start of the April moon's first quarter**

30 repeat the marigold sowing at **the start of the April moon's second quarter**

31 space the two sowings from each other as when making the March sowings

32 place the total April parsnip-plus-marigold development so that it aligns with the March development in the parsnip section and is 10cm away from it.
[*Considerations:* **1** — *an important result of this is that, in due course, a double row of marigolds stands between the March and April sowings of parsnip seeds;* **2** — *the 10cm spacing enables the double row of marigolds to develop without crowding*]

33 comprehensively repeat the March and April developments in May, June and July. Do not protect these three parsnip sowings with twigs. The protection is not necessary in these Summer months.
[*Consideration:* *the overall end product of this at the height of the season is an attractive, fly-resistant, single-row marigold perimeter encasing, at best, five monthly sowings of parsnips divided one from the other by a double-row bank of marigolds. Ideally, abutting this is an identical development of carrots, if that crop is being grown*]

TIP 93
➜   **Chives make an excellent substitute for pot marigolds as an anti-parsnip-fly barrier. Sow them in the same defensive positions in relation to the drills of parsnip seeds, and at the same moon times as the pot marigolds.**

34 from the earliest moment of sowing the parsnip seed, add a few spring onion and pot marigold seeds here and there to the surface of the empty ground between the parsnip rows and between the parsnip and marigold rows. Do so at **the start of the sowing month's second quarter**. Cover them with a dusting of sieved soil. Use a 6mm garden sieve.
[**Consideration:** *this intermixed development helps to confuse further the parsnip fly as it seeks egg-laying opportunities*]

35 do not harvest the spring onions. Leave them in the parsnip section, to retain the benefit of their anti-parsnip-fly aroma

36 when, as the season progresses, germination of the parsnip seeds takes place and there is visible growth above ground

— remove the protective, bushy twigs as these threaten to inhibit development

— remove the two weakest-looking of the three young parsnips at each posting in the rows. Do so carefully, so as not to disturb the strongest-looking plantlet

— thin in this way with minimum disturbance to soil and plantlets. Remove the thinnings from site immediately, to remove a parsnip-fly attractant

37 maintain hoeing throughout the season to prevent weed development and to raise

residual moisture to where the developing roots await it

38 extract parsnips from the soil for the kitchen as soon as they reach usable size. Use a garden fork to do so without root breakage.
[**Consideration:** *a March sowing can, in ideal conditions, result in roots which are usable in late August/very early September. Frequent test checks at the end of August/very early September are well worth the time spent making them*]

39 at **the start of the November moon's fourth quarter**, lift the whole crop without breakage, as far as possible. Use a garden fork.
[**Consideration:** *this is when*

TIP 94
➔ **Frost does no harm to the parsnip; many gardeners believe that it enhances the root's flavour and natural sweetness. For this reason (and noting that the parsnip is resistant to pest attack), it is often left in the soil through Winter until March, when it is removed before it can set seed and attempt to continue its life cycle. Unhappily, the practice disrupts the crop-rotation system, for the all-important BED/1 and/or BED/2 and BED/3 cannot be installed where parsnips continue in residence from November onwards. As a compromise, to obtain the benefit of the frost-improved flavour, the July parsnip row can be positioned where it creates no big obstacle to the continuation of the crop-rotation system. This requires planning at the earliest stages.**

roots and tubers contain the least amount of moisture and, hence, are at their driest. This increases the length of their life during storage. The reduced moisture is caused by the falling water table. This falls during the moon's third and fourth quarters, reducing the moisture content of the top soil and of all that is in it]

40 lift the roots at the end of the day, when the sun is at its lowest ebb.
*[**Consideration:** the exposed parsnips must not be subjected to the heat of the sun. If they are, they become limp and unlikely to store successfully]*

41 immediately de-top them. In each case, leave 5cm or so of the top growth attached to the parent root

42 immediately clean each one by very gently brushing the earth from it. Do not wash it. Do not attempt to clean it by rubbing it.
*[**Consideration:** dirty roots store better, all things being equal, than cleaned roots. This is because they are unbruised and with unbroken skins, not having been rubbed clean by hand or by an implement]*

43 immediately separate the undamaged from the damaged parsnips.

44 without delay, pack the undamaged parsnips for storage in layers in boxes. Place a thickness of dry peat or dry sand between the layers. It does not matter if the roots touch each other within the layers

45 lodge the filled boxes in a cold, dry, frost-free place. Expect the parsnips to store perfectly throughout the Winter and into the next Spring until March or April

46 uproot and remove from the section what is left of the marigold and spring onion developments. Place these in the compost bin or heap or in the trench that awaits development into a deep-trench bed (*BED/1*) or a shallow-trench bed (*BED/2*)

47 consign the removed parsnip tops to the trench.
*[**Considerations: 1** — at this time of the year — late November — the parsnip fly is no longer present to be attracted. The entrenched parsnip tops are buried beneath a depth of other matter by the time the pest re-appears in the following late Spring; **2** — the standard practice is to compost the parsnips' redundant vegetation. The head gardener does not do so. He believes that the material almost certainly harbours pests. Also, it may carry the beginnings of disease — and not only disease related to the parsnip. These conditions may not be destroyed by the composting process. Better and safer, he is certain, to dispose of it as suggested above]*

48 send the damaged roots to the kitchen for use or secure disposal

49 the moment that the parsnips are out of the bed, fork over its surface. Leave it

thus for a day or two, so that the birds can investigate its insect life

50 before the November moon's fourth quarter ends, install in the defunct parsnip section and associated other defunct sections fresh, single-dug (*BED/3*), shallow-trench (*BED/2*) or deep-trench (*BED/1*) beds. These are in readiness for the commencement of a new, four-year rotation cycle in accordance with the head gardener's crop-rotation programme.
[*Consideration: the alternative is to install the new beds in unfriendly December at the start of the December moon's third quarter. At this time, weather/ground conditions are likely to be unfavourable.*]

for background information, see
COMPOST: vegetable waste, FERTILISER, MOON, ROTATION.

PEA/1 — **preparation, sowing, management, harvesting.** The head gardener makes an almost continuous operation of pea production, designing it to result in harvesting which is interrupted only by the worst of Winter.

He sows seeds and plants plantlets at monthly intervals from March to July. He makes a final seed sowing in November, which is aimed at producing a very early Spring crop.

He uses a section of his single-dug bed (*BED/3*) in the first year of its four-year life span. This is when the nutrients and the moisture of its 30cm-or-so thickness of fully-composted animal manure, placed a spade's depth beneath its surface, are untapped.

REQUIRED FOR *PEA/1*

●A section of a year-one *BED/3* for use as a pea producer.

●Early pea seeds sown 5cm apart in 10cm-wide double-rank rows spaced 30cm apart in March and April at the **start of the moon's second quarter.**

●Mid-season pea seeds sown in the same way in May and June at the same moon time.

●Maincrop pea seeds sown in the same way in July and November at the same moon time.

●115g to the square metre of fish-blood-and-bone fertiliser, applied to the pea section at **the start of the February or March or April moon's fourth quarter**, prior to seed sowing in the following month.

●1:40 comfrey solution, applied to the pea section at **the start of the July moon's fourth quarter.**

●A garden fork, a compost bin or heap, a trench for a deep-trench bed or a shallow-trench bed (if possible), a rake, a hoe, a four-tined cultivator (if possible), a garden line, stakes, garden string, labels, fine-mesh wire netting, copper wire or tubing (if possible), secateurs or garden shears.

For the complete instruction, see *PEA/1* to -/3.

Accompanying the pea in the first-year *BED/3* are broccoli, the cabbage family, cauliflower, kale, kohlrabi, leek, savoy, spinach, swede and turnip as well as this manual's highlighted onion and dwarf french bean and — for a part of the tenure of these two — the

---

106

The pea has been cultivated for human consumption since 9,000-to-10,000 BC. Where it began and what were its antecedents is not known. It is likely that it has been in use worldwide for most of that time — first, and for millenia, in the dried form. It dries readily and easily on the plant, and then keeps almost endlessly. It is only comparatively recently that it has been used as a fresh vegetable.

In Britain, introduced — like so many of 'our' vegetables and fruits — by the Romans, it occupied a very important place in the national diet for centuries. This is not surprising: dried, it provides protein and a concentrate of essential vitamins and minerals.

---

broad bean sown in the previous Autumn. Each is in its own, adjacent section of first-year *BED/3*.

Inter-planted between the pea plants' rows (and those of the dwarf french bean) are catch crops, which include this manual's highlighted lettuce.

Adopting the head gardener's method, proceed as follows

1 at the earliest moment in the New Year, procure the chosen seeds of the three types of pea — the early pea, the mid-season pea and the maincrop pea

2 at **the start of the February moon's fourth quarter**, earmark a section of a first-year *BED/3* for use as a pea producer

---

For the starting dates of each month's moon quarters see almost any diary — but it is essential to consult *MOON* first of all.

---

3 ensure that the section to house the pea plants

— is no more than large enough to accommodate the desired number of double-rank pea rows. [***Consideration:*** *the pea plants deliver a harvest that extends through Summer and then, after the Winter break, into the Spring that follows. This is thanks to six successive monthly sowings. For working purposes, assume — until a harvested result declares a firm weight — that a single, successful plant produces about 500g of de-podded peas. The pea plants are posted 5cm apart in two parallel rows which are 10cm from each other and form a double rank. In turn, the double-rank rows are spaced 30cm apart (60cm if lettuce inter-planting is planned). The calculation that decides how much ground is earmarked for pea production takes account of the weight of produce required also for the freezer and for giving away*]

— has access to each of its four sides for management and harvesting. The access takes into account that

---

TIP 95
➜ **For variety, sow also the deliciously sweet sugar pea (sometimes known as snap pea or mangetout). The pods of this legume, as well as the peas, are eaten. Both are best when young and raw. The cultivation regime is as for peas.**

107

Determined to miss no opportunity to recreate Tresillian's Victorian heyday, R J Harris grows the old-fashioned asparagus pea — so called because of its slightly asparagus flavour. It is an early 1800s legume and has a pod which bears three elongated, crinkly-edged ribs. This is why it is also known as the winged pea. The whole of it is eaten when very young, for then the pod tastes as good as the pea.

The Victorians took it to their hearts in the first place because of its very attractive, brownish-red flower. It was grown in their flower gardens long before it found an additional home among the vegetables.

adjacent sections for other crop production are demarcated within the first-year *BED/3*

— is, if possible, sheltered in part to provide protection against Winter's winds for the Winter-developed pea plants

4 the February-initiated pea-section-to-be almost certainly bears a few Winter-grown weeds. Remove these. Use a garden fork. Dispose of all of them off site. [**Consideration:** *it could be considered that these weeds are too few in number to merit the time that has to be given to separation into matter for composting and matter for destruction. However, if every available scrap of vegetable matter is prized for composting or other re-use, the time is*

found to separate them and apply them appropriately]

5 a March- or April-initiated pea-section-to-be (unfriendly weather/soil conditions having enforced a postponement of gardening) almost certainly bears weeds which have potential as vegetation for re-use or destruction. If so, remove the weeds. Use a garden fork to do so

6 compost the annual weeds that have not set seeds, together with their roots. Or place them in the trench that awaits development into a deep-trench bed (*BED/1*) or shallow-trench bed (*BED/2*), if there is one in the garden

7 off site, destroy or dispose of the annual weeds that have set seeds, together with their roots, the perennial weeds and their roots, and the grass growth and its roots

8 at the same time as de-weeding the pea section-to-be, use the garden fork to level its surface. Break up the large clods formed by the use of a garden spade when *BED/3* was created, and that have thwarted Winter's attempts to reduce them in size

TIP 96
➔ **Mix two or three dwarf-french-bean plants and/or seeds into the monthly planting up of the pea section. The general management involved is the same as that of the pea. See *DWARF FRENCH BEAN/1* and -/2.**

9 follow by using a rake. Move the surface of the ground backwards and forwards with the rake's tines. Criss-cross it in the process. Use the full length of the rake's handle. Aim for a rake-tine depth of very coarse earth crumbs, evenly laid out

10 de-earth the rake frequently, to keep its tines unblocked

11 remove the stones that are trapped by the rake's unblocked tines. Store these for use in connection with other projects in the garden. [*Considerations:* **1** — *cost-conscious gardening aims always to conserve useful resources that may be difficult to obtain at some point in the future. Sometimes, stones are an irreplaceable ingredient in garden projects, and merit the small amount of storage space that they occupy when conserved;* **2** — *the stones that slip through the rake's unblocked tines are of the size that is required by the soil. They are an aid to drainage. They act as a moisture-retaining mulch. At all times, but especially in Summer, they release during the night the heat that they absorb during the day, relatively warming the section and its contents;* **3** — *the stones that are gathered by the rake's regularly de-earthed tines are likely to be too large to be wanted in the soil;* **4** — *generally, if no stone removal is desired, use a hoe when a bed's surface is being turned. The hoe's*

shape prevents it from gathering stones of any size]

12 still at **the start of the February moon's fourth quarter**, dress the raked-level surface of the pea section with 115g to the square metre of fish-blood-and-bone fertiliser. Work it in lightly. Use the rake. Restore the level surface

13 achieve a less coarse tilth on the pea section's surface. Do so by re-applying the rake if no other tool is available. Move its head in all directions methodically. Seek a greater breaking down of the coarse particles of surface earth

14 for a better, more easily achieved breaking down of the surface particles, use R J Harris's preferred four-tined cultivator. Do so as if it were a rake. Reduce the coarse crumbs of the soil to crumbs which are as fine as the four-tined cultivator is capable of producing. Whether a rake or a cultivator is applied, penetrate the surface with it

---

If further explanation is required, e-mail
R J Harris on
rjh@moongardening.fsnet.co.uk

TIP 97
➔ **Leave a special crop of peas to dry on the plant, pick them, hull them, store them in paper bags for a few days to complete the drying and then store them in air-tight jars. Nutritionally, they are a marvel. Pre-soak them and steam them as if just from the plant, or put them, as they are, into stews and casseroles. Buy seed that is stated to be designed for this purpose. Or, instead, for a lower purchase price, get dry, unsplit peas from a supermarket.**

as deeply as its tines permit. [**Consideration:** *of the many manually-operated cultivators that are available for this purpose, the head gardener uses the long-handled tool that has three, four or five long, curved tines. In the hands of a practised operator, the three-tined cultivator provides a coarse tilth, the four-tined a less coarse tilth, and the five-tined a fine tilth. Also, being much less prone to clogging and having far fewer and more widely-spaced tines than the rake, all three cultivators ignore the essential small stones that the initial raking leaves in situ*]

15 at **the start of the March moon's second quarter**, (or of the second quarter in the month immediately after applying the fertiliser), position a garden line on the section's surface where the first sowing is to be made

16 using the garden line as a guide, create a 10cm-wide, 5cm-deep channel of the required length. Use a garden hoe. Deposit the removed soil as it arises to one side of the channel for the whole of the channel's length, for relatively effortless reinstatement later on

17 still at **the start of the March moon's second quarter**, post a row of the early pea seeds in the channel along each of its two edges. Space the seeds 5cm apart in the two rows

18 stagger the seeds' postings in relation to each other, so that each seed is opposite to a blank space

19 backfill the channel. Use the hoe. Cover the posted seeds carefully with a 5cm thickness of soil, so that they are not dislodged from their postings

20 compress the channel's top gently and slightly with the back of the rake. Create a shallow, rain-collecting depression along the length of the double-rank row for the full width of the row

21 mark the double-rank row at one end with a durable label stating what has been sown and when

22 place low arches of fine-mesh wire netting over the double-rank row immediately after sowing, to ward off future bird attack

23 insert a stake at least 30cm into the earth at each end of the double-rank row, in between the two rows of sown seeds. The two stakes stand 70cm above the earth's surface

24 tie lengths of garden string tautly from stake to stake.

TIP 98
➔   **Sow the dwarf pea. It produces a plant of less than 60cm in height, which reduces the labour of harvesting and maintenance. Also, at that height, the mature plant casts the least shadow and offers the least wind-contesting bulk. R J Harris's recommendation is** *Meteor.* **Fully grown, it is little more than 45cm high.**

Vertically space the lengths 10cm apart

25 as the season progresses, remove the anti-bird guards the moment they threaten to hamper plantlet development

26 be alert, also, as the season progresses, for when the plantlets need to be guided onto the string ladder support. Carefully and gently introduce their tendrils to the first string rung

27 in the pea section generally, place short lengths of bare, heavy-duty copper wire or copper tubing to ward off the slugs and the snails

28 after the first pea-seed sowing is made, repeat the sowings monthly until and including July. Use

— early pea seeds for the March and April sowings. [*Consideration: forgo the March and April early pea seed sowings if the weather/soil conditions render it impossible to work in the garden*]

— mid-season-pea seeds for the May and June sowings

— maincrop-pea seeds for the July sowing

29 harvest the pea pods when they are young and just short of being fully-formed. Test by opening one or two to establish the size of the contained peas. Harvest them every other day whether or not they are required in the kitchen. Pick

from ground level up. [*Consideration: the peas' cropping season is only six weeks or so in length. This is from when the first young pod is ready to be picked. The pods' contents develop rapidly. As they mature, the plant devotes most of its energies to them. This induces a general reduction in the plant's ability to bear pods. At the same time, its quickly over-maturing pods are of reducing interest to the kitchen. Harvesting aims never to permit the pea- or bean-bearing plant to bring its seeds to the stage of fulfilment*]

30 give away, freeze or compost-bin the unwanted surplus. Or place it in the bottom of the trench that awaits conversion into a deep-trench bed (*BED/1*)

TIP 99

➜ **With the pea section of first-year *BED/3* prepared and sown/planted according to the R J Harris system, it makes sense to get an extra return from all of the involved hard work. One way to do so is to plant quickly-maturing salad catch crops between the developing plants' rows, and to harvest them as rapidly as possible so that they can be replaced by successive catch crops. The extra return — apart from the bonus catch crop/s — is the economy in ground use and reduction in physical effort, for no additional area of soil has to be dedicated to the production of the chosen catch crop. Lettuce lends itself excellently to this (as do spring onions and radishes). See *LETTUCE/1*.**

or shallow-trench bed (*BED/2*), if there is one in the garden

31 hoe regularly from start to finish to keep the pea section weed-free. [***Consideration:*** *this prevents weed-seed germination. As a result, it makes nutrients available to the plants alone. It also deprives the slugs and the snails of food. Additionally, hoeing raises extra moisture to the surface, where the developing plants' roots await it*]

32 at the start of **the July moon's fourth quarter**, drench the surface of the pea section with comfrey solution in the ratio of one part of comfrey stock to forty parts of water. Ideally, do so in the cool of the end of the day. Use a can with a medium rose, to reduce splashing onto the plants

33 when the pea plants are denuded of pods, cut their stems at ground level. Use secateurs or garden shears. Leave their roots in the ground, so that their nitrogen remains in the top soil

34 dismantle the string/stakes support. Clean the stakes and return them to store

---

Visit *R J Harris's Moon Gardening's* companion web site
   www.moongardening.fsnet.co.uk
to keep in touch with the results of the head gardener's latest experimental archaeological projects and developmental work in the walled kitchen garden at Tresillian in Cornwall.

35 either

— burn the pea-plant vegetation on unused ground or an empty bed and turn its cold ashes into the ground's or the bed's surface

or

— destroy it off site

or

— place it in a trench that awaits development into a deep-trench bed (*BED/1*) or shallow-trench bed (*BED/2*).
[***Consideration:*** *the standard practice is to compost this kind of vegetation The head gardener does not do so. He believes that the material almost certainly harbours pests. Also, it may carry the beginnings of disease — and not only disease which is related to the original plant. These conditions may not be destroyed by the composting process. Better, he believes, to turn it to good account in the ways suggested above*]

TIP 100
➔ **The March- and April-sown early peas require at least twelve weeks to develop from sowing to first harvesting. The May- and June-sown mid-season peas require fourteen to sixteen weeks, as do the July-sown maincrop peas. If March's weather/soil conditions are unsuitable for gardening, miss out the March sowing and its associated activities. Sow for the first time in April at the start of the April moon's second quarter.**

36 methodically fork over to the depth of a garden fork that part of the pea section that has ceased production. If the peas' roots are lifted by this process, turn them back into the depths of the soil

37 do not apply feed to the cleared part of the pea section. It bears no more crops until the new season. Then, it embarks upon its second year in the R J Harris crop-rotation system. Meantime, until Autumn arrives, hoe it regularly, to prevent weed-seed germination

38 at **the start of the November moon's second quarter** — provided that the ground is not waterlogged or frozen — sow maincrop-pea seeds in the unused part of the pea section. Do so, in total, as when the earlier seeds were sown

39 support the over-wintering pea-seed sowings with a stakes-and-string 'ladder', as described above. [*Consideration: their developments especially need support against Winter's driving winds and rain*]

40 also in November — ideally at **the start of the moon's third quarter** — give the surface of the cleared part of the pea section its pre-Winter dig. Use a garden spade. Dig to the full length of the spade's blade. Make this a part of the total BED/3 Autumn, fertility-enhancing dig. Aim for the surface finish that resembles the surface finish of a ploughed field. Aim to

complete the dig by **the start of the November moon's fourth quarter**

41 harvest the over-wintered pea crop in early Spring the moment it is acceptable to the kitchen. Then clear the section in which it has grown. Leave the plants' roots in the ground and process the redundant pea-plant vegetation as indicated above

42 fork over the section's surface. Earmark the ground — along with the remainder of what is now a second-year BED/3 — for second-year employment within the R J Harris crop-rotation programme.

for background information, see COMFREY/1 to -/3, FERTILISER, LETTUCE/1 and -/2, MANURE, MOON, ROTATION.

PEA/2 — **plantlet production in plastic roof guttering, planting out, management.** The head gardener uses pea plantlets to secure a four-week start in pea production (see PEA/1). He combines their use with the first sowing of pea seeds.

He produces the plantlets in two ways: 1) seventeen assembled in a single row in compost in planting-out mode in a length of plastic roof guttering; 2) nine double-ranked and turf-based, in planting-out mode (see PEA/3).

For the former, proceed as follows

1 as soon as possible early in the year, procure the seeds of the chosen variety of early pea

2 at the beginning of February (the moon plays no part at

REQUIRED FOR *PEA/2*

- The section of the first-year *BED/3* that has received its first sowing of pea seeds as described in *PEA/1*.

- Early pea seeds for sowing 5cm deep at 5cm postings in plastic roof guttering filled with John Innes No 2 potting compost and for planting out as plantlets at **the start of the March moon's second quarter**.

- 100cm-long lengths of plastic roof guttering, newspaper plugs, sticky tape, John Innes No 2 potting compost, a watering can with a fine rose, water, a cold frame or cold greenhouse, sacks, fleece or redundant blankets, stakes, soft string, a hand fork.

For the complete instruction, see *PEA/1* to -/3.

this stage), and working under cover, clean a 100cm-long length of plastic roof guttering. Ensure that its inner surface is perfectly smooth and offers no protrusions.
[**Consideration:** *half-round guttering is best. Guttering with a shaped profile can be equally suitable, depending upon the extent and complexity of the profile*]

Visit *R J Harris's Moon Gardening's* companion web site
www.moongardening.fsnet.co.uk
to keep in touch with the results of the head gardener's latest experimental archaeological projects and developmental work in the walled kitchen garden at Tresillian in Cornwall.

3 place the guttering length flat on a workbench top

4 block its two ends with plugs of newspaper

5 secure the plugs to the guttering with sticky tape

6 fill the guttering between the two plugs with John Innes No 2 potting compost

7 bang the guttering gently yet firmly, two or three times, on the workbench top to consolidate the compost

8 add more compost and level off with the hand, if that is necessary

9 moisten the compost thoroughly. Use a watering can with a fine rose

10 cover the guttering assembly with sheets of folded newspaper, reduce evaporation

11 leave the assembly and the seeds for 24 hours in a protected place, so that the compost moistens comprehensively

12 insert the seventeen early-pea seeds 5cm deep in the centre of the compost at 5cm postings. Begin and end the seventeen postings 5cm or so away from the two newspaper plugs

13 produce two or four or a greater even number of these assemblies

14 lodge the sown plastic-roof-guttering assemblies in a cold frame or a cold green house. Balance good ventilation against cold

infiltration in accordance with the weather's performance. In the case of the cold frame and the very small greenhouse, be ready with coverings such as sacks, fleece or redundant blankets to increase the night-time — and, if necessary, the day-time — protection. Weigh down the protective covering against the force of the wind

15 do not attempt to develop them in a conservatory or any other 'in doors' location. [**Consideration:** *the result of this kind of over-friendly environment is soft, weak young plants, which have few prospects of becoming successful adult plants*]

16 keep the compost in the guttering assemblies moist all the time as the pea plantlets develop and reach the stage at which they bear at least four leaves

17 **at the start of the March moon's second quarter**, transfer the guttering assemblies to an earth surface. Gently water them thoroughly. Use a can with a fine rose. Ensure that the surplus water drains wholly onto the earth, not also — accidentally — onto hard standing. [**Consideration:** *by this means avoid creating a habitat for disease and/or pest development*]

18 do this at the same time as making the first sowing of pea seeds in the pea section of the first-year *BED/3*. See *PEA/1*

19 park the drained, watered guttering assemblies for a few hours in a protected place for their compost to become comprehensively moistened

20 still **at the start of the March moon's second quarter**, take the guttering assemblies to the sown pea section that is described in *PEA/1*

21 in a spot on the section's surface that is 30cm away from, and parallel to, a sown double-rank row of peas (30cm if no lettuce inter-planting is intended; 60cm if it is), trowel out a guttering-shaped excavation

22 place an empty length of the plastic roof guttering in the excavation. Adjust the excavation's depth, if necessary, so that the top of the guttering levels with the level of the surrounding ground

23 firm the earth around the empty length of guttering

24 remove the empty guttering length

25 leave a channel formed in the section's surface that has the shape and size of each of the guttering assemblies

26 loosen the floor of the formed channel to ensure adequate drainage. Use a hand fork, with care

27 lay a plastic guttering assembly into the formed channel

If further explanation is required, e-mail R J Harris on *rjh@moongardening.fsnet.co.uk*

28 remove one of its newspaper plugs

29 cut the sticky tape around the other newspaper plug

30 hold this plug firmly with one hand. With the other hand, raise the plugged end of the plastic guttering a few centimetres above the floor of the formed channel. Permit the unplugged end to remain upon the floor of the formed channel

31 carefully and gently slide the plastic guttering away from beneath the length of compost and the pea plantlets growing in it

32 at the same time, hold the newspaper plug stationary. Permit the gutter-shaped length of moistened compost and its seventeen plantlets to emerge from the unplugged end of the guttering and to settle unbroken into the formed channel. Place the empty length of guttering to one side.
[**Consideration:** *the successful outcome of this operation is due to the comprehensive moistening of the compost and the smoothness of the interior of the plastic guttering. It underlines the importance of the watering stage. Dry or insufficiently moistened compost is unable to quit the plastic guttering without crumbling and breaking and dislodging the plantlets rooted in it*]

33 place the contents of another guttering assembly immediately alongside and parallel to the first

seventeen plantlets. Install it 10cm away from them. Position this second set of plantlets so that they are staggered in relation to the first set. The result is a double-rank row of thirty-four staggered pea plantlets

34 gently press the combined surfaces of the two lengths of plantlet-bearing compost to a slightly lower level than that of the surrounding surface, to create a rain-catchment area at the base of the plantlets' stems. Do so without touching and possibly damaging the plantlets' stems

35 treat the remaining pairs of guttering assemblies in the same way. Continue the double-rank row until it is of the required length. Or create a new row. Leave a 30cm space between the rows, whether they are sown or planted

36 if the plantlets appear to be vulnerable to bird attack, protect them with arches of fine-mesh wire netting

37 erect a stake-and-string ladder over the plantlets, as described in *PEA/1*. Be alert, subsequently, to guide the plantlets' tendrils onto the first rungs of the string ladder. Remove the wire-netting guards to make this possible

38 manage the pea section generally, and harvest the crop, as described in *PEA/1*. Note, especially, the need to drench the surface of the pea section with a 1:40 solution of comfrey stock at **the start of the July**

moon's fourth quarter.
[**Consideration:** *a crop that is one month advanced can be expected, thanks to the addition of the pea plantlets to the initial sowing of pea seeds.*]

for background information, see
COMFREY/1 to -/3,
COMPOST: *John Innes/1* and -/2,
MOON, ROTATION.

PEA/3 — **plantlet production in turf, planting out, management.** The head gardener uses pea plantlets to secure a four-week start in pea production (see *PEA/1*) at the beginning of the season. He combines their use with the first sowing of pea seeds. He produces the plantlets in two ways: 1) nine double-ranked and turf-based, in planting-out mode; 2) seventeen assembled in a single row in compost in planting-out mode in a length of plastic roof guttering (see *PEA/2*).

For the former, using head gardener Harris's method, proceed as follows

1 as soon as possible early in the year, procure the seeds of the chosen variety of early pea

2 at the beginning of February (there is no moon-quarter involvement at this stage), remove from a field, or from an unimportant part of a lawn, a 30cm-square, 10cm-thick turf of grass

3 take the turf to a workbench and turn it upside down on the workbench top

4 place it, upside down, on a smooth baseboard of timber or rigid plastic sheeting

REQUIRED FOR *PEA/3*

• The pea section of the first-year *BED/3* that is described in *PEA/1.*

• Early pea seeds for sowing 5cm deep at 5cm postings in rows 10cm apart in grass turfs and for planting out as plantlets at **the start of the March moon's second quarter.**

• John Innes No 2 potting compost, a watering can with a fine rose, turfs of grass, smooth baseboards of timber or rigid plastic sheeting, a cold frame or cold greenhouse, fleece, sacks or redundant blankets, fine-mesh wire netting, stakes, garden string.

For the complete instruction, see *PEA/1* to -/3.

5 insert the early pea seeds 5cm deep into the earth of the turf in two parallel rows which are 10cm apart. Post them 5cm from each other in the two rows

6 post five seeds in one row, and four in the other. Stagger the seeds in the two

TIP 101
➜ **Pea plantlets can be developed in individual small pots containing John Innes No 2 potting compost and no drainage stones. The total process is more demanding in time, materials and resources than is R J Harris's technique with plastic guttering and grass turfs. It also brings the awkwardness of securing a 5cm spacing between the plantlets as they are inserted into the soil.**

rows in relation to one another.

7 produce several of these sown, baseboarded turfs

8 lodge the sown, baseboarded turfs in a cold frame or a cold greenhouse to over-winter. Balance good ventilation against cold infiltration in accordance with the weather's performance. In the case of the cold frame and the very small greenhouse, be ready with coverings such as sacks or fleece or redundant blankets to increase the night-time — and, if necessary, the day-time — protection. Weigh them down against the force of the wind. Keep the turfs moist all of the time as the pea plantlets develop and reach the stage at which they bear at least four leaves

9 **at the start of the March moon's second quarter**, (and/or coinciding with the first sowing of pea seeds in the pea section of the first-year *BED/3)*, transfer the sown turfs to the sown pea section that is described in *PEA/1*

10 on the day that the first pea seeds are sown, make a row of joined-up indentations in the pea section's surface parallel to and spaced 30cm or 60cm in from the sown pea seeds (30cm if no lettuce inter-planting is intended; 60cm if it is). Each indentation matches the shape, size and thickness of a plantlets-bearing turf

11 slide the turfs from their baseboards into the

indentations. Press the turfs home. Slightly depress the level of their surfaces below that of the surrounding ground to create a rain-catchment area at the base of the plantlets' stems. By this means establish a double-rank row of the required length

12 if the pea plantlets, however inserted into the section, appear to be vulnerable to bird attack, protect them with arches of fine-mesh wire netting

13 erect a stake-and-string ladder over the plantlets, as described in *PEA/1*. Be alert, subsequently, to guide the plantlets' tendrils onto the first rung of the string ladder. Remove the wire-netting guards to make this possible

14 manage the pea section generally, and harvest the crop, as described in *PEA/1*. Note, especially, the need to drench the surface of the pea section with a 1:40 solution of comfrey stock at **the start of the July moon's fourth quarter**. [*Consideration: a crop that is one month advanced can be expected, thanks to the addition of the pea plantlets to the initial sowing of pea seeds.*]

Visit *R J Harris's Moon Gardening's* companion web site ***www.moongardening.fsnet.co.uk*** to keep in touch with the results of the head gardener's latest experimental archaeological projects and developmental work in the walled kitchen garden at Tresillian in Cornwall.

for background information about
PEA/3, see
COMFREY/1 to -/3,
COMPOST: John Innes/1 and -/2,
MOON, ROTATION.

pH

The p stands for potenz, the H for Hydrogen. Hence, pH stands for potenz of hydrogen, or, translated, the power of hydrogen. The term refers — not especially helpfully, so far as the practical, non-scientist gardener is concerned — to the presence of hydrogen ions in the soil. More usefully, when shown on a seed packet as a pH number, the term answers the gardener's question: May I or may I not sow these seeds at a given spot in my garden? — the pH of that spot being known to me because I have found out what it is.

R J Harris endorses this practical view of what very easily can become a horticultural mystery.

"Each plant has a pH preference," he says.

"That preference can be ascertained without difficulty.

"If it is not printed on the seed packet it is recorded in any number of manuals obtainable at the local reference library.

'So," states head gardener Harris, "when you find that the declared pH requirement of your chosen plant matches the pH of your soil, you know that you are off to a flying start."

No matter what a given plant's, shrub's, vegetable's or tree's role in the grand gardening scheme happens to be, its pH preference is bound to be in the range pH1 to pH14.

"Soil at pH1 is soil at its most acid," says Mr Harris. "You find it in bog conditions.

"Soil at pH14 has hardly any acid at all. You go to the beach to find that.

"The important one is pH7.

"This is the neutral level. It is the pH of most soils. Luckily, most plants prefer it."

The matter, R J Harris points out, can be finely balanced, and he offers, as example of this, the case of the potato.

Potatoes are at their best grown

108

Statement: pH is a logarithm of the reciprocal of the hydrogen ion concentration in moles per litre of a solution, giving a measure of its acidity or alkalinity. The gardener who is neither chemist nor mathematician nor puzzle solver loses little by not expending valuable gardening time trying to make sense of this. He or she is advised to apply R J Harris's practical interpretation and use pH as a simple means of finding out whether or not a chosen seed or plant is likely to prosper in a selected area of soil.

A perfect match between ascertained pH and plant pH preference promises best results. An absolute mis-match promises worst results. Between the two extremes are opportunities for horticultural judgement and experimentation

The required measuring instrument is an inexpensive pH soil-testing kit, obtainable at most garden centres complete with working instructions.

---

not in the more common pH7 but in the less common pH5-to-pH6. Growing in pH7 or over, they incur small warts on the skin known as potato scab.

"This is in no way detrimental, of course; it just affects the look of the tuber."

A pH soil-testing kit for general use has been a weapon in the head gardener's horticultural armoury for many years.

"Any garden centre will sell you one," he says. "It is not expensive and it is a very simple item.

"You are given a test tube. You put in it a pinch of the soil that you want to test. You add the liquid that is supplied with the test tube, you shake it all up and you leave the test tube to stand as directed by the kit manufacturer's instructions.

"In a short time, a colour appears in the soil in the test tube," the head gardener says.

"You then hold the tube against a supplied chart of colours, find a colour match, read across a simple scale, and there you are, that is the pH of the part of the garden that the soil came from."

The head gardener stresses: "When all is said and done, pH identification using one of these kits cannot be established with pin-point precision.

"Fortunately, most crops and plants grow in most conditions and produce some sort of a result, and I am the first to sympathise when the sparetime gardener decides that life is too short to fiddle about with testing and trying to find out why a small p stands alongside a capital H.

"In my experience, it is either the perfectionist or the one who has to feed a family through the year from an allotment who — before putting seed in ground — looks for an exact match between a plant's pH requirement and the growing medium's pH content."

P LANTS: *compatible*. Head gardener R J Harris's forty-plus years in horticulture have shown him that many vegetables help or harm each other when grown in each other's company. Equally, he has found that flowers and herbs have a beneficial or harmful effect upon

109

I n the plant world there are friends and enemies and, in the head gardener's opinion, allying knowledge of which is which to knowledge of the moon's impact upon preparation, planting, feeding and harvesting — and applying that combination — can make the difference between adequate results and superlative results. This reality is demonstrated season after season at Tresillian.

For the individual applications of the laws of compatible planting consult the sections on named plants.

other plants. In general, for improved results, he twins

all beans with asparagus, borage, buckwheat, the cabbage family, carrots, cauliflowers, celery, cucumbers, leeks, peas, poached egg flowers, potatoes, squashes, strawberries, sweet corn, sweet peas, turnips

all herbs with the cabbage family

all peas with all beans, carrots, celery, cucumbers, leeks, radishes, swedes, sweet corn, turnips

asparagus with all beans, parsley, tomatoes

basil with tomatoes

beans (all) with asparagus, borage, buckwheat, the cabbage family, carrots, cauliflowers, celery, cucumbers, leeks, peas, poached egg flowers, potatoes, squashes, strawberries, sweet corn, sweet peas, turnips

beetroots with kohlrabi

borage with all beans

buckwheat with all beans

cabbage family with all beans, all herbs, cucumbers, marigolds, potatoes

calendula (marigolds) with the

cabbage family, carrots

carrots with all beans, chives, garlic, leeks, lettuce, marigolds, onions, parsley, peas, sage, turnips

cauliflowers with all beans

celery with all beans, dill, leeks, all peas, potatoes

chives with carrots, cucumbers

corn (sweet) with all beans, lettuce, peas, potatoes, pumpkins

cucumbers with all beans, the cabbage family, chives, peas, potatoes

dill with celery

garlic with carrots

herbs (all) with the cabbage family

horse radish with potatoes

kohlrabi with beetroots, onions

leeks with all beans, carrots, celery, lettuce, peas, turnips

lettuce with carrots, leeks, radishes, strawberries, sweet corn

marigolds (calendula) with the cabbage family, carrots

marigolds (Mexican) with potatoes

Mexican marigolds with potatoes

mint with the cabbage family

onions with carrots, kohlrabi

parsley with asparagus, carrots, tomatoes

peas (all) with all beans, carrot, celery, cucumbers, leeks, radishes, swedes, sweet corn, turnips

peas (sweet) with all beans

poached egg flowers with all beans

potatoes with all beans, the cabbage family, celery, cucumbers, horse radish, Mexican marigolds, peas, radishes, strawberries, sweet corn

pumpkins with sweet corn

radishes with lettuce, peas

radish (horse) with potatoes

sage with carrots

squashes with all beans

strawberries with all beans, lettuce, potatoes

swedes with peas

sweet corn with all beans, lettuce, peas, potatoes, pumpkins

sweet peas with all beans

tomatoes with asparagus, basil, parsley

turnips with all beans, carrots, leeks, peas.

Plants: *non-compatible.* Certain plants fail to thrive in each other's company. When positioning plants that he wishes to see flourish, the aware gardener avoids such pairings. When his aim is natural weed control, he exploits them. In the Cornish head gardener's experience, the most common of these pairings are

all beans and beetroots, garlic, kohlrabi, onions,

all peas and garlic, onions, shallots

asparagus and garlic, onions

beans (all) and beetroots, garlic, kohlrabi, onions,

beetroots and all beans

cabbage family and garlic, onions, rue, strawberries, vines

camomile and potatoes

couch grass and lupins, tomatoes, turnips

garlic and all beans, asparagus, the cabbage family, all peas, strawberries

ground elder and Mexican marigolds

ground ivy and Mexican marigolds

kohlrabi and all beans, tomatoes

ivy (ground) and Mexican marigolds

lupins and couch grass

marigolds (Mexican) and ground elder, ground ivy

Mexican marigolds and ground elder, ground ivy

mint and potatoes

TIP 102
➔ **Plant mixed aromatic herbs in profusion around vegetable beds to confuse and thus discourage unwelcome insects — as well as to add colourful, decorative planting to the work-a-day kitchen garden.**

oak tree and olive tree
olive tree and oak tree
onions and all beans, asparagus, the cabbage family, peas, strawberries
peas (all) and garlic, onions, shallots
potatoes and camomile, mint, pumpkins, rosemary, sunflowers, thyme, tomatoes

---

110

' **B**eware the walnut tree," counsels R J Harris. "It is a wonderful tree; there are several on the Tresillian estate. But be very, very careful where you plant it. It is the king of the 'non-compatibles'. The ground it grows in becomes sterile. Few plants thrive in its vicinity.

"Even the oak would rather be somewhere else."

---

pumpkins and potatoes
rosemary and potatoes
rue and the cabbage family
shallots and all peas
strawberries and the cabbage family. garlic, onions
sunflowers and potatoes
thyme and potatoes
tomatoes and couch grass, kohlrabi, potatoes
tree (oak) and olive tree
tree (olive) and oak tree
turnips and couch grass
vines and the cabbage family.

POTATO — **preparation, sowing, management, harvesting, storage.** Using R J Harris's method, proceed as follows

1 in the Autumn, earmark for potato production any or all of the beds that are made according to *BED/1*, *BED/2* or *BED/3* and that have completed two years of their four-year life span. Ideally,

REQUIRED FOR *POTATO*

● A third-year area comprising all or any one of the crop-rotation-oriented beds made according to, and for, the R J Harris crop-rotation system.

● Approved first-early and second-early seed potatoes for sowing at **the start of the April moon's first quarter**, and maincrop seed potatoes for sowing at **the start of the May moon's first quarter**.

● A compost bin or heap, a sharpened garden spade, seed trays, a storage point for seed trays, a garden fork, a trench that awaits completion as a deep-trench bed (*BED/1*) or shallow-trench bed (*BED/2*), a rake, fish-blood-and-bone fertiliser applied 115m to the square metre at **the start of the March moon's fourth quarter**, a three-tined cultivator (if possible), a garden line, fully-composted leaf mould (if possible) or wilted comfrey leaves (if possible), a hoe, Bordeaux mixture, a pressure sprayer, paper sacks or timber boxes for storage purposes, a dark, frost-free, unheated, dry potato-storage point.

the general area created by the combination or selection of these beds

— occupies an open, sunny situation

— is not low-lying and, thus, not liable to become water-logged in very rainy conditions

— offers a medium, well-drained soil

The POTATO, the head

The **POTATO**, ¹¹¹ the head gardener is convinced, is the most valuable of the vegetable garden's products. "It rates alongside the apple," he comments. "Probably, too, the pair of them are the most taken for granted.

"Through the years, many a family has been reared on not much else, grown just outside the back door or at the end of the garden. They have done well on them, and have given to society some notable men and women."

Mr Harris's own plantings can be seen as a tribute to this heritage. He produces all three groups: the first-early, the second-early and the maincrop. He chooses from among the scores of available types some of the oldest. Among these is the waxy potato (known to all potato salad makers and lovers), which, in today's shops, is a rarity.

"The *Duke of York* is one of the old ones," he says. "It appeared in 1891. It was the result of crossing the even older *Early Primrose* and *King Kidney* — neither now any longer seen. It is an oval-long tuber, with yellow skin and pale yellow flesh and excellent flavour.

"The oddest is the *Pink Fir Apple*.

"All we know about it is that it was first shown in the catalogues at the end of the 1800s.

"It is a long, oval tuber with yellow, waxy flesh. It keeps its new flavour for a very long time."

This variety holds comparatively less water, so it fries well.

— is not close to, or overhung by, large trees

2 decide on the most effective way to use this general area. Note that

— a row of growing potatoes begins as a trench that is as wide as the width of a spade's blade

— several such trenches, set parallel to each other, are 60cm apart

— seed potatoes are posted 30cm apart in the trench

3 at **the start of the September or October moon's fourth quarter,** clear the two-year-old area's surface of growth that may have survived from the season just ended. [*Consideration: if the R J Harris way of gardening has been followed fully during the previous two years, this growth includes little or no weed material. It is treated, therefore, as eligible for the compost bin or heap and/or for the trench that awaits completion as a future BED/1 or -BED/2*]

4 immediately subject the area to its end-of-season, pre-Winter, fertility-enhancing dig. Use a sharpened garden spade. Dig as deep as the full length of the spade's blade. Achieve a surface finish similar to that of a ploughed field. [*Consideration: this meets the R J Harris requirement that at the end of year one, year two and year three of the head gardener's four-year-based crop-rotation programme, the beds' surfaces are opened as much*

as possible (hence the deep digging with a garden spade) to Winter's worst. The surface is penetrated by Winter's rain, frost and air, which increases its fertility and goes some way towards dealing with the pest problem]

5 be alert as from the following January for the arrival in the suppliers' premises of first-early, second-early and maincrop seed potatoes

6 buy the three types the moment they appear, to be sure of having the widest range from which to choose

7 for the best results, choose the varieties stated to be

— of reputable origin

— free from virus diseases. [**Consideration:** *this is guaranteed by an official certificate number, which the purchaser is advised to secure*]

— blight resistant. [**Consideration:** *this quality, plus the blight-preventive spraying at a later stage that the head gardener strongly recommends, offers as reliable a guarantee as it is possible to get against the onset of crop-destroying blight*]

8 decide how many of each of the three types of seed potato to buy. Do so by

For the starting dates of each month's moon quarters see almost any diary — but it is essential to consult *MOON* first of all.

— establishing the length of the row to be filled with the selected type

— dividing the length by 30cm and then adding two or three to cater for unexpected eventualities

— multiplying the result by the number of rows to be filled with the selected type

9 without delay, house the seeds in trays. Place them so that they support each other in an upright position

10 do not mix the types. Separated one from the other in its own tray or trays. Label each tray, indicating which type is in it

11 position each seed potato in its tray so that the end showing eyes is uppermost. Usually, this is the broadest end of the seed. The eyes take the form of pronounced indents, or dimples

12 locate the filled trays in a protected, *unheated*, frost-free location

13 ensure that the seeds receive full daylight — but

TIP 103
➜ **In Autumn, when the potato-section-to-be becomes available, apply soot from a coal fire to that part of it that is to be used for the maincrop potatoes. Fork it in. Leave it to over-Winter. It deters the black keel slug, which is a potato pest. Do this at the start of the moon's fourth quarter.**

not direct sunlight. Do not stack their trays

14 examine the trays regularly. Remove and dispose of any seed that shows signs of rotting

15 otherwise, leave the trays undisturbed as each seed produces dark-green or purplish sprouts from its eyes. This process occupies at least one month or six weeks.
[*Consideration: doing this enables the growing process to begin well before the still Winter-bound garden is ready to receive the seed tubers. It gives the gardener a lead growing time of up to sixteen weeks. It also permits the gardener to wait for non-frosty growing conditions without risking deterioration of the seeds. The process also, in R J Harris's view, results in crops that are superior to those obtained by the planting of undeveloped seed tubers*]

16 at **the start of the March moon's fourth quarter**, clear the potato-area-to-be of weeds. Use a garden fork.
[*Considerations: this is if weather/soil conditions permit. If they do not, postpone the commencement of operations until the same moon time in April*]

17 compost the annual weeds that have not set seeds, together with their roots. Or place them in the trench that awaits development into a deep-trench bed (*BED/1*) or shallow-trench bed (*BED/2*), if there is one in the garden

18 off site, destroy or dispose of the annual weeds that have set seeds and their roots, the perennial weeds and their roots, and the grass growth and its roots

19 at the same time as de-weeding the potato-area-to-be, use the garden fork to level its surface. Break up the large clods formed when the area was given its Autumn spade dig, and that have thwarted Winter's attempts to reduce them in size

20 follow by using a rake. Since potato planting is contemplated, do not aim for any kind of tilth. Aim, simply, for a level, manageable ground surface

---

TIP 104
➜ **New potatoes for Christmas Day is a R J Harris favourite: 1) in September's first week, place drainage stones in a 25cm pot; 2) cover them with a 6cm-thick layer of compacted John Innes No 2 potting compost; 3) sit a sprouted tuber on top of the compost; 4) fill with compacted compost, leaving room for watering; 5) keep constantly, correctly moist — ie, always slightly under watered, which is better than over-watered; 6) place the pot in a cold frame, unheated greenhouse or conservatory and keep it protected from the frost; 7) ignore the moon's phases, this being crop production minus garden-soil connection. *Arran Pilot, Duke of York* and *Sharp's Express* are R J Harris's favourites for this treatment.**

21 de-earth the rake frequently, to keep its tines unblocked

22 remove the stones that are trapped by the rake's unblocked tines. Store these for use in connection with other projects in the garden. [**Considerations: 1** — cost-conscious gardening aims always to conserve useful resources that may be difficult to obtain at some point in the future. Sometimes, stones are an irreplaceable ingredient in garden projects, and merit the small amount of storage space that they occupy when conserved; **2** — the stones that slip through the rake's unblocked tines are of the size that is required by the soil. They are an aid to drainage. They act as a moisture-retaining mulch. At all times, but especially in Summer, they release during the night the heat that they absorb during the day, relatively warming the section and its contents; **3** — the stones that are gathered by the rake's regularly de-earthed tines are likely to be too large to be wanted in the soil; **4** — generally, if no stone removal is desired, use a hoe when a bed's surface is being turned. The hoe's shape prevents it from gathering stones of any size]

23 still at **the start of the March moon's fourth quarter**, dress the raked-level surface of the potato-section-to-be with 115g to the square metre of fish-blood-and-bone fertiliser. Work it in lightly. Use the rake. Restore the level surface. [**Considerations: 1** — for

perfection in surface preparation for potato planting, apply the R J Harris-preferred, three-tined cultivator instead of a rake. This is the long-handled tool that has long, curved tines. For generations of professional horticulturists it has been available with three, four or five tines. In the hands of a practised operator, the three-tined version provides a coarse tilth (which is perfect for potato planting), the four-tined a less coarse tilth, and the five-tined a fine tilth (which is perfect for seed sowing in drills). Also, being much less prone to clogging and having far fewer and more widely-spaced tines than the rake, all three cultivators ignore the essential small stones that the initial raking leaves in situ. It is used as if it were a rake; **2** — whether a rake or a cultivator is applied, penetrate the surface with it as deeply as the tines permit]

TIP 105
➔ **Insert Mexican marigold plantlets into the 60cm spaces between the rows of potatoes, coinciding with the planting of the potato seeds. Post these half-hardies 3m to 4m from each other in all directions. Their roots protect the developing tubers from eelworm, the black keel slug, mice and moles, and the bed from couch grass, bind weed and ground elder for the length of the season. They grow to 2m to 3m in height. They reach life's end when Winter's frost strikes them. See *MARIGOLD: Mexican/1* to *-/3*.**

24 at **the beginning of the April moon's first quarter**, position a garden line where the first row of first-early seed tubers is to be grown. [*Consideration: sowing occurs about ten days after the incorporation of fertiliser. R J Harris recommends as general, good practice a ten-day pause between fertilising and sowing/planting to ensure the fullest possible assimilation of feed by soil prior to seeds or plant life being introduced*]

25 ideally, but not essentially, position the line so that it extends from north to south. [*Consideration: this ensures that no fully-developed potato top blocks out sunlight from its neighbours*]

26 create a spade-width trench one side of which abuts the garden line. Make the trench as deep as the spade blade's length. Make it long enough to accept the first-earlies spaced 30cm apart

27 deposit the removed earth evenly along the side of the trench that is removed from the garden line by the width of the trench

28 ideally, line the bottom of the completed trench with a 7cm thickness of fully-composted leaf mould. [*Considerations: 1 — potatoes do best in soil possessing a very low pH. Placing leaf mould in the trench first of all reduces the prevailing pH better than any other vegetable matter; 2 — a bonus is that the leaf mould gives the crop skins which are clean and minus unsightly scab*]

29 if fully-composted leaf mould is not available, use comfrey leaves first left to lie on the ground for several hours after being cut, so that they wilt and then settle unprotestingly into the bottom of the trench. [*Consideration: whatever is used, it traps and retains essential moisture where the developing, moisture-craving young potatoes need it*]

30 spread a 2cm thickness of top soil on top of the installed vegetable matter. Take it from the excavated top soil parked alongside the edge of the trench

31 place the seed tubers on top of the added soil, sprouts uppermost. Give them a 30cm spacing. Position them firmly. Take care not to damage the sprouts as this is done

32 cover the seeds — by spade or by hoe — with a 5cm-to-7cm thickness of earth. Leave the balance of the removed soil where it is, at the trench's edge

33 still at **the beginning of the April moon's first quarter**, complete the planting of the

TIP 106
➔ **Seed tubers are sold by weight. Choose the smaller seeds when buying a required number — each about the size of an egg — and, thus, reduce the price of the purchase. The bigger seed, if it must be bought, can be cut into two or four pieces lengthwise just prior to planting. First, it must be fully sprouted. Each piece must bear two or three sprouts.**

112

Exactly where the potato came from has been discussed hotly, and with no little disagreement, since horticultural records first named it. Page 49 of Webbs's 1888 Spring Catalogue sustained a long-running debate by stating that there was no doubt that it was an American plant cultivated by the Peruvians or Chilians long before the advent of the Europeans. It reached Ireland in about 1586, courtesy of Thomas Heriot, one of Sir Walter Raleigh's companions, who was on his way back from Virginia. Whether it was a sweet potato or a common potato Webbs's catalogue did not question, although it added that the tuber was believed to have been sent to Europe before 1586, and by the Spaniards.

A picture of the plant appeared in Britain in 1597; it illustrated a specimen known to have been sent from Virginia.

There is, today, agreement that the potato is one of the few plants that can be said to have helped to mould the shape of history, and to have brought us to where we are at present.

first-early seed tubers. Leave a 60cm gap between their rows' trenches

34 as green shoots appear through the soil in the incompletely-filled trenches, cover them with further soil pulled in from the excavated soil parked at the edges of the trenches. Use a hoe

35 at the same time, remove and re-use or destroy appropriately the fresh weed growth.

[*Consideration: as the potato top growth gets higher and thicker, the weeds are smothered and find it less and less easy to appear and to flourish*]

36 continue to earth up in this way as the first earlies continue to produce green shoots. Eventually, the trench is filled and most of the surplus soil is reinstated.
[*Consideration: earthing up ensures that no young potatoes are developed close to the surface of the soil and, thus, exposed to sun and air. Permitted to be so exposed, they become green and unfit to eat*]

37 still earth up as more shoots appear, using a hoe or a rake to draw up earth from both sides of the row.
[*Consideration: the result is ridges where once there were trenches. The top growth emerges from the top and the sides of the ridges. The ridges direct rain water to where the developing young potatoes await it*]

38 protect the newly-emergent shoots when frost threatens. Do so by placing over them a layer of the soil that is at the trenches' edges.
[*Consideration: no harm is*

TIP 107
➜ **Potato varieties differ in moisture content. Choose according to what happens to the harvested tuber once it gets into the kitchen. Eg, if frying is a culinary practice, plant a variety that has a high dry content. It splutters less in the frying pan.**

113

Over the years, R J Harris's choice of seed tubers for cultivation has narrowed to

First earlies

Arran Comet, a 1927 waxy type
Arron Pilot, a 1930 floury type
Duke of York, an 1891 floury type
Epicure, an 1897 floury type
Homeguard, a 1942 floury type
Red Duke of York, an 1891 floury type
Sharpes Express, a 1901 floury type
Ulster Chieftain, a floury type of unknown vintage

Second earlies

Belle de Fontenay, a waxy type of unknown date
Catriona, a 1920 floury type
Edzell Blue, a pre-1900 floury type

Maincrop

Dunbar Standard, a 1936 floury type
Golden Wonder, a 1906 floury type
Kerrs Pink, a 1917 waxy type
KIng Edward, a 1902 floury type
Majestic, a 1911 floury type
Pink Fir Apple, a pre-1900 waxy type.

---

done by thus anticipating the earthing up that is an essential part of potato production. The aim, ideally, is to have protection in place before the arrival of the frost]

39 repeat the above overall activity in respect of the second-early seed tubers, Do so immediately the initial planting of the first-earlies — a one- or two-day task, at most — has been completed. [***Consideration:*** *by doing so,*

retain the advantage of planting on or about the commencement of the moon's first quarter]

40 at **the beginning of the May moon's first quarter**, one month later, repeat the complete planting programme in respect of the maincrop seed planting

41 complete the sowing of all of the seed potatoes by the end of May at the latest

42 at seven- or ten-day intervals as from early June, spray Bordeaux mixture on the potato foliage to avert the onset of potato blight

43 use a proprietory Bordeaux mixture. Follow its maker's instructions precisely. Use a pressure sprayer. Spray, especially, the undersides of the potatoes' foliage. Spray in the cool of the end of day. [***Consideration:*** *the cool of the end of the day is when the least number of insects — including the beneficial insects — is present]*

44 include any nearby, outdoor tomatoes in this spraying. [***Consideration:*** *potatoes and tomatoes are related, botanically. Either can attract and transmit the disease to the other. Blight comes with heavy, humid, thundery weather]*

45 continue spraying for as long as the potato tops massed above the potato ridges are bright green in colour. Stop spraying when the green changes to yellow. This indicates that the potato plants are at the end of their lives and that

developed potatoes are underground, waiting to be lifted.
[**Consideration:** *the first-earlies yellow first, then the second-earlies, then the maincrop*]

46 twenty weeks after planting the early potatoes, excavate carefully at one end of a row to reveal one or two of the underground tubers to find out whether or not this first crop is ready to for use

47 investigate daily. Begin to lift when unearthed specimens pass muster. Then take as required for consumption. Otherwise, leave these new potatoes where they are, still growing, with the excavated earth replaced to make sure that they are not exposed to the light.
[**Consideration:** *consumed daily, the first-earlies are exhausted before there is need to consider storing them, and before there is risk of them being infested by earth-bound, potato-loving pests*]

48 repeat with the second-early crop. In this case, make the initial inspection twenty-two weeks after planting

49 at the same time, watch for the tops of the second-earlies to change in colour from green to yellow and to droop and, thus, to begin to die. This is a signal that the crop is ready to be harvested; the unexcavated tubers are left in the ground until required for consumption

50 when the maincrop tubers reach their twenty-sixth to twenty-eighth week in the soil, check them for suitability

51 lift them in their entirety when the end-of-row excavations reveal that the tubers are ready to be harvested — and when, at the same time, the plants' tops have died completely and collapsed to the ground

52 ideally, make the harvesting coincide with **the beginning of the moon's fourth quarter**. Make it coincide, also, with a dry, fine day.
[**Consideration:** *the aim is excavated tubers that enter the above-ground world in a non-muddy state. Storage is aided when the least amount of surface moisture is present on the lifted tubers*]

53 lift the tubers with a carefully-applied garden fork. If any tuber is speared in the process, isolate it and send it to the kitchen. Do not attempt to store it

54 immediately, and gently, remove by hand any earth that clings to the tubers. Do not use any kind of implement to do this. Do not bruise and scrape the skin of the individual tuber

55 withhold any diseased potatoes and destroy them

56 the moment the maincrop potatoes are judged to be perfect, place them in stout (ideally, double-walled), dry paper sacks or timber boxes. Seal the sacks or place a close-fitting lid on the boxes. Do not add any other materials to the sacked/boxed potatoes

57 lodge the filled sacks/boxes in a *dark*, cool, frost-free, dry, accessible place for storage.
[*Consideration: the paramount need, at this stage, is for darkness and frost-free dryness. Light turns the tubers green, making them unfit to eat. Dampness induces rot. This is why, contrary to some gardeners' practice, the head gardener does not expose his tubers on the earth's surface to the daylight for a period when they have been lifted. Dryness is not an issue, because of his combining at the moment of harvesting of a) a fine, dry day and b) the start of the moon's fourth quarter*]

58 do not use plastic sacks or containers for storage purpose

59 dispose of the dead potato tops off site. Do not attempt to compost them. Do not add them to the trench that waits completion as a deep-trench bed (*BED/1*) or a shallow-trench bed (*BED/2*) bed.
[*Consideration: there is every possibility that this dead vegetation harbours pests and/or disease. No risks may be taken with it*]

60 lift and consume or store any potatoes that are still in the ground at the beginning of October

61 at **the start of the October moon's fourth quarter**, subject the potato-growing area to its pre-Winter, fertility-enhancing deep dig with a sharpened garden spade.

62 as time passes, examine the stored tubers regularly. Extract and destroy any that show signs of deterioration.

for background information, see *BED/1 to -/3, COMFREY/1 to -/3, FERTILISER, ROTATION, SUPPLIERS.*

RHUBARB/1 — **to prepare to plant a rhubarb root.** In the walled kitchen garden at Tresillian this 16th-century introduction to British horticulture — which has been used medicinally by the Chinese for thousands of years — is inserted into a specially prepared bed. It remains there for seven years. It is then lifted and separated into several pieces each bearing a growing point. The best of these is replanted in a different location to occupy the following seven years in becoming a mature, full-size root ready for separation once again. The unused pieces may also be planted elsewhere or are presented to other gardeners or destroyed off site.

Rejuvenation by this means is a main cause of the Tresillian rhubarb's continued existence as a producer of splendid stems.

Overall, extended harvesting through the year is achieved by planting varieties that produce early and late in the year, and at mid season.

Head gardener R J Harris's procedure in making ready to plant a single root is as follows

TIP 108
➜ **The pH content of soil that is perfect for rhubarb production is between 6.0 and 6.5. A reading that is close to this is almost as good. Happily, rhubarb is not a fussy plant, and — managed correctly — makes a satisfactory return in almost any garden soil.**

REQUIRED FOR *RHUBARB/1*

- A 1m-square plot of suitable ground located outside the garden's crop-rotation system and earmarked for double-dug bed commencement at.**the start of the October moon's third quarter**.

- Composted farmyard manure for light soil, composted stable manure for heavy soil, or composted vegetable-waste or composted leaf mould inserted into the bed by **the start of the October moon's fourth quarter**.

- A garden bucket, a garden fork, a garden spade or shovel, a rake, a wheelbarrow, four short timber stakes.

For the complete instruction, see *RHUBARB/1* to -/3

1 choose a site at which rhubarb has never before grown

2 ensure that the site

— appears to be well drained

— is in an open, airy situation

— is well exposed to the sunlight

— offers sufficient adjacent space for the temporary parking of excavated top soil and materials, and for the manoeuvring of a wheelbarrow

— is not located in those areas of the garden that are subject to the crop-rotation system.

[*Consideration: being semi-permanently established, the plant cannot be moved — and does not need to be moved annually — in order to meet the requirements of a rotation system*]

— is within striking distance of a point at which sub soil may be deposited permanently

3 in October, when **the moon is at the start of its third quarter**, mark out on the ground at the chosen site a square each side of which is each about one metre long

4 remove the top soil within the square. First use a fork to loosen the soil. Then use a spade (or, better, a shovel, in the Cornish style) to lift the soil and heap it nearby. [*Consideration: at its parking point, the removed soil can be retrieved easily to be returned when the square bed is re-instated*]

TIP 109
➔ **Never plant rhubarb in water-logged soil. The condition is likely to bring on this semi-permanent plant's only killer disease, crown rot. The only cure for crown rot is root removal followed immediately by destruction or disposal off site. The place where the diseased plant was grown is never used again for rhubarb development. Be warned that the disease has arrived when 1) the plant's leaves are yellow in colour and generally anaemic in appearance, and 2) its stems are small, weak, spindly and few in number and grow mainly at the edge of the crown.**

114

Cornwall's privileged gardeners harvest outdoor rhubarb as from the middle of January. It is a pleasure that is enjoyed by few elsewhere in a Britain that is bitterly chilly at that time.

"It is in absolute abundance," comments the head gardener.

"Once, when I had more time at my disposal, I used to lift a couple of crowns from the garden in October and put divisions of them in a light-proof box without soil. I would cover them with a 60cm thickness of clean straw and close the lid shut tight. Then there would be fresh, pink stems for Christmas.

"The crowns seldom survived the experience, but next season there were always plenty more to lift, so that was no problem."

The commercial growers have used this method on a vast scale for years. notes the head gardener. They pack thousands of unplanted crowns close together inside darkened buildings in which heat and humidity are mechanically controlled.

"When you go into these buildings you can actually hear the crowns cracking as they are forced to grow the lovely-looking stems that you see in the supermarkets when the naturally-produced stuff is not available."

and remove it from site to its designated disposal point

8 from both extractions, as they are performed, segregate grass, rubbish, perennial weed roots and top growth, annual weed roots and top growth, and large stones

9 wheelbarrow the rubbish, perennial weed material and annual-weed top growth that is in seed from site and dispose of it. Conserve the grass, annual weeds that are not in seed and their roots. Conserve, also, the large stones. [**Consideration:** *cost-conscious gardening aims always to conserve useful resources that may be difficult to obtain at some point in the future. Sometimes, stones are an irreplaceable ingredient in garden projects, and merit the small amount of*

5 dig to a depth that equals the length of the spade's blade. In most gardens, this caters for the top soil

6 dig down a further spade blade's length

7 as the second removal of material is accomplished, separate any sub soil that may arise. Place the sub soil in a wheelbarrow

If further explanation is required, e-mail R J Harris on rjh@moongardening.fsnet.co.uk

TIP 110

➔ **Plant several rhubarb roots 75cm apart. "When full maturity is reached, a rhubarb crown can be as big as a bicycle wheel," points out Mr Harris. "Some of those lifted in the kitchen garden at Tresillian have each filled a wheelbarrow with divisions for re-planting. That is after about seven years in the ground. Our policy is to lift and divide after that time and start all over again."**

storage space that they occupy when conserved]

10 loosen the sub soil in the bottom of the excavation with the garden fork to a depth of about 10cm. By this means, obtain good drainage

11 spread the conserved weed material on the bottom of the excavation. If there are grass turfs, turn them upside down

12 on top of the added vegetable material evenly spread a thickness of fully-composted farmyard manure, if the soil is a light soil or fully-composted, well-strawed horse manure, if the soil is a heavy soil. Make the thickness equal in depth to the length of a spade blade. Tamp it down gently with a garden rake held vertically, to eliminate air pockets and to level it

13 mix the same kind of composted manure into the parked top soil. Aim for a 50:50 mix. Use a garden bucket as a unit of measure. Empty it into — and do the mixing in — a wheelbarrow. [*Considerations: 1 — adding manure is not essential. Undiluted top soil gives an acceptable result. Manure brings an improvement because it is rich in nitrogen. Rhubarb has a high demand for nitrogen. Manure also increases the soil's ability to retain moisture; 2 — failing composted manure, use composted vegetable waste or composted leaf mould or a mixture of the two, in a 50:50 ratio. This improves the soil's*

moisture-retentive powers. Lace the substitute with a small amount of dried manure such as 6X as the mixing takes place]

14 using the wheelbarrow, transfer the neat soil or mixed soil/composted manure/composted vegetable-waste/composted leaf mould to the excavation

15 fill the excavation by this means until its top is level with the surface of the surrounding area

16 gently tamp down the added mixture with a garden rake to remove the air pockets that may have formed within it. Level off with further mixture and gentle tamping down, if that is necessary

17 add a 10cm thickness of the mixture to the levelled bed surface, so that a raised bed surface is created. [*Consideration: by this means, compensate for later bed-surface sinkage*]

TIP 111
➔ **"Rhubarb in the ground never ever wants to be cold," says head gardener Harris. "That is why straw freshly horse-manured — or dressed with fish-blood-and-bone fertiliser — is placed over it as a permanent fixture. Generating heat, it makes and keeps the rhubarb crown warm and forces it into production." The head gardener vetoes composted farmyard manure. "It would sit there on top of the crown and be very, very cold and growth-inhibiting," he says.**

18 insert a short stake into the earth at the each corner of the newly-created bed. Make it protrude by only a few centimetres.

[*Consideration: by this means be able to identify the perimeter of the bed at a later stage, when settlement raises questions about the bed's precise location*]

19 leave the new bed unused until the following October

20 throughout the year, permit weeds to grow. Remove them before they set seed.

[*Consideration: the reward is a bed surface that is as good as permanently weed-free when the time comes to insert the rhubarb root. The benefit extends through the subsequent seven years of bed management*]

21 compost the annual weeds that have not set seeds, together with their roots. Or place them in the trench that awaits development into a deep-trench bed (*BED/1*) or a shallow-trench bed (*BED/2*), if there is one in the garden

22 off site, destroy or dispose of the annual weeds that have set seeds and their roots, the perennial weeds and their roots, and the grass growth and its roots

---

Visit *R J Harris's Moon Gardening's* companion web site

www.moongardening.fsnet.co.uk

to keep in touch with the results of the head gardener's latest experimental archaeological projects and developmental work in the walled kitchen garden at Tresillian in Cornwall.

115

C innamon rhubarb chutney is one way to preserve the over-supply of rhubarb that is sometimes created by the recommended practice of stem pulling the moment that there are stems to be pulled, whether or not the kitchen wants them. It is good with cold meats, and makes a good sandwich spread — especially with cheese. Its recipe has been in R J Harris's family for many years.

Put half an English cup of malt vinegar, 1kilo of sugar and half an English cup of water into a saucepan. Add a tied muslin bag filled with 1.25ml of ground nutmeg, 2.5ml of ground cloves, 5ml of cinnamon and 2.5ml of mixed spice.

Simmer the saucepan's contents for 25 minutes and then remove the bag of spices.

Add 1kilo of washed and de-leafed rhubarb cut into 2cm-to-3cm lengths. Add, also, 250g of washed raisins.

Simmer the whole until it is thick. Stir the mixture from time to time. Put it into warmed jars with metal lids whilst it is still hot.

Screw down the lids when the jars are cold. The chutney keeps well.

23 tread on the surface of the rhubarb bed as seldom as possible. Reinstate trodden-on areas as soon as they are created.

[*Consideration: compacted depressions in a bed's surface collect rain water. Static surface water of this kind provides habitat for pests and disease. It also, minutely but unhelpfully, deprives the bed's contents of their life blood — air*]

24 spread surplus top soil as thinly as possible on the garden's beds.

for background information, see
COMPOST: vegetable waste,
MANURE, MOON, pH.

RHUBARB/2 — to plant a rhubarb root. R J Harris's method is as follows

1 in late September, when the waiting rhubarb bed is one year old, purchase a preferred variety of rhubarb root

2 at **the start of the October moon's second quarter**, finally empty the year-old rhubarb bed's surface of weed growth. Dispose of the weeds as previously

3 excavate a hole in the centre of the bed. Use a trowel. Make the hole generously large enough and deep enough to receive the root that is to be planted

4 place the removed top soil into a wheelbarrow. Mix into it 50g of sterilised bonemeal

5 loosen the soil at the bottom of the hole with a hand fork to a depth of about 10cm. [*Consideration: by this means, ensure good drainage*]

6 add 50g of sterilised bonemeal to the loosened earth at the bottom of the hole. Mix it in

7 fill a garden bucket with soil/bone meal from the wheelbarrow. Position the bucket close to the planting hole

---

REQUIRED FOR *RHUBARB/2*

- The one-year-old, 1m-square double-dug bed that has been prepared for rhubarb development.

- 50g sterilised bonemeal mixed into the soil removed when a root-planting hole is excavated.

- 50g sterilised bonemeal mixed into the loosened soil at the bottom of the root-planting hole.

- 90g to the square metre of fish-blood-and-bone fertiliser applied at **the start of the October moon's second quarter** to a 30cm-thick, straw mulch placed on the planted-up rhubarb bed's surface.

- A trowel, a hand fork, a garden bucket, a wheelbarrow, wire netting.

For the complete instruction, see *RHUBARB/1* to -/3.

8 place the root in the hole. Position it in one hand so that the growing tip at its top is well exposed above ground level. [*Consideration: in doing*

TIP 112
➔ **Rhubarb's stems have a high content of oxalic acid. This inhibits the digestive system from ingesting the iron content of consumed food. It is unwise to consume the plant more than once per week, advise the nutritionists. Bottling and freezing are the best ways to make the whole of a root's annual production available to the kitchen.**

116

Bottling is the old-fashioned way to give rhubarb (and other garden fruits) a long pantry life:

01. save any redundant 2lb jars with metal screw-on lids that come into the kitchen. Failing this size, collect the more common 1-lb jam jars with metal lids

02. wash the jars and lids thoroughly. Rinse and dry them well

03. wash unblemished rhubarb stems. Cut them into 3cm-long pieces

04. pack the pieces as compactly as possible into the jars, without crushing them together. Fill the jars to the very top

05. fill the packed jars almost to the top with syrup. Make this by dissolving 500g of any kind of sugar in a litre of hot water. Use it cold

06. place as many prepared jars as possible in a large saucepan. Sit their lids *loosely* on top of them

07. place cold water in the saucepan until it reaches to a little below the jars' tops

08. cover the saucepan tightly with its lid. If the height of the jars prevents this, turn another saucepan of the same size upside down and use it as a lid

09. place a weight on top of it

10. bring the whole to the boiling point slowly, over a very low flame

11. when boiling point is reached, instantly reduce the heat to its lowest point, so that the water merely simmers

12. simmer for 15 minutes

13. remove the bottles from the saucepan and screw down their tops as tightly as possible

14. permit the bottles to cool. Label them, stating bottling date

15. use the rhubarb straight from the bottle without added sweetening. Limit the amount of syrup that is used when preparing pies and crumbles, etc. Expect to have a surplus, which makes a delicious if highly oxalic-acid-charged drink.

this, it is better to err. and to have an over-visible growing point than to have a buried one — which is almost certain to develop into a crown with rot problems]

9 with the other hand, add soil/bone meal from the bucket to the hole. Firm it in around the root. Ensure that no air pockets are created between the inserted root and the earth surrounding it. Complete the earthing in. Ensure that the root's growing tip is raised above the level of the rhubarb bed's surface

10 cover the entire bed's surface — and the root's very visible growing tip — with a 30cm-thick layer of very loosely distributed straw. If the straw is removed from a farmer's bale or from a similarly compressed unit, loosen it well before placing it on the bed's surface

11 spread 90g to the square metre of fish-blood-and-bone fertiliser on the top of the straw overlay

TIP 113
➔ **Do not, R J Harris advises, place end-of-season rhubarb stems and leaves in the compost bin or heap when they are cleared from the plant's bed prior to the Winter sleep. "This material does not compost well with other vegetable matter, being so acid in nature," he says.**

12 position a square metre, or thereabouts, of wire netting on top of the straw to ward off wind, cat and blackbird attack

13 leave bed, inserted rhubarb root and straw mulch to over-Winter undisturbed.

for background information, see *FERTILISER, MANURE, MOON, pH.*

RHUBARB/3 — to **maintain and manage a planted rhubarb root.** The head gardener's procedure is as follows

1 at **the start of the moon's fourth quarter** in the February or March after the October planting of the rhubarb root — before the root develops top growth — remove the protective wire netting from the straw mulch and the straw mulch from the surface of the root's bed

2 remove and scrap the few weeds that have developed through Winter

3 return the removed straw. Add more straw, if necessary. Loosen it well first of all. Complete the covering of the whole of the bed's surface with loosened straw to a depth of about 30cm

4 apply fish-blood-and-bone fertiliser to the straw's surface at the rate of 90g to the square metre

5 if wind/bird attack is to be expected, replace the wire-netting on top of the straw mulch. Use pieces of wire netting, so that there is an

REQUIRED FOR *RHUBARB/3*

● The one-year-old, 1m-square double-dug bed into which a rhubarb root has been inserted.

● Annually, 90g to the square metre of fish-blood-and-bone fertiliser applied to the straw mulch at **the start of the February or March moon's fourth quarter**.

● Annually, 90g to the square metre of fish-blood-and-bone fertiliser applied to the straw mulch at **the start of the following October moon's fourth quarter**.

● Wire netting, straw for mulch renewal.

For the complete instruction, see *RHUBARB/1* to *-/3*.

uncovered area at the centre of the mulch through which the rhubarb's leaves can develop without being impeded by the netting

TIP 114
➜ **The purist, advises R J Harris, excavates the rhubarb-root hole in the new bed and adds sterilised bonemeal to the loosened earth at its bottom at *the start of the September moon's fourth quarter*. The same purist then inserts the rhubarb root at *the start of the October moon's second quarter*, when the rising water table brings increased moisture to the top soil and, hence, to the moisture-deprived, traumatised, newly-planted root. "Of course," comments the head gardener, "not everyone can afford the time to be a purist."**

6 permit the rhubarb root to develop fully and undisturbed throughout its first year. Its stems and their leaves push the straw apart and to one side as they develop

---

117

'Freeze rhubarb," R J Harris suggests, "the quick, simple way."

He itemises:

1) wash and dry the de-leafed stems

2) cut them into 2cm-to-3cm-long pieces ("kitchen scissors are the best for this job," he recommends)

3) place the rhubarb pieces in a transparent plastic bag

4) tie the bag with a wire tie

5) date the bag

6) place and store it in the freezer

7) wait a day or so for the rhubarb to freeze into stonelike chunks.

"Use it in pies and crumbles etc, in its frozen state, and bake or cook as if it were fresh rhubarb."

---

7 do not pull stems from the plant during its first year of growth. Permit it to use all of its resources to become fully established in the new bed

8 at **the start of the next October moon's fourth quarter** after the year of uninterrupted growth, remove the wire netting and straw mulch. Remove also the dead and dying rhubarb leaves and stems and dispose of them off site. If there are usable stems, take them to the kitchen. Weed

the bed. Dispose of the weeds in a proper manner

9 replace the straw layer, loosened. Add more straw, well loosened, if that is necessary. Completely cover the bed to a depth of about 30cm

10 dress the top of the straw layer with 90g to the square metre of fish-blood-and-bone fertiliser

11 replace the wire netting as previously. Leave the bed to over-Winter undisturbed

12 in the following year, in February or March, repeat the previous year's management programme in every respect

13 in this first year, take stems from the plant each time they attain a height of 30cm. Dispose of their leaves off site.
[*Consideration: the standard practice is to compost this kind of redundant vegetable matter. The head gardener does not do so. He believes that the*

TIP 115

➔ **The recommended straw and fertiliser overlay for the planted-up rhubarb bed is a version of what head gardener R J Harris prefers to use. His straw comes from a nearby stable. It arises out of the stable's daily clean out. It has been slept on only once by the horses. Hence, it contains the urine (high in nitrogen) and droppings of only one night. Mr Harris applies no fertiliser to it when he overlays it on the rhubarb bed.**

material almost certainly harbours pests. Also, it may carry the beginnings of disease — and not only disease which is related to the original plant. These conditions may not be destroyed by the composting process. Better and safer, he is certain, to destroy it]

14 continue harvesting throughout each of the following five years of the root's life

15 pluck the ready stems whether or not they are required for use by the kitchen. Do so as often as possible, ideally, when the moon is full.
[***Consideration:*** *this is when the fully-raised water table fully charges the top soil and all that is in it with moisture under pressure. Hence, the rhubarb's stems are at peak moisture content and, consequently, peak flavour*]

16 do not permit the plant to develop stems which are coarse and, thus, unusable by the kitchen. This can lead to the development of flowers and seed. The plant then gives up being a provider of kitchen-fit stems. If the stems coarsen, remove them and their leaves and dispose of them off site

17 pluck each stem fully from the root. Grasp it as close as possible to the root to do so, prising it away from the root with the fingers at the same time

18 if the stem breaks when it is pulled, detach its stub fully from the root. Do not leave a broken end of stem exposed to the atmosphere, with the broken end itself still attached to the root

19 freeze or bottle the stems that are not required immediately by the kitchen

20 progressively reduce taking the stems immediately after the year's longest day on June 21. Do so until hardly any are being taken in October. By this means, permit the plant to recover before dormancy sets in

21 each year, as from **the start of the October moon's fourth quarter**, repeat the annual maintenance programme

22 make **the start of the October moon's second quarter** the time at which a seven-year-old and exhausted rhubarb root is

— taken out of its bed

— divided with a sharp, long-bladed knife into several parts each bearing a single growing point

— replanted in its several parts in other beds according to the method described in *RHUBARB/1*

23 ensure that the original place of planting is not re-used for the growing of rhubarb.

If further explanation is required, e-mail R J Harris on
rjh@moongardening.fsnet.co.uk

for background information, see
FERTILISER, MOON.

ROTATION. Correctly carried out, four-year crop rotation ensures that a given vegetable, root, tuber, legume or annual flower is not grown in the same place twice until after an interval of three years. The gap reduces considerably the risk of pest and disease becoming permanent residents in the garden's vegetable/flower beds. It also reduces the burden that is imposed upon given growing medium by the requirement that it produces the same crops year in, year out.

R J Harris's rules of crop rotation are his own. They combine with his rules of moon gardening and with the traditional horticultural methods that he has revived. For as long as there is growing season in the year, they dictate what happens, and when and why, in the four 15m by 34m rectangular areas that occupy approximately two-thirds of the three-quarters of an acre of space that is enclosed by the four walls of the Tresillian estate's kitchen garden.

When there is no growing season, the unemployed soil is kept in what the head gardener refers to as a naked state.

In this state, the soil is hoed constantly. This is done to prevent weed germination and to remove before seeds are set the weeds that manage, somehow, to germinate.

Thus is depleted the hidden army of weed seed that awaits constantly the opportunity to invade, to occupy and to pillage nutrients and moisture.

The unrelenting hoeing also revives and continues the ancient tradition of manual manuring. The old-time horticulturists knew this as 'manoeuvring'. It encourages and maintains and enhances soil fertility without the addition of specific fertilisers and manures.

The walled kitchen garden has been treated in this fashion almost since its soil was first turned in the mid 1800s. The head gardener is committed to restoring such old practices.

"The modern approach is to cover ground with mustard or cress the moment its crops have been cleared, to dig this in as a green manure before it sets seed, and then to repeat the process, weather and season conditions permitting," he notes.

"It is a good way, too, and I recommend it to today's sparetime gardeners. They require such quick, safe, low-cost, undemanding solutions to the problem of restoring or increasing fertility — solutions, moreover, that demand little in the way of appreciation of the basics of horticultural practice."

118

"Give serious thought," urges the head gardener, "to exactly what is and is not to be grown in the vegetable beds *before* drawing up the crop-rotation plan."

"If ever a matter called for a family discussion, it is this.

"If everyone hates cabbage, there is no point in growing cabbages — no matter how handsome and caterpillar-free they are.

"If everyone likes the idea of sweet-tasting sugar peas, make sure these are included.

"Equally, if the cos lettuce is preferred to the other types, note this and get the appropriate kind of seed."

Quantities is a related consideration.

"Too much of a given vegetable or salad crop is likely to lead to waste — of soil, seeds, feeds and effort," comments Mr Harris. "And of money."

He adds: "They *could* make this particular solution even more effective by sowing their green manure at the most beneficial moon time — which is at the start of, or during, the moon's second quarter.

"That is when there is maximum moisture in the top soil at the very moment when the sown seed wants to germinate."

Each of Tresillian's four highly-productive, crop-rotation-controlled areas incorporates traditional deep-trench beds and single-dug beds constructed according to this manual's *BED/1* and *BED/3*. Elsewhere, inside and outside the kitchen garden, double-dug beds cater for specific needs arising outside the crop-rotation system.

The crop-rotation beds are installed in the Autumn by the start of the September, October or November moon's fourth quarter. They endure for four years. They are renewed in the Autumn of the fourth year, after which another four-year cycle begins.

In design, they are the head gardener's versions of the beds of the ancient Romans and Greeks. Theirs were beds for their times. The trenches were at least two metres deep, not a mere one, being excavated by an unlimited supply of free, easily-replaced labour and being filled with the product of efficient sewage- and night-soil-collection systems, extensive animal-intensive farming and the ubiquitous horse and mule.

In two particular respects, the beds of those times were exactly as those of today's walled kitchen garden at Tresillian: 1) they considerably reduced the need for water and watering; 2) they were reliant upon the availability of copious quantities of manure.

After a revival programme occupying almost two decades, the four crop-rotation areas of the kitchen garden in Cornwall now produce as follows

AREA ONE

Year One: broad beans, broccoli, cabbages, cauliflowers, dwarf french beans, kale, kohlrabi, leeks, onions, peas, savoys, spinach, swedes and turnips, all grown in the *BED/3* that was created in the previous Autumn. Runner beans, climbing french beans, marrows, courgettes, pumpkins and sweet peas, all grown in the *BED/1* that was created in the previous Autumn.

Year Two: all annual flowers and flowers the tubers and corms of which are lifted annually to safeguard them. They are grown in *BED/1* and *BED/3*, now two years old.

Year Three: potatoes — grown in *BED/1* and *BED/3*, now three years old.

Year Four: beetroots, carrots, celery, parsley and parsnips, all grown in *BED/1* and *BED/3*.

TIP 116

➔ **A crop-rotation system is possible in the garden that is large enough to provide only one vegetable/annual flower production area. With meticulous planning and annual record keeping, the single area can be devoted to the head gardener's four-year regime. By this means, a given set of crops returns to it only after the required three-year pause. The growbag can be added to extend the growing area (for strawberry and daffodil production, for example). This can be converted into an organic aid by being moistened and fed only with comfrey solution.**

These are now four years old and almost completely spent.

Year Five: produces Year One's crops; begins to repeat the four-year cycle. *BED/1* and *BED/3* are new and in use for the first time. They were created in the previous Autumn at the end of Year Four's season.

AREA TWO

Year One: beetroots, carrots, celery, parsley and parsnips, all grown in *BED/1* and *BED/3*. These are now four years old and almost completely spent.

Year Two: broad beans, broccoli, cabbages, cauliflowers, dwarf french beans, kale, kohlrabi, leeks, onions, peas, savoys, spinach, swedes and turnips, all grown in the *BED/3* that was created in the previous Autumn. Runner beans, climbing french beans, marrows, courgettes, pumpkins and sweet peas, all grown in the *BED/1* that was created in the previous Autumn.

Year Three: all annual flowers and flowers the tubers and corms of which are lifted annually to safeguard them. They are grown in *BED/1* and *BED/3*, which are now two years old.

Year Four: potatoes — grown in *BED/1* and *BED/3*, which are now three years old.

Year Five: produces Year One's crops in four-year-old *BED/1* and *BED/3*; in Autumn, receives new *BEDs/1* and *BEDs/3*, to begin a fresh four-year cycle.

For the starting dates of each month's moon quarters see almost any diary — but it is essential to consult *MOON* first of all.

AREA THREE

Year One: potatoes — grown in three-year-old *BED/1* and *BED/3*.

Year Two: beetroots, carrots, celery, parsley and parsnips, all grown in *BED/1* and *BED/3*. These are now four years old and almost completely spent. In Autumn, receives new *BEDs/1* and *BEDs/3*, to begin a fresh four-year cycle.

Year Three: broad beans, broccoli, cabbages, cauliflowers, dwarf french beans, kale, kohlrabi, leeks, onions, peas, savoys, spinach, swedes and turnips, all grown in the *BED/3* that was created in the previous Autumn. Runner beans, climbing french beans, marrows, courgettes, pumpkins and sweet peas, all grown in the *BED/1* that was also created in the previous Autumn.

Year Four: all annual flowers and flowers the tubers and corms of which are lifted annually to safeguard them. They are grown in *BED/1* and *BED/3*, which are two years old.

TIP 117
➔ **A three-year rotation system utilising three vegetable-growing areas is almost as beneficial as a four-year/four-area system which includes flower production. Equally, advises R J Harris, in a four-area system the flowers can be omitted, with an area being given over each year to old-fashioned, fertility enhancing 'manoeuvring' or, with much less physical effort, a cress or mustard green manure sown in Spring and turned into the soil in Autumn.**

Year Five: produces as in year one in three-year-old *BED/1* and *BED/3*.

AREA FOUR

Year One: all annual flowers and flowers the tubers and corms of which are lifted annually to safeguard them. They are grown in *BED/1* and *BED/3*, which are now two years old.

Year Two: potatoes — all grown in three-year-old *BED/1* and *BED/3*.

Year Three: beetroots, carrots, celery, parsley and parsnips, all grown in *BED/1* and *BED/3*. These are now four years old and almost completely spent. In Autumn, receives new *BEDs/1* and *BEDs/3*, to begin a fresh four-year cycle.

Year Four: broad beans, broccoli, cabbages, cauliflowers, dwarf french beans, kale, kohlrabi, leeks, onions, peas, savoys, spinach, swedes and turnips, all grown in the *BED/3* that was created in the previous Autumn. Runner beans, climbing french beans, marrows, courgettes, pumpkins and sweet peas, all grown in the *BED/1* that was also created in the previous Autumn.

Year Five: produces as in year one in two-year-old *BED/1* and *BED/3*.

The below-the-surface plants are sown/planted at the start of the moon's first quarter. The above-the-surface plants are sown/planted at the start of the moon's second quarter.

The sowing/planting is done in the appropriate Spring month. Invariably, each follows a standard feed of fish-blood-and-bone fertiliser applied at the start of the moon's fourth quarter. Invariably, too, when 'watering' is carried out in the open garden — which happens rarely — the water incorporates comfrey solution in the standard ratios of 1:40 and 1:80. Generally, 1:80 is applied at the start of the season; 1:40 is applied for specific reasons to do with feeding.

for background information, see
COMFREY/1 to -/3, FERTILISER, MANURE, MOON, SOIL.

SOIL. So far as head gardener R J Harris is concerned, the soil of Earth's crust is in two types: that which has been cultivated for more than one year by farmer or by gardener; that which permanently bears grass in the form of meadow, pasture or lawn.

"Fundamentally," says Mr Harris,

TIP 118

➜ "The secret of obtaining good soil in the garden," says R J Harris, "is to change its colour to as dark a shade as possible. The darker the soil, the more warmth it retains. And warmth is the key to increased fertility and better plant life. Light soil loses its heat, which causes reduced bacteria activity and, hence, reduced fertility." Added decomposed vegetable matter — as much as possible, and mulched on or turned in during the moon's third or fourth quarter — leads to a darkening "and so does soot and ashes from the coal fire," adds Mr Harris, "which was one of the ways grandad achieved the lovely rich, dark-brown loam and tilth that enabled him to feed his large family right through the year."

"soil is the product of rock which has been broken down by weather activity during millions of years. In that time it has been augmented by the by-products of the growth and death of living creatures and vegetation."

Today's soil is in many types, worldwide, because rock has always existed in a similarly considerable number of types.

In practical, gardener-friendly terms, soil is in two categories: light and heavy.

Light soil has comparatively coarse particles.

Heavy soil has comparatively fine particles.

The difference accounts for the difference in weight between the two, volume for volume — a reality to which any spade-wielding, earth-hefting gardener can testify.

Heavy soil's particles are packed more closely together than are light soil's, volume for volume. Hence, heavy soil retains moisture more effectively than does light soil. It also, in given conditions, becomes more caked and sticky when wet than does light soil, and — with its greater concentration of particles — forms into harder lumps when dry than does light soil.

LIGHT soil is more sand-laden than is heavy soil. Sand particles do not readily adhere to each other. As a consequence, moisture passes through light soil more readily than

it does through heavy soil. That is why light soil requires to have moisture-retaining material added to it, such as heavy manure

---

119

In true horticulture, the traditional way to tame previously unused, unworked soil has not changed, notes Mr Harris.

"Old-fashioned double digging — or bastard digging, as it was sometimes known — consists of trenching down as deep as twice the length of a spade's blade for the whole of the area that is to be turned into a bed.

"The trenches are dug right alongside each other, so that not one cubic inch of soil is unturned.

"The bottom of each trench is thoroughly loosened with a fork, and then the trench is reinstated with the earth from the next trench as that one is dug."

Traditionally, too, this preparatory work is done in the Autumn, so that the rains and the frost and the winds of Winter can have impact upon the deeply-turned soil and help to produce a generous depth of loosened, aerated, workable medium which features, eventually, a good surface tilth. It is done, too, during the moon's third quarter. This, thanks to the failing water table, is when the soil is at its most receptive to air and rain

"Depending upon what is to be done with the completed bed, a depth of fully-composted manure is placed into each of the trenches before it is reinstated," says the head gardener. "So there are nutrients as well as enhanced drainage just where the plants' roots expect to find them.

"Indeed," he adds, "the other chief main reason for double digging is to cure drainage problems. Which it does, and very effectively."

(farmyard, not stable) or leaf mould.

Grit or sand or stable manure containing much straw (horse manure) opens up heavy soil's particles and, thus, reduces its tendency to retain moisture unhelpfully. These lightening additives are at their most effective when applied in Autumn. They then have time in which to penetrate the top soil and to become absorbed by it in readiness for the commencement of the following growing season.

Chalky soils are limey soils. Usually, they are positioned above solid chalk, Their high lime content is counteracted by the addition of acid, organic matter such as fully-composted leaf mould.

Acid soils contain decomposing plant fibre and little or no lime. Natural conditions such as centuries of leaf drop or peat-marsh origins give rise to these soils. Their acidity is counteracted by the addition of lime.

In their uncorrected states, these two extremes — the lime-laden and the acidic — support widely differing kinds of plants. Hence, it can be argued that it is the wise gardener who finds out beyond question what is in his or her garden, does not devote resources to trying to alter its character, and is content to grow in it what it is best suited to grow.

FORTUNATELY, the vast majority of gardens do not call upon their users to arrive at this kind of decision making. They possess the medium that holds a co-operative balance of lime and acid. It responds enthusiastically to repeated, traditional deep digging plus the age-old way of making calculated, purposeful additions of manure. As a result, it converts itself into the holy grail of gardening, that which is known as loam or marly soil.

"Gardens which are kept alive with nothing other than artificial fertilisers are no gardens at all," comments R J Harris.

A feature of the healthy garden is a gardener-created, gardener-maintained combination within the soil of warmth, air and moisture. It provides the habitat in which beneficial bacteria turn decaying vegetable matter into the essential component, humus.

Overall, this ideal growing medium is seldom without its very minor disadvantages, but — again — it is the wise gardener who knows what these are and adapts to them.

STRAWBERRY/1 — year one of strawberry production: preparation and planting. Head gardener R J Harris's Tresillian strawberry plants begin as plantlets inserted into a section of a single-dug bed (*BED/3*) that is in the first year of its four-year life span. This is when the nutrients and moisture of its 30cm or so thickness of fully-composted stable or farmyard manure, placed a spade's depth beneath its surface, are untapped.

The plants live in the section through four Summers and give the head gardener three harvests and the next generation of strawberry plants. They then reach the end of their lives and are uprooted and destroyed.

Extended harvesting is achieved throughout the individual year by planting early-, mid-season- and late-fruiting varieties.

Apply the head gardener's system for first-year development in the following way

1 as soon as a single-dug bed made according to *BED/3* has been established in September or October, earmark a section of it for strawberry production. Ideally, the section

— is no more than large enough to accommodate a small number — twelve, say — of young plants inserted 30cm apart in no more than two rows which are 45cm apart. [*Consideration*: *two rows*

REQUIRED FOR *STRAWBERRY/1*

- A section of a first-year *BED/3* , for use as a strawberry producer.

- Four early, four mid-season and four late-season strawberry plantlets certified to be virus-free and planted out at **the start of the August moon's second quarter**.

- 60g to the square metre of fish-blood-and-bone fertiliser applied to the strawberry section at **the start of the July moon's fourth quarter**.

- A garden fork, a compost bin or heap, a trench that awaits completion as a deep-trench bed (*BED/1*) or a shallow-trench bed (*BED/2*), a rake, a four-tined cultivator (if possible), a trowel, a hand fork, garden labels, a watering can with a medium rose, water, a hoe, scissors or secateurs.

For the complete instruction, see *STRAWBERRY/1* to -/5.

makes it possible to manage the plants and their ground with ease from either side of the section. Better still are two rows which can be reached into from an established path running parallel to one of the long sides of the section. Three rows, or more, creates a need to tread on the soil in order to reach the inner row or rows. This entails working in discomfort and almost certainly

For the starting dates of each month's moon quarters see almost any diary — but it is essential to consult *MOON* first of all.

compressing the soil — especially when the strawberry section is not adjacent to an established path or hard standing]

— provides access to each of its four sides for management and harvesting.
[**Consideration:** *the access makes allowance for the fact that adjacent sections within the BED/3 are, or are to be, earmarked for other crop production*]

— is an unshaded, protected sunny area

2 between earmarking the bed section and filling it with strawberry plantlets (in the following August), permit it to produce weeds. It does so throughout Winter, Spring and early Summer

3 remove each development of weeds once its members are large enough to handle and before they set seeds. Use a garden fork to do so.
[**Consideration:** *the aim is to deplete the top soil's weed population as much as possible before planting takes place in August. The reward is a piece of ground which suffers only slightly from weed growth during its*

TIP 119
➔ **August is the perfect month for strawberry planting. It ensures maximum fruit bearing the following year. September is almost as good. October-planted (or later) strawberries bear reduced quantities of berries the following year.**

four years of commitment to strawberry production]

4 compost the annual weeds and their de-earthed roots. Or place them in the trench that awaits completion as a deep-trench bed (*BED/1*) or a shallow-trench bed (*BED/2*), if there is one in the garden

5 off site, destroy or dispose of the perennial weeds and their roots, and the grass growth and its roots

6 at the first time of de-weeding the strawberry-section-to-be, use the garden fork also to level its surface. Break up the large clods formed by the use of a garden spade when *BED/3* was created, and that have thwarted Winter's attempts to reduce them in size

7 at **the start of the July moon's fourth quarter**, make the final removal of weed growth and dispose of it as before

8 rake the section's surface level. Move the surface of the ground backwards and forwards with the rake's tines. Criss-cross it in the process. Use the full length of the rake's handle. Aim for a rake-tine depth of very coarse earth crumbs, evenly laid out

9 de-earth the rake frequently, to keep its tines unblocked

10 remove the stones that are trapped by the rake's unblocked tines. Store these for use in connection with other projects in the garden. [*Considerations:* **1** — *cost-*

conscious gardening aims always to conserve useful resources that may be difficult to obtain at some point in the future. Sometimes, stones are an irreplaceable ingredient in garden projects, and merit the small amount of storage space that they occupy when conserved; **2** — *the stones that slip through the rake's unblocked tines are of the size that is required by the soil. They are an aid to drainage. They act as a moisture-retaining mulch. At all times, they release during the night the heat that they absorb during the day, relatively warming the section and its contents;* **3** — *the stones that are gathered by the rake's regularly de-earthed tines are likely to be too large to be wanted in the soil;* **4** — *generally, if no stone removal is desired, use a hoe when a bed's surface is being turned. The hoe's shape prevents it from gathering stones of any size*]

11 still at **the start of the July moon's fourth quarter** in the single-dug bed's first

TIP 120
➜ **Watering is of paramount importance when growing soft fruits. Keep the strawberry section moist throughout the growing season. Use a can with a medium rose. Direct the water onto the soil, not onto the plants. Do so at the very beginning or the very end of the day. Then, soil and plants are at their coolest and there is least loss of moisture due to evaporation. A seep-hose system used during the night is excellent for strawberry beds.**

year, dress the surface of the section with 60g to the square metre of fish-blood-and-bone fertiliser. Work it in lightly. Use the rake. Restore the level surface

12 achieve a less coarse tilth on the strawberry section's surface. Do so by re-applying the rake if no other tool is available. Move its head in all directions methodically. Seek a greater breaking down of the coarse particles of surface earth

13 for a better, more easily achieved breaking down of the surface particles, use R J Harris's preferred four-tined cultivator. Do so as if it were a rake. Reduce the coarse crumbs of the soil to crumbs which are as fine as the four-tined cultivator is able to produce. Whether a rake or a cultivator is applied, penetrate the surface with it as deeply as its tines permit.
[*Consideration: of the many manually-operated cultivators that are available for this purpose, the head gardener uses the long-handled tool that has three, four or five long, curved tines. In the hands of a practised operator, the three-tined cultivator provides a coarse tilth, the four-tined a less coarse tilth, and the five-tined a fine tilth. Also, being much less prone to clogging and having far fewer and more widely-spaced tines than the rake, all three cultivators ignore the essential small stones that the initial raking leaves in situ*]

14 in early August, place an order with a reputable supplier for strawberry plants certified to be virus-free. Or buy plants of the same certified quality from a garden centre. Buy four early, four mid-season and four late-season strawberry plants.
[(*Consideration: This range makes possible ripe berries from June to November. Buy only a small number of each, because from these, in due course and if so desired, springs progeny enough to populate the whole garden*]

15 at **the start of the August moon's second quarter**, in the coolness of the end of the day

— in the case of bare-rooted plantlets, place the roots in water for at least two hours, so that they absorb as much moisture as possible

— in the case of potted plantlets, stand the pots in water for at least two hours, so that the

TIP 121
➜ **Strawberries planted where sunshine is limited bear fruit later than the same variety planted where sunshine is abundant. Hence, the shady parts of the garden can be seen as offering the opportunity of an extended season, rather than the problem of difficult cultivation. The early- and mid-season varieties are the best for this kind of phased harvesting — the success of which must depend, to an extent, upon the strawberries' place in the overall rotation programme.**

compost absorbs as much moisture as possible

16 whilst waiting, mark out on the section's surface with stones or short sticks the points at which to insert the young plants. Space them 30cm apart in two rows 45cm apart. Use a staggered planting-out pattern

17 for each bare-root plantlet, make an excavation in the ground that is of sufficient diameter to accept its roots fully and carefully spread out. The excavation is also only deep enough to ensure that the plantlet's central growing point (from which grow its leaves' stems) is positioned slightly above the ground's surface. With these two conditions met, insert the roots, spread them out and cover them with soil drawn in from the section's surface

18 for each potted plantlet

— trowel an approximately pot-sized, pot-shaped hole in the appropriate place

— place in the hole an empty pot that is the same size as the pots in which the plantlets grow (or, instead, and with very great care, use one of the received pots)

— adjust the depth of the

hole so that the rim of the empty pot's top levels with the surrounding ground surface

— firm gathered-in earth around the empty pot

— remove the empty pot,

120

Strawberry Sticks offer a different kind of propagation exercise and a different kind of strawberry, suggests R J Harris.

He recommends raising them through seed, plantlet and planting-out stages, applying the method he uses to raise Mexican marigolds (see *MARIGOLD: Mexican /1* to *-/3*). He says that they grow to a metre high, each being covered from tip to toe with small, Alpine-type strawberries.

"It was always known as the fruit and veg plant," he says.

"The leaves could be plucked off and cooked and eaten like spinach, to be followed by the fruit as dessert."

Mr Harris gets his Strawberry Stick seeds from Suffolk Herbs.

See *SUPPLIERS*.

---

with care. Leave a pot-shaped, pot-sized hollow in the ground

— loosen the earth at the base of the hollow. Use a hand fork.
[**Consideration:** *this prevents poor drainage. Poor drainage results in accumulated water, which is anathema to the developing plantlets' roots*]

— working as close as possible to the waiting

If further explanation is required, e-mail R J Harris on *rjh@moongardening.fsnet.co.uk*

hollow, place a potted plantlet upright in the palm of one hand

— place the fingers of the other hand over the top of the pot. Spread the fingers, so that they pass around the stem of the plantlet. By this means avoid touching and possibly damaging what is the plant's most sensitive feature — which, if harmed, will cause the plantlet's death

— grip the top of the pot with the tips of the spread fingers. Turn the pot upside down

— supporting the surface of the compost, still with the fingers spread out to avoid touching the plantlet's stem, permit the pot's contents to slide out slowly. If necessary, initiate this and encourage it to happen by first tapping the upturned base of the pot gently once or twice

— hold and support the pot-shaped, glistening compost root ball upside down in the palm of the hand. Place the empty pot to one side

— using both hands, turn the compost root ball upright. Do so with utmost gentleness and without compressing it. Immediately slip the root ball into the waiting hollow. It fits the hollow perfectly

— gently firm in the compost root ball

— depress its surface slightly below that of the surrounding ground in order to create a rain-collecting depression

19 name each plantlet on a durable label inserted nearby. Note, especially, if the plant is an early, mid-season or late bearer

20 water well the earth around the inserted plantlets. Use a can with a medium rose

21 keep the strawberry section weed-free from this moment. Do so by regular hoeing. [*Consideration: this both prevents weed-seed germination and raises moisture to the surface, where it is needed by the plantlets' roots.*]

22 do not expect to harvest berries during this first year of strawberry development

23 at the end of the strawberry section's first year, in Autumn, give the section's surface a final weeding. Also remove the dead plant foliage and the few runners that may have been produced by the young plants. Cut off both as close as possible to the parent. Use scissors or secateurs. Do not wrench them from the plant. Transfer the redundant, unwanted vegetable matter from site and burn it or otherwise dispose of it securely. [*Consideration: the standard practice is to compost this kind of redundant vegetable matter. The head gardener does not do so. He believes that the material almost certainly* harbours pests. Also, it may carry the beginnings of disease — and not only disease which is related to the original plant. These conditions may not be destroyed by the composting process. Better and safer, he is certain, to destroy it]

24 leave the strawberry section to over-Winter undisturbed.

for background information, see *MANURE, MOON, ROTATION.*

S TRAWBERRY/2 — year two of strawberry production: managing the bed and taking the first harvest. Continue year one's work as follows

1 at the start of **the April moon's fourth quarter** in the strawberry section's second year, remove the Winter/Spring weed growth. Dispose of the weed vegetation in a proper manner, as before. From this moment on, prevent weed germination. Use a hoe. Do so without harming the roots of the strawberry plants. These are close to the surface of the soil in the section

2 dress the de-weeded section's surface around the inserted strawberry plants with 60g to the square metre of fish-blood-and-bone fertiliser. Work it in lightly. Use a hand fork or a hoe

3 acquire a supply of straw. Keep it in dry conditions. [**Consideration:** ideally, the straw has not been subjected to pesticides and insecticides. Also, it has not

REQUIRED FOR *STRAWBERRY/2*

- The section of a second-year *BED/3* that is stocked with first-year strawberry plants.

- 60g to the square metre of fish-blood-and-bone fertiliser applied to **the strawberry section at the start of the April moon's fourth quarter**.

- 1:80 comfrey solution applied to the strawberry section at **the start of the moon's fourth quarter** prior to strawing down.

- A hoe, a hand fork, a supply of straw applied to the strawberry section after blossom drop, water, a watering can with a medium rose, scissors or secateurs.

For the complete instruction, see *STRAWBERRY/1* to -/5.

been stored by its supplier alongside hay. Straw that is placed along side hay at the retail outlet is likely to be contaminated by the hay's

TIP 122
➔ **Keep the slugs and snails out of the strawberry bed by laying short lengths of copper wire or copper tube in amongst the plants. For copper wire use redundant power cable of the kind that connects domestic power outlet points. Strip off the insulating materials.**
R J Harris has used the method successfully for many years, and not only in strawberry beds. He learned about it early on in his career "from a wonderful old Australian gardener who'd been organic gardening long before I ever thought about it."

121

The growbag is excellent for strawberry production. Place up to ten plantlets in the one bag, position the bag where there is plenty of sunlight, and feed it throughout the whole of each of its three years of employment.

Use tomato feed. Better, convert the exercise into an organic one by using comfrey solution.

Make this by adding eighty parts of water to one part of comfrey stock

Without fail, add the solution each time the bag's compost shows signs of drying. Wait for that signal as a way not to over-add or to add too often. Inspect daily.

Whether in a bag or a garden bed, a properly-managed strawberry plant bears, on average, about 300g of berries in its first-year, and about twice that weight in its second year. Expect a decrease in size and weight in the third and final year.

seed content. This results in the probability of grass-seed transference to the surface upon which the straw is laid, and consequent grass development]

4 as soon as the strawberry blossom has ended and the very young, small berries show themselves (in May, probably), water the strawberry section thoroughly with comfrey solution (water and comfrey stock in the ratio 1:80). Use a can with a medium rose. Do so at the end of the day. [*Consideration: the application of cold water to plants and/or soil is always*

best done when both have been cooled by the lower temperatures of the end of the day. The plants are less likely, then, to suffer health-damaging trauma as the cold water falls upon them and upon the earth over their root systems]

5 immediately, and with great care, cover the section's surface around the plants with a layer of the straw, placed loosely. Mask the bed's surface as completely as possible.
[*Consideration: the straw keeps the berries clean as they form and ripen. It also limits the evaporation of moisture from the bed's surface. Improved moisture retention improves size and flavour in the berries*]

6 cut off the plants' runners as they appear. Do so as close as possible to the

TIP 123
➔   **Black plastic netting offers the simplest and lowest-cost way to protect ripe strawberries from bird attack. Made by Netlon, it is available in rolls from the gardening areas of DIY stores. Lay it gently on top of the plants — a one-person task when R J Harris's two-row planting-out system is applied. Being feather light and inflexible, it does not crush them. Being fine-meshed and of a slippery construction, it does not entangle itself in them. Also, its fine, rigid mesh is bird-beak proof, so that the berries upon which it rests are as safe as those that are not in contact with the netting. It is easily folded back or removed at harvest time and for weeding.**

parent plant. Use scissors or secateurs. Do not wrench off the runners. Aim for runner-free plants throughout the season

7 harvest the fruit as it ripens. Do not leave ripe berries to rot on the plants

8 at the close of the season, de-weed the strawberry section. Also uproot the overlooked runners that have taken root in the section. Immediately remove the redundant vegetation from site and dispose of it securely
[*Consideration:* *all redundant plant material is seen as potential habitat by the strawberry's ever-ready diseases and pests. These must be kept at bay. Immediate material removal and disposal is the best course*]

9 leave the now two-year-old strawberry section to over-Winter undisturbed.

for background information, see
COMFREY/1 to -/3, MOON, ROTATION.

S **TRAWBERRY/3 — year three of strawberry production: managing the bed and taking the second harvest; securing the next generation of plants.**
Continue year two's work as follows

1 at the start of **the April moon's fourth quarter** in the strawberry section's third year, clean the section of weed growth. Dispose of the weed vegetation in a proper manner, as previously. Keep the section in this condition at all times.

REQUIRED FOR *STRAWBERRY/3*

● The section of a third-year *BED/3* that is stocked with twelve second-year strawberry plants.

● 60g to the square metre of fish-blood-and-bone fertiliser applied to the strawberry section at **the start of the April moon's fourth quarter**.

● 1:80 comfrey solution applied to the strawberry section prior to strawing down.

● A supply of straw applied to the strawberry section after blossom drop.

● A hoe, a hand fork, a watering can with a medium or fine rose, water, the required number of 8cm pots, John Innes No 2 potting compost, staples made of garden wire, labels, a cold frame (if possible).

For the complete instruction, see *STRAWBERRY/1 to -/5.*

Use a hoe. Do so to prevent weed germination. Do so, also, without harming the roots of the strawberry plants, which are close to the surface of the section

2 dress the section's surface around the inserted strawberry plants with 60g to the square metre of fish-blood-and-bone fertiliser. Work it in lightly. Use a hand fork or the hoe

3 acquire another supply of suitable straw

4 as soon as the strawberry blossom has ended and the very young, small berries show themselves (in May,

probably), water the strawberry section thoroughly with comfrey solution (water and comfrey stock in the ratio 1:80). Use a can with a medium rose. Do so at the end of the day

5 immediately, and with great care, cover the section's surface around the plants with a layer of the straw, placed very loosely. Mask the bed's surface as completely as possible

6 as the season progresses, reduce the runners appearing from each of the plants to one or two per plant. Select the strongest-looking runners for this purpose

7 cut off all of the others as close as possible to the parent plant. Make all removals with scissors or secateurs. Do so as often as unwanted runners appear as the season progresses. Do not wrench the runners from the plants. Do not develop more than two runners per plant, to maintain plant quality.
[**Consideration:** *the suggested starting stock numbers four early fruit bearers, four mid-season fruit bearers and four late-season fruit bearers. Leave one or two runners on each plant according to how many replacement plants will be required*]

8 wait for each conserved runner to grow to about 20cm in length and to develop a point at which leaves appear

9 sensibly anticipating this stage, and choosing a convenient moment (the

---

122

Strawberries are sometimes harvested in the old style in the walled kitchen garden at Tresillian. Gathered on a dry day at mid-day, when the sun has been at its height for two or three hours, they are arranged on a bed of strawberry leaves placed in a broad. shallow basket.

"The head gardener of the time would have sent up none but the best to the big house," comments R J Harris. "They would have been put on the table about half an hour before they were required, so that the diners could admire them and savour their aroma."

Royal Sovereign is a favourite of Mr Harris's for this kind of presentation.

"It is a very old, very reliable variety, with a fine flavour," he says.

"It bears large berries, fruits early and fruits for a long time. It can give crops of enormous volume.

"It is not at all difficult to raise when the proper preparation has been carried out, and when there has been proper management of the developing crop."

---

moon plays no part at this stage), prepare as many 8cm pots for strawberry-plantlet production as there are runners to be accommodated. Working under cover, in the case of each pot

— loosely fill it with John Innes No 2 potting

compost. Do not place drainage stones in the pot first of all.
[**Consideration:** *in so small a pot, a drainage aid is unnecessary*]

— brush a hand across the top of the pot to level off the compost

— tap the base of the pot gently yet firmly, two or three times, upon the workbench top. By this means, settle the compost until its surface is level with the base of the rim that is moulded into the top of the pot

— add more compost, if necessary, to raise the level of the compost's surface

— gently add water to the compost's surface until it threatens to overspill from the top of the pot. Use a can fitted with a fine rose. Do not disturb the surface of the compost as the water is added

— put the pots to one side for at least two hours, in order to achieve comprehensive moistening of the compost

10 station the watered, compost-filled pots in the strawberry section, one per runner and sensibly close to the parent plant

11 pin the runner to the centre of the surface of the pot's John Innes compost. Do this at the best-looking and most conveniently-placed leaf-growth point on the runner.

Improvise a pin by bending a length of garden wire into a long-legged, narrow staple

12 label each pot, making clear that it contains either an early- or a mid-season- or a late-fruiting plantlet.
[**Consideration:** *the labelling of the parent plants when they were inserted into the ground as plantlets makes a simple task of this*]

13 settle the individual pot firmly into the straw and adjacent to the parent plant. Do so in such a way that the pinned-down runner is not under strain and, thus, is able to sink roots into the pot's compost

14 cut off the extensions that may develop from the pinned-down runners. Do this as close as possible to the pinned-down point on the pinned runner. Use scissors or secateurs

TIP 124
➔ **Straw is out of the reach of many gardeners (except from pet shops, where buying it in quantity can be an expensive undertaking). Supports to keep the developing bunches of berries off the soil can be fashioned out of thin, galvanised wire. Combined with positioned copper wire or copper tubing (see STRAWBERRY/2) they keep the slugs and snails at bay. Small mats cut out of roofing felt and positioned appropriately are an alternative. These improvisations leave the surface of the strawberry bed unmulched and, consequently, prone to moisture evaporation.**

15 regularly water the pots. Use a can with a fine rose. Never permit them to dry out

16 harvest the section's fruit product as it ripens. Do not leave ripe berries to rot on the plants

17 at **the start of the September moon's fourth quarter**, detach the potted young strawberry plants from their parents. Do so as close as possible to the parent plants. Trim off from the potted plantlets the now redundant lengths of runner. Use scissors or secateurs.
[*Consideration: do so in the cool of the end of the day, to reduce the stress to parent plant and potted plantlet that is caused by the surgery*]

18 immediately transfer the pots to a cold frame or some other unheated, well-sheltered place. Lodge them there until they are wanted for planting out in their own section. The new section will succeed the section that is now three years old and approaching its demise

19 keep the compost in the plantlets' pots moist at all times. Adjust the pots' storage point, day by day, so that adequate protection is

---

⌨ Visit *R J Harris's Moon Gardening's* companion web site
www.moongardening.fsnet.co.uk
to keep in touch with the results of the head gardener's latest experimental archaeological projects and developmental work in the walled kitchen garden at Tresillian in Cornwall.

balanced by adequate ventilation

20 complete the season just before Winter sets in by removing the straw from the established strawberry section and finally weeding its surface

21 dispose of the removed straw and other vegetable material off site

22 leave the section and its plants — and the general crop-rotation area of which it is a small part — to over-Winter undisturbed and to enter their fourth and final year.

for background information, see *COMFREY/1 to -/3, MOON, ROTATION.*

S TRAWBERRY/4 — year four of strawberry production: managing the bed and taking the third harvest. Continue year three's work as follows

1 at the start of **the April moon's fourth quarter**, clean the strawberry section of weed growth. Dispose of the weed vegetation in a proper manner, as

---

TIP 125
➜ A long-gone head gardener under whom R J Harris trained gave him two tips to improve the flavour of strawberries: 1) mix finely-crushed fir cones, gathered in the Autumn, into the strawberry bed just prior to the plants coming into flower; or, 2) mix lime into the bed — 60g to the square metre — also just before the blossom appears.

REQUIRED FOR *STRAWBERRY/4*

● The section of a fourth-year *BED/3* that is stocked with third-year strawberry plants.

● 60g to the square metre of fish-blood-and-bone fertiliser applied to the strawberry section at **the start of the April moon's fourth quarter**.

● 1:80 comfrey solution applied to the strawberry section prior to strawing down.

● A supply of straw applied to the strawberry section after blossom drop.

● A hoe, a hand fork, a watering can with a medium rose.

For the complete instruction, see *STRAWBERRY/1* to *-/5*.

---

previously. Keep the section in this condition at all times. Use a hoe. Do so without harming the roots of the strawberry plants, which are close to the surface of the ground

2 dress the section's surface around the strawberry plants with 60g to the square metre of fish-blood-and-bone fertiliser. Work it in lightly. Use a hand fork or a hoe

3 acquire another supply of suitable straw

4 as soon as the strawberry blossom has ended and the very young, small berries show themselves (in May, probably), water the strawberry section thoroughly with comfrey solution (water and comfrey stock in the ratio 1:80). Use

a can with a medium rose. Do so at the end of the day

5 immediately, and with great care, cover the section's surface around the plants with a layer of the straw, placed very loosely. Mask the bed's surface as completely as possible

6 keep the section weed-free. Do not devote time to removing runners

7 when it is certain that fruiting has come to end, uproot the now redundant strawberry plants. Empty the section of all other growth and the straw. Immediately remove all of this potentially harmful material from site and dispose of it securely

8 return the one-time strawberry section to when, four years previously, it was a part of a single-dug bed installed to grow a range of

---

TIP 126

➜   The head gardener urges: "Should disease or pest show itself in a given strawberry bed, have the plants out and destroyed off site immediately. Do not keep a single one of them. And do not waste time and money trying to 'cure' the problem. Culling is the simplest, cheapest, most reliable way if the attack is to be contained." Mr Harris adds: "When starting over again with new plants, establish them in their own section of the next single-dug bed to be made as a part of the crop-rotation programme. This way, be sure of starting again in a different place in the garden."

vegetable plants.

[*Considerations:* **1** — *the single-dug bed is now at the end of its four-year life span. It is to be replaced in the present Autumn by a new single-dug bed, to begin a new round of R J Harris's four-year, crop-rotation system;* **2** — *the precise matching of the strawberry plant's life span and that of the special beds indicates a strength of the head gardener's system of gardening. Were there to be a difference between the two, rotation would be impeded by the presence in a four-year-old and redundant area of a plant requiring either less or more time in the ground.*]

for background information, see
COMFREY/1 to -/3, MOON, ROTATION.

STRAWBERRY/5 — **strawberry production continuity.** To achieve the next harvest, and successive strawberry harvests, proceed as follows

1 earmark a section of a new single-dug bed for strawberry production. Do so in the September or October that follows the second harvest of the current strawberry development

2 in this new section begin a new generation of strawberry plants. Repeat STRAWBERRY/1 to -/4. In doing so

3 use the plantlets produced by the current development as it produced its second harvest. Hold these potted plantlets in a cold frame

until they are inserted in the new section in the following August. Manage the cold frame so that adequate ventilation is balanced against adequate insulation against the cold and the frost. Manage the moistening of the plantlets' compost so that it never dries out

4 alternatively, use bought-in strawberry plantlets, obtained in the early August before planting time and as explained in STRAWBERRY/1. In this considerably more expensive case, the current strawberry section is not permitted to convert runners into plantlets in compost-filled pots. Equally, the runners are not permitted to take root in the soil of the strawberry section. Each season, the runners are removed from the parent plants

5 mark every second strawberry harvest by taking this step. Throughout, adhere to R J Harris's overall moon-quarter-oriented feeding and planting times, and crop-rotation principles.

for the complete strawberry instruction, see also
STRAWBERRY/1 to -/4.

SUPPLIERS. The suppliers and organisations with which head gardener R J Harris deals for the resources that he applies on behalf of the Tresillian estate — and from which he receives advice — are listed in this section. Their products and services are indicated, as that information is required, elsewhere in the manual.

123
At 2002, the member companies of the **John Innes Manufacturers' Association**, which produce the John Innes soil-based composts, were

Eden Park Ltd
Crown Quay Lane Sittingbourne Kent ME10 3JJ tel 01795 471583 fax 01795 428011
www.edenpark.co.uk
sales@edenpark.co.uk

Gem Gardening
Brookside Lane Oswaldtwistle Accrington Lancashire BB5 3NY tel 01254 356635 fax 01254 356677
www.gemgardening.co.uk
sales@gemgardening.co.uk

Wessex Horticultural Products Ltd
Wessex House Hill Top Business Park 1-3 Devizes Road Salisbury Wiltshire SP3 4UF tel 01722 337744 fax 01722 333177
www.wessexhort.co.uk
wessex@wessexhortgrp.co.uk

Westland Horticulture Ltd
14 Granville Industrial Estate Granville Road Dungannon Co Tyrone BT70 1NJ tel 02887 727500 fax 02887 723800
www.westlandhorticulture.com
SMcGrane@westlandhorticulture.com

William Sinclair Horticulture Ltd
Firth Road Lincoln LN6 7AH tel 01522 537561 fax 01522 513209
www.william-sinclair.co.uk
chris.turner@william-sinclair.co.uk

The John Innes Manufacturers' Association is at PO Box 8, Harrogate, HG2 8XB (*tel* 01423 879208; *fax* 01423 870025; *e-mail* BDunsby@ntlworld.com). Contact it for a helpful, illustrated brochure on the benefits and uses of the John Innes loam-based composts. The brochure is free in return for a stamped and addressed envelope.

Chase Organics Ltd, Riverdene, Molesey Road, Hersham, Surrey, KT12 4RG
01932 253666
chaseorg@aol.com until 2004
sales@chaseorganics.co.uk
wef October 2002
www.organiccatalog.com

E W King & Co Ltd, Monks Farm, Pantlings Lane, Coggeshall Road, Kelvedon, Essex, CO5 9PG
01376 570000
sales@kingsseeds.com
www.kingsseeds.com

Edwin Tucker & Sons Ltd, Brewery Meadow, Stonepark, Ashburton, Newton Abbot, Devon, TQ13 7DG
01364 652403
tuckersseeds@agriplus.net
www.tuckersseeds.agriplus.net

Heritage Seed Library, an initiative of HDRA

HDRA, Ryton Organic Gardens, Coventry, CV8 3LG
(024) 7630 3517
enquiry@hdra.org.uk
www.hdra.org.uk

Organic Concentrates Ltd, Chesham, Buckinghamshire, HP5 1EN
*01494 866768 (**fax** 01494 792199)*
organic6x@aol.com
www.6-x.co.uk

Peter Grayson, Sweet Pea Seedsman, 34 Glenthorne Close, Brampton, Chesterfield, Derbyshire, S40 3AR
0124 627 8503 (also fax number)

Simpson's Seeds, The Walled Garden Nursery, Horningsham, Warminster, Wiltshire, BA12 7NQ
01985 845004
simpsonseeds@aol.com

Suffolk Herbs, Monks Farm,
Pantlings Lane, Coggeshall
Road, Kelvedon, Essex, CO5
9PG
01376 572456
sales@suffolkherbs.com
www.suffolkherbs.com

The Seed Swap Register, an
initiative of HRDA

The Tomato Growers Club, an
initiative of Simpson's Seeds

Thomas Etty, heritage seedsman
and bulb specialist, 45 Forde
Avenue, Bromley, Kent, BR1
3EU
02084 666785

TRESILLIAN/1 — the walled garden. The head gardener is charged with the revival, maintenance and management — and overall productivity — of the walled kitchen garden that is a feature of the privately-owned 200-acre Tresillian (Cornish for *House in the Sun*) estate that is located near to Newquay in Cornwall. It is one of Britain's few fully-operational Victorian walled gardens. Unlike so many of its peers throughout the country, it has been rescued from wall-to-wall grass, forgettable shrubbery and forgotten orchards.

It extends over some three-quarters of an acre.

It was established in the early-to-mid 1800s to feed and delight the family and servants of a country house which was built upon the foundations of a thirteenth-century dwelling.

Now, in 2002 and after some twenty years of head gardener Harris's influence, the garden's cold frames, potting and tool sheds and ancillary buildings have been returned to their original state and are as essential, horticulturally, as ever they were.

Its four red-brick walls stand unchanged at about 4m high. Facing

The walled kitchen garden at Tresillian offers a month-by-month, all-year-round demonstration of Victorian horticultural development.

JANUARY
Begonias, lobelias sown in heated greenhouse.
Lettuces, cauliflowers, vegetables sown in unheated greenhouse. Peas, beans sown in cold frame. Early camellias bloom.

FEBRUARY (the first of early Spring in Cornwall)
Peaches, nectarines, apricots in early bloom. First daffodils, first violets show.

MARCH
Primroses, snowdrops and other Spring flowers start to show their early Spring colour.

APRIL
Flowering shrubs bloom. Early leaves show on trees. Daffodils bloom in abundance. Tulips and other Spring bulbs show. Bluebells, foxgloves, campanulas begin to break colour.

MAY
A wonderful month, with many wild flowers in the adjacent woodland walks. Red and white broad beans flower. Blue, white and red peas flower. Early Victorian potatoes harvested. Apple blossom at its peak in wide range of colours, with the bees by now working overtime. Cornish gooseberry standards (each almost 2m high) flower. Wisteria flowers. Herbaceous flowers — especially the over-wintering Brompton stocks — in full blossom. Sweet peas being picked; at their best through June, July, August (there is no
continued on 243

north, south, east and west, their internal and external surfaces created — as they create now — the micro climates that made possible the severely organised, maximum production that Mr Harris's predecessors sought with such determination and achieved with such apparent aplomb and demonstrated success.

These were the bowler-hatted, winged-collared, horticultural overlords of severe mien and tightly-buttoned, chain-festooned black waistcoats. Their skills embraced not only the management of vegetable, fruit and flower output. Supremely, they were managers of men and time. Often, as well, they were masters of whatever order of household politics dictated the quality of life where they practised — for if any estate employee's livelihood was constantly under threat of curtailment, it was that of the provider of the year round food.

The Tresillian kitchen garden's layout is as simple in 2002 as it has always been: a 90cm-to-120cm wide bed stretches along the foot of each of the four 50m length walls. The four wall beds meet the broad path that establishes the perimeter of the garden proper and forms a box within which lie four rectangular beds of equal size separated by two paths forming a cross.

In season, these inner beds are filled with potatoes, peas, beans and other vegetables dating from the early-to-mid-1800s, and cultivated in accordance with head gardener R J Harris's four-year crop-rotation cycle. The crops are supported by special plantings of pollinator-attracting sweet peas that date from the late 1600s.

The width of the paths, and their layout, facilitate harvesting in the unsullied conditions that the people from the big house insisted on and which the head gardener of the day secured by the unbending appli-

from page 242

better perfume on a still summer's evening than that to be experienced walking beside a row of very, very old-fashioned sweet peas).

JUNE
A continuation of May, with fruit blossom almost gone. Lupins, delphiniams, pinks, border carnations in bloom. Early vegetables and salad crops harvested.

JULY
Peaches, nectarines, apricots on the south-facing walls. Cherries and red currants for the cook pot on the north-facing wall. Ripe gooseberries adjacent to north-facing wall. Strawberries, raspberries, loganberries, tayberries ready for picking. Apples, pears develop on east- and west-facing walls. Victorian shrub roses in bloom. Honey suckle, clematis, roses bloom on pathway arches. Victorian sweet peas on show. Victorian white and pink runner beans in flower (especially the old-fashioned white one called Czar, and the pink-and-white one, Painted Lady).

AUGUST
The whole of the fruit garden is just a wonderful, wonderful aroma of ripe fruit. Apples, pears, medlars, figs in development. Blenheim orange melons ripen in heated greenhouse. Globe artichokes in flower.

SEPTEMBER (when the head gardener's year ends)
1700s' and 1800s' Cornish apples ripen. Plums, peaches ripen. Onions, mixed vegetables harvested: vast array of colour in garden. Pumpkins, squashes, marrows ready. Wild-berry trees
concluded on 244

cation of demanding regimes and stern discipline.

This was especially the case so far as the wall beds were concerned.

These were, and are now, filled with the kinds of flowers that appear year after year ("perennials such as lupins," says Mr Harris), and with those that are seed-sown one year to flower and then die in the following year ("biennials such as wallflowers, honesty and sweet rocket").

There would have been, as there are still, annually-planted, highly-scented flowers: "Wherever there was a seating area it was traditional," comments the head gardener, "for there to be beautiful-smelling, fragrant plants such as night-scented stock or lavender or sweet peas.

"Perfume in abundance for the ladies and their guests was the order of the day.

"Even the north-wall bed that gets little more than a mere half an hour's direct sunlight at each end of the day is productive," says the Cornish chief gardener. "It is stocked with shade-loving perennials such as primroses, foxgloves, sweet rocket, honesty, violets and aquilegias."

At the centre of the walled garden, where the two inner paths cross, is a collection of the culinary,

---

from page 243

(rowan, elder, etc) begin to change colour.

OCTOBER (when the head gardener's year begins)
Woodland trees don their Autumn colours, especially the chestnuts. Quinces, medlars are full-bodied. Fruit, vegetables selected for competitive showing in county shows.

NOVEMBER
Chrysanthemums and other flowers still add colour. Fruit trees and bushes pruned. Herbaceous borders tidied.

DECEMBER
The garden sleeps, the seedsmen's catalogues arrive, the next season's plans are laid.

---

aromatic and medicinal herbs that were so prized by the head gardener's forbears and their forbears.

The tree fruits supported by the walls — peaches, apples, cherries and pears — are festooned against the red bricks in the old style.

Notably, the unwarmed north-facing wall stands guard over soft fruit destined for the kitchen, being required unripened.

This wall's outer face looks south and until early 2001 transmitted the heat of the sun to an adjacent, mature 15-metre-long bed of figs, outdoor grapes, raspberries and gooseberries. These ripened fully and were used for dessert purposes. The gooseberries were in bush form and in 150cm-high, mop-like standard form "growing side by side," comments R J Harris. "They made very good bed mates."

This external area has been re-organised, so that loganberries and cultivated blackberries, tayberries

---

124

The garlic (the name is a derivation, it is thought, of the Saxon words for spear and leek) that is cultivated in the Cornish walled garden's centrally-placed herb bed was almost certainly brought to Britain by the Romans.

R J Harris's notes, made in his teens during his apprenticeship in the 1950s, tell him that it was then believed to have fed the slaves that built the Egyptian pyramids.

125

The walls of England's first walled gardens, established in the late 1700s, were built of that century's traditional wall-building material, stone. Stone lacks red bricks' ability to absorb the day's heat and then release it during the night. Once that fact was ascertained, stone was abandoned. Indeed, so rapidly did the technology of horticulture advance during that highly pressured period, the red-brick garden wall's performance was often enhanced by the addition of iron pipes of considerable bore. They were threaded through cavities in the walls — which were enlarged and strengthened to accommodate them — and were supplied with water heated in sunken boiler houses.

Alternatively and at lower capital cost, cavities within the walls were filled with boiler-house-heated air.

Horticulture during the winter was transformed. So were both the standards of cuisine in the big house and the working lives of the head gardeners and their under gardeners. In many significant ways, the winters of the land-owning gentry became as productive, horticulturally, as the kindlier times of the year.

and raspberries, trained on horizontal wires, are now posted where they enjoy the uninterrupted breezes and unsheltered positions that help to protect them from mildew and disease.

Remarkably, the erstwhile figs, grapes, raspberries and gooseberries were not protected against the birds.

"We had no noticeable loss of crop," says Mr Harris.

"Partly, this was because of the vast amount of soft fruit that was grown. We could afford the comparatively small amount that the birds took. In any event, we found that they did not touch the gooseberries and the grapes.

"The figs, yes, and the rasp-berries. They would take a few of those — especially the figs when they turned a dark-purple-to-black colour.

"That was when the blackbirds appeared. They loved them.

"But we never lost to the point where we had a complete failure.

"Of course, there is so much natural habitat and food for the birds elsewhere on the estate due to our tree planting — much of it especially for the birds."

During 2001 the map of this soft-fruit area and of the orchard of which it was a part was re-drawn. As a result, the area was emptied and then turned over to stone-fruit production, and considerable soft-fruit replanting took place at a greater distance from the south-facing outer surface of the garden wall.

"Now, in another location, we have 50m-long rows — spaced 2m from each other — of wire-trained blackberries, black currants and red currants, loganberries, tayberries, gooseberries and raspberries," says the head gardener.

"Fruit in one form or another is scheduled to be produced for the first time by Tresillian's newly-planted fruit garden in the Summer of 2002."

TIP 127
➜ **The head gardener gathers seeds from his plants for use the next season. Also, he is one of the growing band of rare-seed collectors and preservers. He keeps his seeds in good condition by storing them in labelled tins in the company of dried laurel or bay leaves.**

The wall's heat-absorbing, heat-radiating outer surface continues to be employed, in that fig trees and outdoor grapes have been trained against it.

Fruit production in general at Tresillian makes but one unwelcome demand upon Mr Harris. This is imposed by a particular member of the neighbourhood's fauna.

"The grey squirrel," says the head gardener.

"It steals fruit and damages the plants, which is probably more serious where the apple trees are concerned.

"The male squirrel de-barks the apple tree and urinates on it at mating time in January/February to mark its territory.

"We put on plastic protectors at ground level to stop that. The protectors are there to stop the rabbits, too, which are very destructive creatures."

Facing outwards, the exteriors of the kitchen garden's walls support, in the antique manner, figs and cordons of historical varieties of apples, pears, peaches and cherries. Nearby are freestanding espaliers of both current and ancient apples and pears.

"When I took over the walled garden I found that not only had it been neglected for more years than I cared to think about," comments R J Harris, "but also in certain places there was a thickness of no more than about 15cm of top soil.

"This was because over a long period gardening had not been done as it should have been done. One of the results of correct gardening is increased top soil.

"Soil had to be brought in and placed where the bad gardening had thinned it.

"Now, after years of four-bed, four-year rotation involving the deep-trenched incorporation of composted manure and vegetable matter — the whole managed in accordance with the phases of the moon — our soil, probably, is unique."

Since professional gardening began in Britain, the aim of all conscientious head gardeners has been to leave, on retirement, a garden at least 30cm deeper in good top soil than when they were appointed.

"This was achieved — and still is achieved," explains Mr Harris, "by the planned scattering around the garden of the top soil left over after the digging of deep trenches and their reinstatement with vegetable matter of one kind or another in readiness for planting up."

Adjacent to the walled kitchen garden is Tresillian's main greenhouse, which is unheated. It is a new structure and replaces the original, which, over the years, was

---

126

The cherries that the Victorian owners had grown for them on the north-facing walls of their kitchen gardens were known to them as 'sour' cherries.

"Cooking cherries, in other words," says R J Harris. "*Morello* was a favourite. It is still used today for jam making on a commercial scale. It is rich, juicy and self-fertile.

"It harvests in July/August, and has a good dark colour and a good flavour when turned into jam. Also, it puts up very well indeed with the lack of sun on north-facing walls.

"A snag is that it is prone to the brown-rot fungus disease, which can be a problem.

"*Stella* was another Victorian cherry," notes Mr Harris, "and just as welcome to Cook up at the big house."

The head gardener grows both varieties on Tresillian's two north-facing wall surfaces.

127

R J HARRIS: "For me, February, April and September mark the annual highlights of bird life in the walled garden.The blackbirds begin it all. Towards the end of February, year after year, without fail, they nest in the potting shed at a spot where once there was a brick. It has been missing since times gone by and when I restored the shed after ages of neglect and soon after taking up my appointment I deliberately left that brick out. Sure and behold, the very next season, there they were, and starting to nest. The blackbirds — and the thrushes — are two of the reliables of the English garden. They are the earliest of the British birds to begin nest building.

"The swallows tell me that April has arrived. Without fail, every year at about the middle of the month, they swoop into the garden. It happens always at that time and with very, very few arriving either before or after.

"What a wonderful feat it is: such tiny mites travelling thousands of miles to come back to the same nest in the same out-buildings in and around the same locations.

"Then, without fail between the 19th and the 22nd of September or thereabouts, they all line up for two or three days on the fruit wires just outside the gardens — scores of them, packed close together. And then, suddenly, without warning, they are gone, disappeared for another season.

"Very few people see them go. They seem to know exactly when the wind currents are the right ones for the long, long journey that they have to make.

"They leave an emptiness.

"One can only look forward to them returning when April is back."

neglected to the point of irrecoverability.

It complements Tresillian's heated greenhouse, which is within the kitchen garden. Like the heated greenhouse of every estate's kitchen garden in the 1800s and 1900s, it was built against the inward-looking, south-facing wall.

Light is thrown, indirectly, upon rural Victorian employer-staff relationships by the typical siting of Tresillian's potting and tool sheds. These are positioned against the north-facing outer surface of one of the garden's four walls.

In estates throughout the country, such service premises were routinely located at this inhospitably sunless spot. They included, as well, the so-called ice house for keeping fruit, the boiler house, the storage sheds and the head gardener's office.

The employer saw no reason to commit any of the warm, productive areas to gardeners' work premises. Installed heating, too, was not seen as necessary — other than a small, open grate for the head gardener.

"It was a way to keep the staff busy," says R J Harris. "In winter this spot was so cold they had to keep working to keep from freezing.

"As a youngster," he recalls, "I spent many, many winters scrubbing flower pots hour after hour in an old shed against a north-facing wall with no electricity and only cold water, a rubber apron and boots. There was no such thing in those days as a pocket radio to keep your mind off it all.

"That was in days long gone, thank goodness. There were some good days, then, but there were some very, very hard and cruel days. It is better now, and a good job, too."

TRESILLIAN/2 — restoration and conservation. A major feature of the extensive area in which are sited the Tresillian estate's Victorian walled kitchen garden and unheated greenhouse is large-scale restoration work. Head gardener R J Harris has managed a formidable amount of tree planting and, as a partial consequence, the walls of the kitchen garden are now hemmed in by an expanse of trees stationed as saplings in 1990 and, in 2002 (the date of this manual's publication), matured to heights of between three and seven metres.

"The garden's immediate landscape looks now very much as it must have looked in the 1840s," says Mr Harris.

"Then, the walls were new, the paths within them were being laid out and the external planting of very young trees was under way.

"By the early 1900s, those trees

128

The head gardener's reclamation and maintenance work in the Victorian walled garden is done, in the main, with yesterday's tools. As well as being accessible in the tool shed for daily use they are displayed there, formally, as a reminder to visitors of an important aspect of the horticulture of bygone years. Once, the tool shed was adjacent to the potting shed. Now, the two are one, the combined areas remaining outside the garden, built against the outer, north-facing surface of one of garden's four walls. The original two buildings were derelict when R J Harris took up his appointment in 1985. Among his most pressing initial tasks was their rehabilitation, for little could be attempted if tools could not be housed securely in appropriate conditions.

In reviving the two offices, and prior to joining them together, Mr Harris improved on the thinking of the garden's designer by opening a doorway through the wall so that the two premises could be entered from within the garden.

"Prior to that, one had to go outside altogether and walk all the way round the north side to get and to replace equipment and materials," comments the head gardener. "It was all very time-consuming and cumbersome and inconvenient. Brickwork three layers thick had be removed to quite a height and width," he recalls, "but it made a tremendous difference."

Posted above the newly-inserted doorway is a notice. The potting shed, it warns, must be kept in a clean condition, with potting bench cleaned nightly and all materials stored away in a proper manner. The tools, too, it reminds, must be washed and oiled after use and replaced in their designated places on the wall-hung display.

"Every night," says R J Harris, "they are checked, to make sure that none is left lying around and unseen to." Behind the potting shed's door is pinned a current moon-phase chart. It is the head gardener's year planner for preparation, sowing/planting, maintenance and — in great part — harvesting. Related to the activity that it dictates is the ordering of resources.

129

Probably, the most visible and striking expression of the Tresillian kitchen garden's return to Victorian practices is its intermixing of vegetables and flowers. This was, quintissentially, the way of the affluent Victorians. They admired contrasted colour and texture in their vegetable beds. They loved to transfer that colour to their plates: peas were often brought to the table decorated with the ruby red flowers of the legume's later sowings. In those days, these would have been the three-sided asparagus peas, steamed or eaten raw in their charming winged pods. Flower petals, too — often those of the old fashioned English pot marigold, the *calendula officinalis* — adorned chosen of their sweet puddings.

of the 1840s or thereabouts had reached maturity and immense size.

"Their huge branches filtered the bitter and often destructive winds of Winter and did a highly useful job of protecting the walls and making the garden a much less cold place than it can be nowadays at the end of the year.

"Unhappily, from about the mid 1900s, those fine old trees diminished.

"They were not cared for. They fell down or they were blown down.

"They died and they had to be taken out.

"Most serious of all, they were not replaced."

"Of course." points out Mr Harris, "all of this was but a tiny part of a national scene.

"Wealth shifted to new people, and many them had different ideas about how to use their money. The families that had both the means and the will to keep land and property in its original state and for its original purposes, and to move forward from those two stages of achievement, became fewer and fewer.

"As more time passed — and especially after World War I, which took so many of the staff away from the gardens, never to return them — those that were left were forced to use reduced incomes in ways other than that of maintaining estates."

The Tresillian walled garden's days of natural protection against the wind will return in the 2040s-to-2050s. Then, the saplings planted by R J Harris in the early 1990s will be between 20m and 30m high.

"They will filter and soften the winds over a distance equal to three

130

The restored Victorian walled garden at Tresillian and the conservation area in which it stands are in the presence of a vast tree-planting scheme that was forced upon the estate by the havoc created by the storm in 1987. This was the storm that Britain's weather experts said could not happen. It was followed by the storm of 1990 that the experts were prepared to acknowledge in advance as possible, and which finished off what was left undone by its predecessor.

The planting scheme has aimed to restore the grounds to their late 1800s' appearance, and has entailed the planting of about 15,000 trees. These replace destroyed beech and oak — English and Turkish varieties — chestnut, mountain ash and holly trees, and many fruiting trees, such as the wild cherry. The latter are being grown for the benefit of the birds and other wild life.

times their height," says Mr Harris, "so the garden will be a snug place once again."

Tomorrow's gardeners at Tresillian will have cause to commemorate R J Harris's efforts, for the prevailing wind in Cornwall is the unkind south-westerly.

"It comes straight off the Atlantic Ocean, with nothing to stop it," observes the head gardener.

An eye-catching element of Mr Harris's contribution to the revival of the Tresillian estate has been the prolific planting of bird-feeding trees. These include the wild cherry and *Gelder Rose*, the latter being given a home on the marginal land that is adjacent to the estate's wetlands.

\`The *Gelder Rose* is a wonderful tree for producing white blossom in the Summer, followed by red berries for the birds in the winter," describes Mr Harris. "With it we have put in beech and decorative whitebeam."

On a wider front, the amount of tree planting being undertaken each Autumn and Winter throughout the estate is formidable in volume and influence.

It includes much oak ("these will reach a height of at least 35m," notes the head gardener), ash, holly ("unbeatable for Christmas-decoration purposes at Tresillian House"), lime, alder and eilder.

Complementing all of this, the estate's ornamental grounds now feature additional magnolias and camellias and specimen trees such as the copper beech.

The latter, now a dotting of slender youngsters, will be mature when most of 2002's generation has passed on. Then, they will have massive trunks and majestic canopies and will be hugely shade-creating. They will express the accomplished purpose of the entire tree-installation programme: a looking ahead to tomorrow's needs — those of animals, birds and insects as well as of human beings.

If further explanation is required, e-mail R J Harris on *rjh@moongardening.fsnet.co.uk*

THE GARDENER'S DAY

In the garden, so peaceful, nature takes its turn to awaken, while some must slumber.

The owl from lofty heights swoops silently upon its prey of mice and vermin, the hedgehog in the undergrowth seeks beetles, worms and slugs.

The new moon shines brightly, so that the gardener, when morn arrives, sees the plants with dew upon their leaves, it is the time to plant the seeds, for all good gardeners work by the moon, with all its phases it is a busy time.

Seed planting must take place, for when with the full moon, harvest will reap a bountiful reward.

The gardener's life is always a busy one, for during the early part of the day he is busy raking, tilling, weeding, pruning, and keeping everything in order, as the heat of the day takes its toll so the gardener finds a shady place to stand and think, more often or not it is under an old oak tree with so many tales it could tell.

The afternoon sun sees the gardener once more busy picking fruits and caring for his ways, for the gardener's life is a never ending toll of things that must be done, evening sunset is fast approaching and the beckoning of another day will soon arrive, so he must shut the door upon this day because his tomorrow will soon be another day.

R J Harris 1998

Tips and information-panel indexes, complementary moon-gardening discussion and a continuing report on R J Harris's horticultural methods and experimentations are available on *www.moongardening.fsnet.co.uk*